David Boyle has been writing about the past and the future, and new ideas in economics, for more than a quarter of a century. He is a fellow of the New Economics Foundation and in 2013 produced an independent review for the Cabinet Office. He is the author of *The Tyranny of Numbers*, *The Human Element* and *Authenticity: Brands, Fakes, Spin and the Lust for Real Life*. He lives in London.

P- 2 30
2 33 - 234

P 264 - 26 5

277 — 2 82

P 290 Left = Right

Broke

How to Survive the Middle-Class Crisis

DAVID BOYLE

FOURTH ESTATE • London

Fourth Estate
An imprint of HarperCollins*Publishers*
77–85 Fulham Palace Road
London W6 8JB

This Fourth Estate paperback edition published in 2014
First published in Great Britain by Fourth Estate in 2013

I

ISBN 978-0-00-749105-6

Set in Quadraat by Palimpsest Book Production Limited, Falkirk, Stirlingshire

Printed and bound in Great Britain by Clays Ltd, St Ives plc

MIX
Paper from
responsible sources
FSC
www.fsc.org **FSC C007454**

For, William

Contents

Acknowledgements

I have had a number of huge advantages which helped me write this book. The first is that I am myself middle-class. I admit it. So are many of my friends. There is nothing quite like writing about yourself to help you get the atmosphere right.

Another advantage has been a hugely supportive agent and friend, Julian Alexander, who shaped this idea right from the start. The third has been a very clever and insightful editor, Louise Haines, who has been an enormous source of strength and imagination. The fourth was the vital help and advice given me by Ruth Yeoman, who helped me with the research and whose conversation helped me with the shape of the argument.

Then there are my colleagues at the New Economics Foundation, who have in so many ways inspired me and helped me think more creatively about the future, both about the problems we are going to face and the potential solutions to them. There are also the people who gave me their time so that I could ask them personal and potentially embarrassing questions about their attitudes, fears and finances. I will not embarrass them by listing them here, but many of them you can see interviewed in the book that follows.

Apart from them, I especially want to thank the people who have read chapters, answered questions or advised or gossiped or made useful suggestions in a whole range of ways, including Amanda Horton-Mastin, Andrew Burns, Andrew Simms, Anna Coote, Anna Crispe, Caroline Payne, Christine Berry, Corinna

Cordon, Dale Bassett, David Kynaston, Glyn Redworth, Helen Kersley, Jane Franklin, Joe Penny, Judith Hodge, Julia Slay, Kate Vick, Lindsay Mackie, Louisa Crispe, Louise Bazalgette, Maria Nyberg, Mike Harris, Molly Conisbee, Penny Godwin, Richard Foreman, Roger Mortlock, Ruth Potts, Sagar Shah, Sonia Purnell, and many others who I haven't listed but am very aware of, I promise – also the many relatives who I have irritated by asking them questions about class. I must also thank my father for his invaluable stream of suggestions and articles, many of which you will find quoted within. And also my mother and stepfather, for showing me what the middle classes can be at their very best. The mistakes, misinterpretations and muddles are all mine.

Finally, I want to thank my wife Sarah, and Robin and William, for being so interested in what I was doing all the while I was locked away at the bottom of the garden, thinking about our future as a middle-class family, when I should have been paying the bills. Beyond anything else, they have taught me what family life could be, and there is not an idea in these pages that has not been influenced, shaped or knocked about by them. I owe them a huge amount. If anything, writing this book has caused me to think back across my overwhelmingly middle-class life and to love and enjoy my family even more.

Prologue

'By the people, I mean the middle classes, the wealth and
intelligence of the country, the glory of the British name.'

Henry, Lord Brougham, 1831

I was born in a corner of central London that wraps itself around
a great grey-green greasy stretch of water called the Regent's Canal.
It was and is known as Little Venice.

As anyone familiar with Little Venice will know, this defines
me inescapably as middle-class. Not just slightly middle-class, but
staggeringly, swelteringly, stratospherically middle-class, as
middle as you can get. And not just by the broad American definition (average income) either, but by the specific British definitions
which are harder to pin down, but which seem to be about attitudes
and upbringing, culture and prejudices.

But there are many kinds of middle class, even in the UK, and
I hope this book will strike a chord with all of them. From the
first-generation middle classes who followed the entrepreneurial
path set out by Margaret Thatcher right through to the crustiest
scion of the landed gentry. From the brand-new estate outside
Bishop's Stortford to the tumbledown off-grid eco-cottage outside
Totnes. I mention Little Venice because anyone reading this book
deserves to know about the niche in the class system I am writing
from, but I am only too aware that there is more than one way of
being middle-class.

In my case, I am also middle-class because my parents are. Both my grandfathers were in the services, one rising to be a colonel in the army and the other to be a captain in the navy. Their service pensions and various modest pots of inherited money and property gave them relatively comfortable retirements. I owe my grandparents a great deal for their resources of love and care, but also perhaps for placing me so unambiguously in such a recognizable spot in the class system.

Neither set of grandparents approved very much when my newly married parents moved into a run-down rented flat in Little Venice, which was not in those days quite what it has become. The canal stank of drowned cats, and was divided from the road by a tall brick wall, like a scene from *Love on the Dole*. All those coloured barges sheltering artists and musicians (and later Richard Branson) were still a decade away.

The flat was in the least respectable half of Randolph Avenue, bending down towards the canal, with peeling white stucco columns and flaking black front doors which looked like the portals of some medieval fortress. But the family disapproval also touched the street's reputation. Only ten years before, this end of the thoroughfare had sported the name 'Portland Road', which had been such a notorious red-light district that the council decided to change it.

Downstairs from our flat was a fearsome Alf Garnett figure, string-vested and with a fluent and foul-mouthed command of the language, who would hammer on the ceiling at the slightest provocation. My uncle had a heavier tread than most (submariners tend to be larger than the rest of us), and he could set off the hammering and oaths just by walking across the room.

We moved closer to the canal, to another rented flat, when I was only about three, and we left Randolph Avenue behind. I never lived there again, though I have wandered down the street many times, and watched the slow transformation of the red-light district, first into respectability, and then into luxury. I ran into a couple at a dinner party a few years ago who lived in a tiny flat at the very top of the very building where I started out. They told me that our flat – which had so shocked my grandparents' families – was now inhabited by the head of Benetton Europe. It had become, through the strange metamorphosis of gentrification, a fitting home for the new class of ultra-rich.

I tell this story to show how, during my lifetime – even my adult lifetime – my contemporaries and I have witnessed an extraordinary revolution in the fortunes of the middle classes, from the widespread doubts in the mid-1970s whether they could survive at all, through to their recent apotheosis under Margaret Thatcher a decade later. It was a revolution that began with DIY and was carried forward – leaping and out of control – into staggering house-price inflation, as previously careful and respectable middle-class investors began to cream off the rewards of the next property bubble. Public policy, under all the prime ministers during that period, has been intended, if often quite wrong-headedly, to promote the middle-class life ever since.

So here is the question at the heart of this book. Given that extraordinary shift in fortunes – and that cascade of money through property and financial services known as Big Bang – why is it that the middle classes feel so threatened? Why have they been sidelined by a new and aggressive international class of mega-rich? Why have their homes and way of life and retirements become virtually unaffordable, with home ownership falling steadily, and now lower than in Romania and Bulgaria? Why are they in such a panic about their children's education? Why has their professional judgement been shunned? And why have they allowed their hard-working duty to career, family and salary to be so futile – given that, however successful they become, there is a banker half their age whose bonus makes them look ridiculous? In short, why are we wondering again whether the distinctive lifestyles of the English middle classes can survive?

Those are the questions I have set out to answer, and finding the solution is a kind of detective story. There were the middle classes – successful, privileged. What flung them into such desperate straits? What were the crucial moments that were to spell disaster, the decisions that went so terribly wrong? Who was responsible?

It is next to impossible to pin down the first cause for this intense crisis, because you can happily follow the strands back generations to find it, perhaps even to the beginnings of the modern middle classes in the 1820s. So I have followed the recent clues as best I can, and pinpointed six critical moments of decision – six moments, all within recent history, when disaster could perhaps have been averted. This is a whodunnit, after all. There are clues and suspects and red herrings. There are motives to be weighed and witnesses to be questioned. By the end, I hope we can begin to agree who struck the fatal blow, and work out whether the victim has any hope of rebirth – and, if so, how.

But before we set out with our deerstalkers and magnifying glasses, there is just a little more I need to say about myself. Because this can never be an objective study, and I don't want to claim that it is. As in the best detective stories, the narrator of this one is involved in the action. I am complicit because I am middle-class myself. I live in a small detached home with a lawn. I have an allotment. I shop at Waitrose, at least when I can afford it. I buy olive oil and have bizarre food allergies. Any detective needs to know how far they can trust the evidence I bring.

There is also something peculiar going on when people talk about the middle classes. In the course of writing this book I carried out a huge number of conversations with friends and acquaintances, and some people I had never met before, about being middle-class. Many of them would 'admit' to it, 'confess' to it, or even apologize at the outset. Yes, they would say, I *am* middle-class – 'I'm afraid', as if they were confessing to alcoholism. It happened so often that I came to expect it.

In the course of writing the book, I thought a great deal about this. I don't believe it is anything new. A generation ago, when the financial journalist Patrick Hutber wrote his book *The Decline and Fall of the Middle Class*, he said that no class in history had been quite so complicit in its own demise. So I have been asking myself this question too: why do we have to apologize? It isn't a rhetorical question but a genuine one, and it seems to me that there are three reasons.

The first is that the term 'middle-class' sounds like 'middle-aged' or 'middlebrow'. It sounds miserably ordinary, and there is a vague implication of smugness about it – as if we don't care how ordinary we are. I think we can discard this one: many of the best artists, sportspeople, scientists, writers, teachers and leaders have been middle-class. It is just silly to write the lot of us off as 'suburban', as if sub-urban meant that we were somehow sub-human. I reject the charge.

The second reason is that saying 'I am middle-class' may seem somehow to embrace all the disapproval and prejudice peddled by middle-class people in all generations. That may be so, and I will return to this later in the book.

The third reason also has some merit. It is the implication that, when we say we are middle-class, we are admitting that we are privileged. It is the same for me. I am a self-employed writer so I am hardly wealthy (I am probably the only person to conduct an independent review for the government on tax credits). But I went to independent school in Bristol, in the days when we still called them 'public schools', and was constantly told that I was privileged

– without being told what that might imply. Yet this only matters if we are exclusively self-interested as well as privileged. By writing about the plight of the middle classes, I am not implying that nobody else is suffering – quite the reverse. I don't want the middle classes to survive at the *expense* of anyone else, but I do want them to survive.

Even so, this book is bound to be dismissed by some people as special pleading by the privileged, and it is true that the middle classes have the huge advantages of capital, inheritance, confidence and political influence. Yet none of those privileges look like providing their next generation with a roof over their heads. I am certainly not suggesting that the plight of the middle classes is anything like the plight of the working classes. If middle-class professionals have suffered from new, narrow forms of efficiency, then the working classes are oppressed all the more by the same forces, timed and regimented, targeted and manipulated, often for a miserable pittance that still keeps them dependent on the state. If the middle-class jobs have been disappearing – and they have – working-class jobs have all but disappeared.

What this amounts to is that I *don't* apologize for writing about the middle classes or for being middle-class. I am not denying that anybody else is in trouble. I am certainly not saying that the middle classes are sinless, or wholly innocent of their own demise. But I make no apology for defending them, or assuming that they are worth defending, because – despite the disapproval and the reserve – I believe there is something about middle-class life in the UK that is worth preserving. Not the privilege, not the snobbery, but the right of everyone to live the kind of independent life that I was brought up with and which I struggle to provide for my own family.

So yes, I am middle-class, 'I'm afraid' – but I'm not really ashamed of it. Because somewhere in this whodunnit are the clues that might prevent us all from sinking into a new proletarian semi-slavery. So in the best traditions of Miss Marple, the most middle-class detective of them all, bring your knitting and your notebook and help me piece together the evidence.

1

The scene of the crime

> 'I still look up to him [the upper-class man] because, although I
> have money, I am vulgar. But I am not as vulgar as him [the
> working-class man], so I still look down on him.'
>
> Ronnie Barker, as the middle-class man,
> in The Frost Report, 1966

Shona Sibary is a Daily Mail columnist who reveals the intimate
details of middle-class life, from the woman's point of view. Her
husband Keith and son Monty have regular walk-on parts in this
everyday story of suburban folk. But none of her revelations
struck a chord quite like the description of losing her £400,000
family home in 2009, after remortgaging four times and seeing
the mortgage payments rise by £3,000 a month.[1]

It was a moving and honest account, as she described the misery
of driving past her old house every day. 'What I could never have
known is how soul-destroying it is to raise children in a house
that is not your own,' she wrote:

Sometimes it feels like we are guests in the one place we should
feel ourselves. So when Dolly draws on the wall with crayon or
Monty spills juice on the carpet, I know at the end of our lease
these normal spots of family life will be totted up as wear and tear
and added to our bill. I miss marking the children's heights on a
wall, to look back on in years to come. And, last year, we couldn't

bury our beloved labrador in the garden when he died. I'm pretty sure that digging graves for family pets is not permitted in the tenancy agreement.

Shona Sibary got into the financial mess she did partly by sticking with such determination to the commitment to educate her children privately, and that made her the target for some criticism. The decision to endlessly remortgage is not in her favour either, as the angry middle-class readers of Mumsnet pointed out in furious terms. Of course, lots of people have to bring up children in a home that is not their own, but there is something about this angst-ridden glimpse that will be recognized at once by home-owners everywhere. The terrifying fall from grace that the middle classes dread in all ages. The submission to the power of the landlord. The loss of freedom to manage your family in your own peculiar way if you want to.

There is familiar horror and fascination about any middle-class eviction, and any painful revelations about the gap between middle-class appearance and desperate reality. That may explain why the media have often returned to this theme since the financial collapse of 2008. There is a thrilling there-but-for-the-grace-of-God feeling about it, a relief that – for all our own money troubles – we have so far avoided that particular pitfall.

But there has been a further element to the media coverage, as if there was a bit of a mystery to be solved. Why is it, asked the *Daily Mail* in another article, headed 'The nouveau poor', that families on twice the average UK household income are in such desperate financial straits? 'We don't put the heating on very much at all, even during that freezing spell in December,' said Christina Reynolds, who runs a catering company in south-east London, and earns £60,000 together with her husband.[2] 'We snuggled under our blankets to watch TV and took the icy chill off the beds with hot-water bottles. Our utility bills are usually about £100 a month and recently they have gone up by almost a quarter.'

There was a parallel here with Shona Sibary. One reason why apparently affluent middle-class couples could hardly afford central heating was that Christina and her husband were determined to go on paying £12,000 a year for their son to go to independent school, as so many do. It was also true of the middle-class blogger Deborah Lane, who has been going online to explain why she was then struggling financially. This deserved closer inspection. When you have a £900,000 home in west London at your disposal, and the endless leafy suburbs of middle-class book clubs, parents' evenings and recycling classes stretching all around, why would you worry about money? I went to see Deborah to find out.

Deborah Lane is something of a bellwether. When she wrote the words 'I'm skint' on her blog, tracking the peculiarities of a middle-class life in London, her readership suddenly went up from double figures to somewhere in the thousands. It wasn't that she was looking for sympathy. It wasn't even that she was claiming that she was particularly unusual or interesting, at least as far as her dwindling wealth was concerned. But it was written as a cry from the heart of the beleaguered middle classes, and those googlers in the ether heard her and responded.

Of course, there are people in the world far worse off than Deborah, even in the London borough of Ealing – probably even in her street. The difficulty when it comes to writing about this is that unearned privilege (which might not be worth saving) and the idea of putting education first, despite sacrifice and struggle (which might), are all inextricably confused.

'I would say I had aspirations,' Deborah tells me as we sip our coffee and tea next to the river in Hammersmith. Her dark glasses glint with reflected elevenses. 'I always wanted to be married. I knew where I was going to live and how I was going to live. I wasn't really driven by how much money I was going to earn,' she goes on, explaining that it hasn't really turned out like that, despite her husband's earnings as a successful photographer.

'I never thought we would be struggling in the way that we are, for every little thing. We do get to do some of the nice things, but not without some kind of anguish. I have to get my loyalty schemes and it goes down each time. We can no longer afford to go away. Our main summer holiday is five days in Majorca in the half-term, when the prices are lower [than in summer itself].'

Of course, a great deal of Deborah's angst is bound up with the banking crisis and the recession that has followed. She agrees that she still leads a 'privileged life'. But there is something about her predicament which is recognizable to the nation's supposedly affluent classes, and exactly the same mixture of frustrated aspirations and threatened values is shared a good deal more widely. 'Just trying to keep where we are, and downshifting a tiny bit; that's what we're aspiring to,' she says. 'I say to my kids: don't break that because can't afford to replace it. We've come off the AA. Our gas boiler is playing up and we can't mend it because our policy still charges a £50 call-out.'

So why is she struggling to educate her two children privately? 'Long, long ago, when we had savings and pensions, holidays and cleaners, we were in the privileged position,' she wrote in her blog, 'not so much to pay for our children to attend a newly founded independent primary school in the next town, as to pay for them not to attend our allocated state version in the next road.'

Once again, this is instantly recognizable. It is easy to disapprove of middle-class parents who baulk at the prospect of sending their children to the school they have been allocated, until it comes to your own children and their welfare – which explains the stressful competition for places in 'good' schools, especially perhaps where Deborah lives in west London.[3] The allocated state school offered to put her son on the 'gifted children' programme just because he could spell a couple of three-letter words at the age of five, she said. It made her absolutely determined not to take up their offer, but the decision costs money. A lot of it.

She describes how she and her husband have stopped paying into a pension in the struggle to keep paying the fees in dribs and drabs. 'They're not even instalments; they are kind of random instalments – here's another £800 to go in the pot. We have already spent £100,000 in school fees, and my kids are only seven and nine, and they are in the cheapest private school in this area.'

It is a huge financial commitment, and Deborah was about to get two jobs to help pay for the summer, when the children would be at home, but here she runs foul of the dilemma haunting all struggling parents. One recent part-time job offer would have paid her £18,000 for the year, but tax and holiday childcare would have gobbled up £17,000 of it.

Only 7 per cent of UK parents pay school fees (much the same as it was a generation ago, though 17 per cent of school places in London are private). The fees at secondary level are beyond all but the very highest-paid, but scholarships and other assisted places are much more available than they used to be. Yet there is something else implied in the conversation with Deborah that is important. It is the fear that this angst, the one described in terms like 'nouveau poor', has nothing to do with the temporary economic downturn, and that there is a fundamental shift going on – a permanent crisis that marks the slow decline of the middle classes as an identifiable segment of British life. The fear is that this marks the end, not so much of privilege, but of what the middle classes believe they stand for – education, culture, leadership. Perhaps also imagination, though that is hardly a traditional attribute of the English middle classes – but at least the ability, however unexercised, to think for yourself.

It isn't that somehow these values belong nowhere else, and – yes, of course – the middle classes are known for a whole range of attributes that most of us could cheerfully consign to the scrapheap. Snobbery, conformity, curtain-twitching suburban dullness, who wants those? But they also stand, traditionally, for other things which we can ill-afford to lose, and education is often at the heart of them. Not just education, but independence and learning for its own sake – and the need to sacrifice wealth and well-being to achieve it. The fear is that this generation will be the last to live the aspirational middle-class life, that the future will be an endless, heartbreaking succession of small shifts downwards towards a precarious existence, dependent on mean employers, short contracts, demanding landlords and state handouts in old age.

'Once we move out of London, we don't have a pension, so we will have to sell to realize some cash,' said Deborah, thinking ahead nervously. 'We will have to move to a much smaller property and move twice, first time so the children can go to school, and for the second time so we will have some money to use as a pension. We're never going to be going up again – we're just going to be going down. My financial planning at the moment revolves around getting a lottery ticket once a week.'

'All my friends are struggling,' she adds, and again she is not alone. Two-thirds of middle-income people in the UK are not saving for a pension. Half of them also struggle with bills every day, but the unease goes deeper than paying the bills in the middle of a global downturn.

Here is the point. The middle classes don't like to mention it too openly, and they find it hard to articulate it even to themselves. But the truth is that they can no longer afford the life they always imagined having. It isn't that they are greedy or want something for nothing. But they did assume, because that is what they were always told, that they would have a life like their parents and grandparents – a comfortable home, a respected professional position, good schools for their children.

They now willingly submit to a quarter of a century of mortgage discipline – in jobs that frustrate them and force them to buy in expensive childcare – just to pay hugely inflated house prices. And no matter how much they earn, there is a banker's bonus somewhere that makes their effort look ridiculous (even in these days of slimmed-down bonuses). Worse, they seem unlikely to be able to fund their own retirement, except by the very house-price inflation that will exclude their children from the housing market.

It wasn't supposed to be like that. Their middle-class parents and grandparents lived respected lives as local doctors, lawyers and as a range of other professionals and managers. Now many of those positions have disappeared outside London, except as unionized supplicants to central government largesse. As a by-product of their own political success, they have also backed the creation of a new privileged class of Übermenschen in the financial sector, who inflate the prices for everyone else – and whose salaries and bonuses make a mockery of the values they were brought up with.

So here is the dilemma for the English middle classes. They are like the proverbial frog in a frying pan, unable to make a leap into the unknown to escape being fried – but knowing it was also them who turned on the stove in the first place. They hate complaining, certainly about losing privileges. But the middle classes believed themselves to be the respectable backbone of a respectable, successful nation. Brought up to stand for something beyond money, they have found their values eroded, misunderstanding the difference between making money and creating wealth. They have colluded in a new dispensation which assumes that shopping is the highest aspiration and which undermines their independence as professionals.

'The middle class, as we knew it, is not long for this world,' wrote the journalist William Leith in the Daily Telegraph, hitting the nail on the head.[4] Leith described the moment the penny dropped for one man when he was looking for a job. 'Everything's changed,' he said. 'Now you have to be talented, or make people think you're talented. Being qualified counts for nothing. I mean, these days, everybody's got a degree.'

Then he described the middle-class credo:

> People could be teachers, or civil servants – not rapacious capitalists, but ordinary, quiet, middle-class people – and still live in detached houses, and buy new cars, and go on holiday to the south of France. And they had decent pensions to look forward to afterwards. That was what being middle class was all about. You passed your exams. You got a job. You stayed out of trouble. In return, you felt safe. And now, it looks like all of that is slipping away. And who knows, soon it might be gone for good.

That description feels right. It is the sheer lack of ambition that used to be such a feature of middle-class life that this captures, and it does indeed feel like it is slipping away. Increasingly, the middle classes are finding that they can't afford it, even when they are earning twice the average income. Why should that be? What went wrong? The answers are in some ways the same as the ones given by Deep Throat in an underground car park during the Watergate affair. The key lies in following the money.

'I feel like I'm stuck, like I can't breathe, like I'm in quicksand,' said Brooklyn Davis, unemployed in Pittsburgh, about his financial plight.[5] Davis was not middle-class, even in the USA, but it is strange, once you start researching the current plight of the middle classes, how this word 'stuck' keeps coming up over and over again.

'We are stuck,' one human resources manager told the *Guardian* newspaper in 2011. 'At the end of the month, what with rent and extortionate costs of travel, we have nothing left. In fact, less than nothing, which is a bit of a shocker.'[6] Shona Sibary used the same word describing the plight of her family when they had their home repossessed. As Deborah Lane implied, this feeling of being 'stuck' emerged before the banking crisis and the downturn. When the Department of Work and Pensions began investigating the so-called 'squeezed middle' in 2006, it found that – even then – a quarter of middle-income earners could not afford a week's family holiday. Six per cent of them couldn't afford to send children swimming once a month. According to the TUC, the same proportion of middle-income people were worried about their jobs as were the very lowest earners. Not all of them paying school fees by any means.

Even by the middle of the last decade – years before the financial crisis – the number of middle-class families earning more than £30,000 who were looking for debt advice had tripled.[7] These were the boom years. It had nothing to do with the global downturn.

When the Bath University professor Guy Standing coined the phrase 'the Precariat' in 2011, to describe those on low to middle incomes that exist in a precarious succession of short-term contracts, my impression is that it wasn't intended to include the traditional middle class (he calls them the 'salariat').[8] But in fact the same precarious existence, struggling with the costs of a respectable, civilized life, while the generous Victorian provision of parks and libraries shrinks before their eyes, is affecting the middle classes too. Perhaps not so corrosively, but as a terrifying future prospect that they can see all too clearly, it is there. The Precariat has no control over its time – that is Guy Standing's definition – and one definition of the middle classes since the Industrial Revolution is that they have leisure time.[9] Of course the middle classes still have some control over their time, over-mortgaged and over-indebted as they are, but it is increasingly uncertain.

There is also no doubt that middle-class life has grown more and more precarious, all part of the complicated relationship between the costs of mortgages, childcare and transport which make all the difference in the Micawberesque calculation that families have to go through these days: mortgage payments, food, fuel, childcare, holidays, credit card bills £4,001 a month; income £4,000 a month – result: penury.

Partly because of the cost of accommodation, the plight of middle-income earners is again not that different from the plight of the lower-income earners. Even those on higher incomes (over £66,600 a year) face housing and fuel bills up 110 per cent during the last decade: 17 per cent of them can't afford holidays and 40 per cent have no savings for retirement.[10] This is, after all, the biggest squeeze in living standards since the 1870s according to the economist Roger Bootle.[11] There is a financial squeeze going on, and this is what it looks like:

The Mortgage Squeeze Until 1988, mortgages worth more than three times the joint salaries of couples were extremely rare. By 2005, a fifth of all mortgages were based on multiples of four times joint salaries or more. Almost a third of Londoners say they expect to be driven out of London by rising housing costs (a typical London deposit is now £85,000).[12] Nor is it just London: Dorset and Wiltshire are actually the least affordable places in the UK. House prices in Truro and Edinburgh have gone up by over 500 per cent in the last quarter of a century.[13] House prices have quadrupled in real terms during my lifetime (I was born in 1958), as I said. If they had stayed steady, the average home would now cost £43,000 at today's prices, rather than £250,000, which is the actual cost.

The University Squeeze The US middle classes have been hit by an unprecedented increase in the cost of going to university, with fees rising from 10 per cent of median income at US public-sector universities in 2005 to 25 per cent now, and the same process is clearly happening here. Already we have £35 billion outstanding in student loans, and the fees look set to burst through the current barrier of £9,000 a year.

The Childcare Squeeze Childcare in the UK is said to be the most expensive in the world, and takes up to 28 per cent of the average income of a two-income family – it costs £5,000 a year for twenty-five hours a week for a single two-year-old in a nursery. This is the main factor forcing a quarter of parents into debt.[14] Part of the problem is that, unlike Scandinavia and North America, we have lost our mutually run nurseries – mainly through misplaced fears about 'safeguarding', and a general and unaccountable feeling that parents are the last people who should be trusted to look after children.

The Pensions Squeeze The stock-market collapse, and the end of the long boom in stock prices, has meant miserable returns for those private pensions so many of us took out in the 1980s and 1990s. Gordon Brown's decision to tax pensions income in 1997 looks as if it also reduced the money going into pensions by about £5 billion every year. The number of 'defined benefit' schemes open to new members has been falling steadily for a decade and has now trickled down to almost nothing. People are left increasingly with the far less valuable 'defined contribution' schemes. Final salary schemes are also being replaced by average lifetime earnings. All this means that most middle-income groups look set to lose 60 per cent of their income in retirement, and low bond yields, low stock-market returns and slowing house prices will put them further at risk.

The Education Squeeze Education is central to the whole idea of the English middle classes, but for a long time now most of them have been priced out of independent education (average fees are now £23,000 for boarders and £11,000 for day pupils, with more for uniforms and extra-curricular activities, and that is for each child) – the 'preserve of the super-rich', according to the former High Master of St Paul's.[15] The result is the extraordinary worry and struggle to get into good state schools, which drives up property prices around the best schools by around 35 per cent (up to £77,000 extra).[16] This is a nightmare labyrinth, according to a report to the Greater London Assembly, where the middle classes 'play the system'.[17] True, but they play it against each other, putting ever more pressure on their poor overstretched children with frenetic after-school CV-building activities.

The Status Squeeze 'I feel stuck' – that familiar cry – said Andrew Schiff, marketing director for the New York brokers Europe Pacific Capital, whose bonus was down to $350,000 and no longer covered private school fees and summer rents. 'People who don't have money don't understand the stress,' explained the New York accountant Alan Dlugash. 'I got three kids in private school; I have to think about pulling them out? How do you do that?'[18] These are extreme examples, but the same is increasingly true in the UK. Our parents' generation could feel reasonably secure once they had reached a certain income. Now it doesn't matter how successful you are – there is always someone paid staggeringly more who can make you feel as if you are struggling, and who pushes up the prices to make it even worse. 'These people never dreamed they'd be making $500,000 a year,' Dlugash said about his clients, 'and dreamed even less they'd be broke.'

There is the middle-class crisis at a glance. It is about money, and about much more than money, but the heart of all this is still house prices, which are the subject of the next chapter. Middle-class homeowners put up with spending between 20 and 40 per cent of their income on mortgages because the prices are rising, and it seems like a more reliable pension than when they invested so nervously and pointlessly in the stock market. Conventional wisdom also suggests that this will at least mean a huge transfer of value from one generation to the next, just in time to pay the vast deposits on their children's houses – and 63 per cent can't buy a house now without help from relatives. And it wouldn't come a moment too soon, because those born after 1985 are the first UK generation not to enjoy better living conditions than those born ten years before.[19]

But we should hardly hold our breaths, because this cascade of wealth down the generations is actually slowing down. Homeowners need the money for other things. For one thing, they are living much longer and their homes are also their pensions. For another thing, about half of them will need their homes to pay for care bills as they get older, and 50,000 homes a year are already sold to pay for care.

There, in a nutshell, is the heart of the fear: that once the middle classes peer towards their children's future, there seems no way that they will be able to afford a home themselves. Halifax, now part of the banking conglomerate HBOS, calls this next generation 'Generation Rent'. They mean children whose parents are homeowners but who will be raising their own children in rented accommodation, and at hugely inflated rents, because rents are also related to the cost of buying property.

How will they ever be able to buy homes or shake off their debts, or even the housing debts of their parents? Especially when policy and economic circumstances have combined to provide an extraordinary shift in resources backwards from the next generation to their baby-boomer parents, the phenomenon outlined by the higher education minister David Willetts in his much-debated book *The Pinch*. Willetts showed how the baby-boom generation benefited from free higher education, low house prices and inflation to eat away at their debts. And now when the debts are almost paid off, they benefit from low income taxes and low interest rates. 'The boomers, roughly those born between 1945 and 1965, have done and continue to do some great things but now the bills are coming in,' he wrote, 'and it is the younger generation who will pay them.'[20]

The middle classes – those that dare to look ahead – see their children being flung into a proletarian struggle to maintain any kind of roof over their heads. 'It is as if your parents die leaving a treasure chest,' wrote Willetts, 'and, when you open it, you discover a pile of IOUs which you are obliged to pay.'[21]

But there is something else going on here which affects the middle classes, however you define them, in many developed countries. Middle incomes in the USA and Canada have flatlined for three decades now. Even in Germany, real monthly incomes have been falling. In fact, the term 'squeezed middle' came originally from the United States, where the term 'middle class' is usually used to mean what it says – those on average incomes – rather than the extra superstructure of values and social aspirations that the term has come to stand for in the UK.

There certainly is a middle-class problem in the USA, where 4 million families are believed to be in danger of sliding into poverty and one in four middle-class households are about to drop down onto the lower rung, spending a quarter of their incomes just servicing debt.[22] It is different over there, but there are important parallels between the UK and USA, which is why the Labour leader Ed Miliband borrowed the American phrase 'squeezed middle' in 2011. The parallel has also been noticed by one of the most important commentators on world affairs. Francis Fukuyama is busily charting the decline of the middle classes in all developed nations.

Into the misty past, the middle classes have benefited from rising above the undifferentiated masses, Fukuyama implies. Now they are being driven back into the undifferentiated mass by a new global elite which is benefiting from the shifts in the financial world over the past generation. Once the middle classes siphoned off wealth to provide themselves with comfortable lives, now they are the victims of the siphoning – and siphoning on a vast scale.

What is happening is most obvious in the USA, where it drove the massive growth of inequality over the past generation. In 1974, the top 1 per cent of families took home 9 per cent of GDP. By 2007, that share had increased to 23.5 per cent. But this isn't just the USA, because the same global and technological shifts are happening everywhere, says Fukuyama, from off-shoring to replacing skilled jobs with IT systems. 'What if the further development of technology and globalisation undermines the middle class and makes it impossible for more than a minority of citizens in an advanced society to achieve middle-class status?' he asks:[23]

The other factor undermining middle-class incomes in developed countries is globalisation. With the lowering of transportation and communications costs and the entry into the global work force of hundreds of millions of new workers in developing countries, the kind of work done by the old middle class in the developed world can now be performed much more cheaply elsewhere. Under an economic model that prioritizes the maximisation of aggregate income, it is inevitable that jobs will be outsourced.

We have become so used to the idea that the middle classes are the winners, as they have been since time immemorial, that it is difficult to get our heads around the fact that this has now changed. The middle classes are no longer winning. They are losing out, and losing out devastatingly, to the rise of a whole new class which has become known as the 'One Per Cent' (1 per cent may be an overstatement: in the UK, 0.6 per cent of the population earns more than £150,000 a year). It was this phenomenon that the great investor Warren Buffett referred to in 2006 when he confirmed the existence of a 'class war'. 'But it's my class, the rich class, that's making war and we're winning,' he said, fearful of the consequences.

The One Per Cent is dominated by people in financial services, and at the top of the global corporations, plus perhaps a handful of global bureaucrats. It is a deeply interconnected world – one study showed 94 directors holding 266 directorships in 22 corporations.[24] But the real point is that they are doing very well. The number of billionaires in the world grew from 225 in 1996 to 946 in 2006. These are the customers for $45 million personal Gulfstream jets. They control two-thirds of the world's total assets. They are the reason why house prices are so high in London and the south-east.

All this explains to some extent the vast transfer of public money to the banks from 2008 onwards, but we all know about that (£1.5 trillion in the UK alone). What is less understood is that there is something bigger going on: a huge transfer of assets from the middle classes to the new elite. Labour's business secretary Peter Mandelson once said that the Labour Party was 'intensely relaxed about people getting filthy rich', but actually it *does* matter. House prices are higher as a result, the salaries of those lower down the food chain are squeezed, pensions are top-sliced, while the financial class has become a new kind of landlord, living off the rents and charges of the financial system which funnel wealth upwards – while real wages, and real salaries, haven't risen in real terms since 1970, and since 1960 in the USA where the process is most established.

This all sounds a little like a conspiracy theory, but the figures are stark. And although the phenomenon is hardly ever discussed in the media, it is discussed among the very rich. In 2005, the first of three reports was published privately by the US banking giant Citigroup, especially for their wealthiest clients; they coined a word to describe the phenomenon and tried to explain it. The first report was called 'Plutonomy', and it explained the idea like this:

> The world is dividing into two blocs – the plutonomies, where economic growth is powered by and largely consumed by the wealthy few, and the rest. Plutonomies have occurred before in sixteenth century Spain, in seventeenth century Holland, the Gilded Age and the Roaring Twenties in the US. We project that the plutonomies (the US, UK, and Canada) will likely see even more income inequality, disproportionately feeding off a further rise in the profit share in their economies, capitalist-friendly governments, more technology-driven productivity, and globalization. In a plutonomy there is no such animal as 'the US consumer' or 'the UK consumer', or indeed the 'Russian consumer'. There are rich consumers, few in number, but disproportionate in the gigantic slice of income and consumption they take. There are the rest, the 'non-rich', the multitudinous many, but only accounting for surprisingly small bites of the national pie . . .[25]

Two more reports followed in 2006, explaining that plutonomy was a result of a kind of *financialization* of the economy – a huge expansion into financial assets, which are the target for investment rather than real assets, and which the financial sector repackages and repackages, inflating their prices each time. When the financial bubbles burst, they buy back the assets again at a lower cost. Even bursting bubbles make the One Per Cent better off. This is helped by the fact that the most powerful governments of the world see the value of those assets – property, bank shares etc. – as the touchstone of economic success, which is why so much of the banking bailout was designed to reflate their value.

Citigroup came to regret publishing these reports, presumably because it encouraged the idea that they were cheerleaders for plutonomy. Over the years, copies began to leak out via the

Internet, much to their horror. There was a concerted attempt to suppress them. By 2010, Citigroup lawyers had managed to remove them all from the Web, only to find them seeping back again. The revelations are important because not only are these vital resources sucked out of the middle classes, just as they are sucked out of all classes, they also affect the middle classes in other ways. Unless they work in the financial sector themselves, they find their factories and real-world businesses starved of investment and their professional skills automated.

Even so, it isn't really a conspiracy. It is a peculiar twist of the way our economy has become unbalanced towards financial products rather than real ones, and it is a real phenomenon. It is a practical acceleration of the division between two worlds – one where money is infinitely elastic and where mistakes get bailed out, and the world of the rest of us, including the indebted middle classes, for whom money is concrete and unforgiving. There is something about the frenetic generation of outsourcing, streamlining and offshoring, and the whole business of permanent restructuring, that has quietly shifted power and profit away from the middle classes. 'Instead of democracy widening and deepening as we had hoped,' writes the eminent Conservative writer Ferdinand Mount, 'power and wealth have slowly and unmistakably, begun a long migration into the hands of a relatively small elite'.[26]

When 1 per cent of the world owns a quarter of all the wealth, leaving the middle class scrambling for the crumbs that fall from the rich man's table, then a different kind of lifestyle becomes necessary. Over the past generation, it slowly began to dawn on the English middle classes – who believed with some reason that the financial service professionals and their institutions were firmly on their side – that it wasn't like that at all. Something had shifted, very quietly, very dangerously, and actually the signs were there a generation back.

* * *

Christopher Stockwell was a successful businessman and property developer. He was the very model of middle-class success, the son of a clergyman and an innovative campaigner for development causes in his youth. But in the mid-1980s he began to be sucked into the peculiar – and now largely forgotten – story of financial incompetence and staggering callousness (and probably worse) at the ancient insurers Lloyd's of London. Within a few years, he had been made bankrupt, lost his home and found himself at the head of a campaign to unravel what had happened to so many ordinary middle-class families, and get them some kind of redress.

Even now, two decades after the events of the Lloyd's Scandal became clear, it has a shock value which seems to speak to the plight of the middle classes today. It is somehow the sheer respectability of the families caught up in the scandal that gives it such a peculiar edge, drawn in because they trusted this apparently respectable financial institution, when actually the world had changed.

Stockwell is a tall, imposing presence, six foot six inches in his socks. His upbringing was impeccably middle-class: born in the shadow of Romsey Abbey. As a young man, he was a Labour councillor in Letchworth and one of the founders of the World Development Movement, but he was also one of those people who seemed hardly able to stop himself making money. He had an antiques business, a reproduction furniture business, up to forty properties and much else besides. He describes his property skills as like a sixth sense, being able to 'see through walls'. 'I can see the possibilities of spaces,' he says.

It was also the property boom, as it was with so many other people, that brought him into contact with Lloyd's of London, which he found had a highly unusual, even archaic, structure. Lloyd's is made up of a whole number of syndicates, known usually by the name of the underwriter in charge, and each one was supported by a whole range of ordinary investors known as

'Names'. These Names would need at least £37,500, a third of which would have to be deposited with Lloyd's, but they would accept a bank guarantee based on the value of your home (£37,500 was worth about £150,000 today). You didn't have to be rich, and this explained why people whose wealth was almost entirely made up by notional increases In the value of their home became caught up in the scandal.

All this meant that becoming a Lloyd's Name was within the reach of anyone with some equity in their homes. It was also considered a safe investment. Thousands of ordinary people signed up to become Names after a recruitment drive in the early 1980s. The problem was that the new recruits were actually signing a guarantee that they would underwrite losses as well as profits made by their syndicate. It included the wholly irrational concept of 'unlimited liability'.

This was a fiction. How could such a thing exist? But the newly recruited Names were assured there was no risk. Nobody had ever been bankrupted and you could sign up for an insurance policy of your own to pay any debts up to £135,000.

'There they were, sitting on a house which had gone up hugely in value,' said Christopher Stockwell. 'They were asset-rich, while their retirement income was going down. They were wheeled around Lloyd's and the agent got a commission and they would get a five per cent return on the value of their house. It seemed totally secure. This was Lloyd's, after all, not a bunch of shyster gangsters.'

Stockwell became interested in Lloyd's as an investment and joined in 1978. The way that Lloyd's works meant that years had to be 'closed', with no more claims expected, before they could distribute the profits. Of course, there might be liabilities to pay for previous years as well – and Names were responsible for previous years before they joined – but, all being well, he would expect his first cheque some time early in the 1980s.

The problem was that all was *not* well with Lloyd's. What Stockwell had not been told was that underwriting mistakes were about to threaten the very existence of Lloyd's – based on a combination of their collective failure to understand how the world was changing, combined with a fatal clubbishness that preferred to shove bad news under the table. Nor had the twenty thousand ordinary Names recruited after 1982 been told either. The establishment had consistently closed ranks to prevent proper regulation of Lloyd's, and this was about to guarantee financial misery for many of those middle-class investors who had been assured that being a Name might be a good way of helping out with the grandchildren's school fees. It was also providing a strange dress rehearsal for the far greater banking scandal and collapse in 2008.

The immediate trigger of disaster was the asbestosis insurance claims in the USA, though there were other disasters as well, natural and predictable. Asbestosis should have come as no surprise either to the companies or their insurers. The fact that exposure to asbestos fibres might cause cancer was first noticed way back in 1918 and confirmed in a series of medical studies in the 1920s. But it was a test case in the US Supreme Court in 1969 that made this directly relevant to the Lloyd's Names and their 'unlimited liability'.

The case concerned a former asbestos worker called Clarence Borel, and was brought by his widow, Thelma. He had been told so little about the little white asbestos fibres that were to kill him that he used to bring them back to decorate the Christmas tree at home. The Supreme Court found in favour of Thelma Borel, and, as a result, the asbestosis claims began to mount and the ultimate insurers – those with the unlimited liability – turned out to be some of the Lloyd's syndicates which specialized in reinsurance. In 1979, the US courts ruled that the insurers were liable for all the years between when the workers were exposed and when they fell ill.

Perhaps Lloyd's could not have reasonably predicted this extension of their liability, or the rise in hurricane damage, though it was clear in the world outside that both cancer liability and climate were changing. But the real problem was how the senior officials at Lloyd's responded. Exactly who was aware of what, and who was informed of what, was to be the subject of a series of legal actions in the UK, but Lloyd's bankers NatWest could see, and wrote a warning report – known since as the Armageddon report – about the terrifying implications for their clients. All copies later disappeared. The losses were small by then, but the line on the graph showing their rising impact was terrifyingly steep and getting steeper.

The appeal court ruled later that there had been a gross misrepresentation to the Names, but not fraud, and – although more evidence has come to light since – that is where matters now rest. The decision was important because the Conservative government of John Major had by that stage rushed through legislation giving Lloyd's immunity for negligence but not for fraud. They were not therefore responsible for ruining so many Names, yet this was another sign for the future. Among the huge privileges of the financial industry, as we have seen more recently, is that they have been so deregulated that they also have immunity for the results of their negligence, though not, so far anyway, for their fraud. In practice, it is hard to distinguish between the two.

The British establishment closed ranks, and for the first time – but definitely not the last – ordinary middle-class investors found themselves on the outside. Even when the implications for the Names should have been growing apparent, Lloyd's continued their recruitment campaign to attract new ones.

In his Oxfordshire home, running his businesses, Christopher Stockwell knew nothing of this. He realized at the start that it made a big difference which syndicate he joined. He met one of the rising stars of Lloyd's, Dick Outhwaite, liked him and joined his syndicate – and then joined others too. The first sign that there might be anything wrong appeared when it came to closing the books on that fateful year of 1982, because the Outhwaite auditors insisted on leaving the year open. Stockwell was angry about it and remonstrated with the auditors. By 1987, it was clear that something was extremely wrong and that losses on other syndicates had somehow been diverted onto one of his syndicates as the bearer of the ultimate risk. The following year, he summoned up his old campaigning experience and formed an action group.

Even so, he wasn't too worried. The losses at the troubled syndicate were being covered by profits from others. Never one to do things by halves, Stockwell was by now a member of many other syndicates, but more accounts for more years were being left worryingly open. Not until the end of 1991 did the penny drop. He had been expecting a cheque for £250,000. Instead, he got a demand for an immediate £500,000. Most ordinary investors would baulk at anything remotely on that scale, but Stockwell was no ordinary investor. The trouble was that, six weeks later, there was a similar letter. By February 1992, in the run-up to the election stand-off between John Major and Neil Kinnock, the demands were pouring in at the rate of £100,000 a week.

'It coincided with the collapse in property values and astronomical interest rates after Black Wednesday, and I was facing total wipeout,' he says. 'I had no income coming in. All my businesses were in receivership. I was spending 30 or 40 per cent of the time with the receivers, just picking up the pieces out of the chaos.'

The Stockwell family lost their home, which was then sold by the bank later in the summer, while they rented a cottage on what had been their land. In July, his bank made him bankrupt too. It was a desperate situation for a self-made man, and a huge strain on any marriage and on the children, especially when the furniture had to be sold.

'It was a catastrophic blow,' he says now. 'It was emotionally traumatic, leaving your home and everything, totally unclear about where the next meal was coming from.'

By then, Lloyd's was threatening 39,000 Names with legal action for failing to pay up. They could have approached the Lloyd's hardship fund they had set up under the fearsome chairmanship of Mary Archer, novelist Jeffrey Archer's fragrant spouse. But like Stockwell, many desperately resisted that fate too, because they would have had to accept all their losses, abandon any appeal over their fairness, and hand over all their other assets to Lloyd's.

Behind that 39,000 figure, the suffering was also now widespread. Elderly couples who had been persuaded to invest their money as Names found themselves evicted from their homes and living in caravans. There were very public suicides and very quiet divorces and evictions. People who had saved for their retirement their whole lives were finding themselves effectively on the street. Yes, they were a privileged class with family to fall back on. Yes, they had been chasing unlimited profits in return for those unlimited liabilities, but they had not been told the risks and were often no wealthier than the theoretical rise in value of their homes.

Within eighteen months there were more than twenty-five action groups, and Stockwell was involved in many of them. At one meeting of the activists, there was a stand-up row between two prominent Names. Stockwell, towering over both of them, told them to sit down and shut up. He attributes to this the decision to ask him to chair the meeting, which led him to chairing the Lloyd's Names Association and made him the obvious choice to chair Lloyd's Open Years Working Party, Lloyd's own attempt to hammer out a compromise.

Either way, it put him at the heart of a whirlwind. The phone rang at home all the time, and his young children had to learn how to deal with the outpourings of fear and betrayal that came down the line.

'I spent hours and hours listening to tales of human misery,' he says. 'From people who had just done what they had been told. Who never intended to take any real risks and who were losing everything. They just couldn't understand how this could happen.'

In that same year, 1992, the Sunday Times concluded that 'the professionals at Lloyd's are not fit to regulate a flea circus, never mind a multi-billion market'.[27]

But it was worse than that. It was quite clear by then that some Lloyd's professionals regularly kept the most profitable business for their own mini-syndicates, for their families and relatives, and shifted the loss-making ones onto the absent Names. It was also clear that the leading underwriters were themselves avoiding the worst-hit syndicates and warning friends and family away from them. They knew, but said nothing in public. The nod-and-wink culture that the English middle classes specialize in was being turned against them. 'Many members of the Lloyd's community in senior positions', concluded the 1986 Neill Report to Parliament, 'were not even vaguely aware of the legal obligations on agents to act at all times in the best interests of their principals, not to make secret profits at their principals' expense and to disclose fully all matters affecting their relationship with their principals.'[28]

The journalist Adam Raphael, himself a Name, described the plight of a secretary who had worked at one insurance brokers for twenty-five years. As a reward, the company chairman had asked her and a colleague if they would like to be Lloyd's Names, promising to provide the guarantee and an insurance 'stop-loss' policy. As her losses began to mount, she contacted the retired chairman, who had completely forgotten her existence. The new chairman replied in 1988: 'I am afraid there is nothing to suggest any sort of commitment to indemnify you against losses incurred by that membership. Indeed it would be highly unusual if any such arrangement did exist.' Her insurance policy would not pay out because the wording was wrong. When, in desperation, she contacted the chairman of Lloyd's, he warned her to do nothing that might 'prejudice the reputation of Lloyd's'.[29]

Julian Tennant attacked the underwriter of his syndicate at a meeting of Names in the Albert Hall in May 1993. 'Our faith in Lloyd's has been totally destroyed,' he said. 'It's bad enough to be forced to move out of your house into a small cottage, but it's even worse to learn that Mr Brockbank's salary [underwriter of his syndicate] was £430,000 last year. That is obscene.'[30] In 1988, the Lloyd's market made a loss of £500 million, but the managing agents and members' agents earned £124 million in commission. As late as 2009, another group of thirty-five Names were bankrupted at the end of their legal process.

Two decades on from the eye of the storm, Stockwell accepts that there were aspects of the experience that provided some compensation for the lost years and lost money. It was fascinating to work at the cutting edge of the law, dealing with some of the cleverest lawyers in the country. But in the end, the establishment shut the door on the Names and bolted it, and, despite the new evidence that he had amassed, the Court of Appeal refused to reopen the case against Lloyd's. Now, viewed with hindsight, the Lloyd's Scandal looks like a curtain-raiser for the banking scandal – the same refusal to provide proper regulation, the same scramble to cover things up, and to provide immunity for the financial community rather than to protect vulnerable people.

'The legal system let us down badly,' says Stockwell now. 'I understand why. I understand their need for the legal system to give some kind of finality. I understand the need to protect the Lloyd's market so that it could get back on its feet. But nevertheless, allowing the establishment to cover up was what made the banking crisis possible.'

Here is the conundrum of the story, and the paradox for the middle classes today. They believe the great financial institutions are on their side, believe they understand the way the world works, pride themselves even on their ability to navigate through it – they had welcomed the deregulation of financial services and all the other changes since the 1980s. But they have been horribly deluded.

The truth is that the world has changed, and the middle classes failed to see it. Their sturdy English conservatism has not served them well in this respect, because the financial sector is not on their side at all, and has not been for some time, and for reasons that go way beyond the shenanigans at Lloyd's. Through no one's fault and no one's conspiracy, their collective failure to see the world clearly has made them vulnerable – so vulnerable that their survival as a recognizable class is now in doubt.

There are two big objections to the thesis I have set out here, and we need to look at them now. Doing so will also force us, and not before time, to look at the other big question: who are the middle classes these days anyway?

There have always been middle classes, right back to ancient times. They were the professionals, the shopkeepers, the tax-collectors and all the rest of the population between the peasants and the aristocracy. There they were in Britain too, through the centuries, running the pubs, owning property, riding to hounds. But the great influx into the middle classes coincided with the development of the railways, so that – for the first time – they could move away from their place of work. They no longer needed to live over the shop. These were not so much gentry as commuters, setting up home in the suburbs, and their emergence coincided with a new kind of middle-class society, dedicated to independence from the tyranny of bosses and landlords. From Mr Pooter to Captain Mainwaring, they thrived well into the twentieth century, but not smoothly or universally. There was always the chance, as they were well aware, of a politician determined to squeeze them until the pips squeaked.

Perhaps the biggest shift came after the war when, thanks to the 1944 Education Act, the upper middle classes began to shift from the grammar schools to fee-paying independent schools, until the prices shot up out of reach at secondary level – while the new middle classes filled their places.

The first objection to the idea that the middle classes are disappearing is that, for as long as they have existed – and even Aristotle warned that it was important that they survived for the good of the state – there have been warnings or bleatings from inside them that their days were numbered. This is a collective peril for anyone who writes about the death of the middle classes. In fact, there have been so many predictions of their demise, all of them premature, that it is hard to imagine them expiring at all – despite everything I have set out so far.

The Marxist critic and novelist Raymond Williams famously talked about an 'escalator' that took every generation back nostalgically to a golden age a few generations before.[31] The same phenomenon seems to work the other way around for the struggling middle classes. For more than three decades I have until now left unread on my bookshelf a book by Patrick Hutber, one of the cheerleaders for Margaret Thatcher, called *The Decline and Fall of the Middle Class*.[32] This was at least subtitled 'How it can fight back', which did imply some hope.

The 1970s were certainly a tough period, especially for anyone practising 'thrift', which Hutber called the defining characteristic of the middle classes. For Hutber, the middle classes were the 'saving classes', which was difficult for them when inflation was then only just down from 25 per cent and the top rate of income tax stood at 83 per cent. He put a note in his *Sunday Telegraph* column asking for people to write to him, and was deluged with accounts of the mid-century middle-class life.

One correspondent described himself as 'up against the wall'. 'I haven't seen a play in London in two years. I only eat in restaurants on business. I can't afford the gardener once a week any more. You start adding it up and it amounts to a social revolution.'[33] 'It is my belief that, the way things are going, the middle classes are doomed to a gradual extinction over the course of the next generation or two,' said another. 'We are mainly living like the camel in the desert does on the fat stored in its hump.'[34] Another reply added, in typical middle-class self-deprecating style: 'I hope to receive the "final call" before the roof falls in.'[35]

Even the great egalitarian playwright J. B. Priestley was worried. 'The full effect in our culture, largely based on the middle class, has not been felt yet, but many of us are feeling gloomy about our prospects.' Who would have thought it: the Sage of Working-Class Bradford brought down to such a level of pessimism?[36] In 1974, the prominent Conservative MP John Gorst set up the Middle Class Association (he sent out a mailshot to people he knew might be interested, but the two or three replies he received back all said that, although they were interested, unfortunately they were upper-class).[37] It was taken over by a small right-wing group who kicked him out, renamed it and allowed it to collapse the following year. The middle classes are not good at political movements at the best of times.

You might think, given Hutber's fears, that the middle classes had never felt quite so embattled. Yet go back on the escalator another generation and you find a fascinating 1949 book by the future playwright and Washington editor of *The Economist* Roy Lewis and the future Conservative cabinet minister Angus Maude, father of the current Cabinet Office minister Francis Maude.[38] Like Hutber, they were writing at the end of a period of Labour government, in the austerity years, immediately after the abolition of most fee-paying in primary schools and grammar schools.

'We thought of calling it "The Decline and Fall of the Middle Class",' they wrote, 'but they are kicking so hard they must still be alive.'[39]

Again, you might think that the late 1940s were a unique

moment of fear and anxiety for the middle classes, because of uniquely high taxation and government on behalf of another class. Not a bit of it. Travel back on the time conveyor belt another generation and there was the *Daily Mail* castigating David Lloyd George's People's Budget, the one that introduced old-age pensions, under the headline 'Plundering the middle classes'. Three years before had seen the launch of the Middle Class Defence Organisation which ran candidates in the London County Council elections and eventually became the Middle Class Union. This was a branch of Middle Class International, though the existence of such an organization does make the mind boggle a little.

Here is a letter written to the *Daily News* just after the First World War, which might have come from Patrick Hutber's files:

> My wife goes 'sticking'. That saves the expenses of firewood, our holidays are generally imaginary. That saves too. My wife gets bargains at remnant sales, and rhubarb from the garden does yeoman service. Also my wife murders her eyes with sewing sewing, sewing. Saving is out of the question.[40]

The truth is that the middle classes have always felt beleaguered, and perhaps that isn't surprising, since they are almost by definition putting their money away for a rainy day, a home or the children's education. They are bound to be fearful of the future. Angus Maude and Roy Lewis talked about the middle classes always approaching the future with a mixture of 'dread and confidence'. What is different now?

Perhaps they were always indebted. Perhaps there have been periods when the middle classes exhausted themselves and their children with the desperate struggle for school places – though I'm not sure of that. Perhaps previous generations doubted that their children could lead a middle-class life. I don't know. But there is something different now. It is that, as we shall see and without their noticing, the very engines of thrift – the savings and financial sector – have turned against the middle classes and are actively funnelling their wealth out of their reach. They have disguised their fears of the future from themselves with ever greater debts, and their education, cars and holidays – core features of a middle-class life – are more often now funded by increasingly big loans.

There is no doubt that the English middle classes have an extraordinary gift for absorbtion and reinvention. Over the centuries they have integrated Roman Catholics, Jews, Nonconformists and a whole range of other domestic and immigrant groups, and are still doing so today. On the other hand, if the middle classes were really dedicated primarily to thrift – an idea that seems to have been banished by the credit card – you might reasonably wonder whether they still exist at all. In my own generation, in a period of rising prices, those who have done better financially are those who borrowed the most. Whatever that amounts to, it isn't thrift.

Which brings us to the other objection. Maybe there is no longer any such thing as 'the middle classes' anyway. Maybe they have long since been subsumed – along with the working classes – into a large lump of Middle England, with our two children each, our front gardens paved, our wii machines churning out the detritus from American and Japanese culture.

Struggling with this same question in 1949, Angus Maude and Roy Lewis suggested, tongues slightly in their cheeks, that the difference between the middle classes and the rest was that they used napkin rings – on the grounds that the working classes never used them and the upper classes used a clean napkin at every meal.[41] It is one definition. I have to admit that, although there may be napkins somewhere in my own house, there is nothing remotely like a napkin ring (though my parents use them). But don't let's dismiss this too quickly. This is one of the respondents to a modern version of the wartime survey Mass Observation talking about class in 1990:

> I was ill at ease . . . when invited to the home of a girlfriend who lived in a wealthy quarter of Wolverhampton. I was there for lunch, and while I was quietly confident my table manners would stand scrutiny, I was disconcerted to find a linen table napkin rolled in an ivory ring on my side plate. It was my first encounter with a napkin and while I knew it should be laid on the lap and not tucked into the shirt collar I could not think what to do with it when the meal was finished. It worried me greatly and finally I laid it nonchalantly on my plate in a crumpled heap . . .[42]

This was quoted in a study by one of the leading sociologists of class in the UK, Professor Mike Savage of York University, comparing how people talked about class then and in the 1940s, in the original Mass Observation surveys. His conclusion was that class is now not so much a designation as a starting point in a long story about your identity. You can try the experiment yourself. Ask someone what class they come from, preferably someone you know well to avoid a clash, and after some agonies – there is still a huge reluctance among the middle classes about declaring themselves as such – they will tell you the story of their life. Researching this book, I found that to be true over and over again.

Despite people's reluctance to say they are middle-class, the Future Foundation's Middle Britain report in 2006 found that 43 per cent identified themselves as middle-class. Another survey concluded that about a quarter of the population were middle-class but preferred not to say so. It is hard to find a lucid definition these days, certainly when we get beyond the napkins. You can't do it in the way people used to.

White collar versus blue collar? Most of our traditional working-class jobs have long since been outsourced to China or India.

Salary versus wage packet? Who gets a wage packet these days?

Homeowner versus renter? Three-quarters of trade unionists now own their own homes.

Even earnings just confuse the issue. One recent study found that 48 per cent of those calling themselves 'working-class' earned more than the average salary and a quarter of them earned more than £50,000 a year. In some cities (Leeds for example) people calling themselves working-class are better off than those who see themselves as middle-class.[43] A third of bank managers in one recent survey identified themselves as working-class.[44]

To confuse things further, those calling themselves 'upper-class' seem to have disappeared altogether.[45]

My own sense, having talked to lots of people while I was writing this, is that there are now many different kinds of middle classes. Sociologists talk about the different wings of the middle class – the conservative and radical wings, the consumerist and the avant-garde middle classes, not to mention the managers and the intellectuals. There is even the London middle class, a different animal again. But it is even more complicated than that. Twenty-first-century middle classes might also include any of these:

The Old Middle Classes These are the old gentry, still the backbone of the community, often with a forces background. They remain understated, modest, and you can tell them immediately because their kitchen units and labour-saving machinery seem to date back decades before anybody else's – they are immune to marketing – and because they keep their regimental photos, and former ships tossing on the high seas, hung firmly in the downstairs loo (a middle-class word, if ever there was one). The pictures are then prominent enough to inform visitors, but not so much as to imply that life stopped dead when their owners became civilians. Caricatures of the English, they hanker successfully for the countryside.

The Designers These are the London middle classes, and as different from the old middle classes as it is possible to be. They are streetwise (or so they believe), sophisticated, early adopters of technology, and have kitchens done out entirely in matt black. They sneer slightly at provincial life, but they keep their eyes glued to the value of their homes, aware that it is also their escape route to a less stressful life, outside the metropolis, where they no longer have to renew their resident's parking permits and can abandon the agony of finding acceptable schools for their invariably talented offspring.

The Creatives Look at most newspaper journalists and writers (this doesn't apply to TV journalists for some reason). Their hair uncombed, their clothes unironed (I speak partly of myself of course), they are not obviously members of the middle classes as we might have understood it in the 1960s, and they often roam widely in and around the class system. They exist as a group because of the huge success of UK export earnings in the creative market, from Shakespeare to Comic Relief via the advertising and film industries, among the biggest export earners for the UK economy. There is an inverted snobbery lurking here that explains why so few films are made about middle-class life. Yet the Creatives are highly educated and are clearly part of the increasingly exotic creature known as the middle class.

The Omnivores This was an aspect of the class system identified by the sociologist Tony Bennett, and it explains some of the hesitancy when you ask people about class these days.[46] These are the people who tasted working-class club culture in their youth, and middle-class classical concert culture in their middle age, and have an eclectic music collection of musicals, country and western and drum and bass. They enjoyed working-class drinking holes in their student days, and posh gastropubs in their affluent middle age. They move quite freely across the class system, but are not quite at home anywhere. Most of us these days are omnivores, to some extent, but some of us get stuck there, half in, half out, uneasy with middle-class values yet clinging to them at the same time, our accents uncategorizable and varying with company.

The Multis I live in south London, the capital city of Multi culture. The first two couples we met through the children's school were a German missionary married to a Ghanaian doctor and a Swedish-speaking Finnish artist married to an Algerian chef. This section of the new middle classes covers those people who live in the UK but were born elsewhere and who find our class nomenclature utterly baffling. Equally, these are often mixed-race couples who have chosen to live in the UK because it is relatively tolerant – and because they met somewhere in the UK melting pot, and the thought of going back to the Middle East or to northern Europe, and dealing with the disapproval there, was too exhausting to entertain. South London is, despite everything, a huge success story in multiracial, multicultural living. It isn't traditionally middle-class, but that is the way it is going.

The Public Servants They don't fit the caricature either, but all those frontline professionals – local government managers, charity executives, nurses, teachers, trading standards officers and all the rest – are plainly a large niche in the middle classes, perhaps usually overlooked because they might vote Labour, Liberal Democrat or Green before Conservative. They are less squeezed financially, though their pensions are not quite what they were, but they have been squeezed in other ways – their responsibilities and dignity eroded by the blizzard of targets, standards, guidelines and directives. Also included are the university lecturers, squeezed in their own way by the Research Assessment Exercise which forces them to publish like crazy to prove their worth. And the new charity and social enterprise managers who deliver so many aspects of public services, perhaps more enslaved by targets than all the rest put together.

The Crunchies These are the British equivalent of the American 'cultural creatives', doyens of what used to be called the 'inner-directed' approach to life.[47] They are people who are no longer interested in keeping up with the Joneses over their material possessions, but are overwhelmingly motivated by health, independence and education. They vote across the political spectrum, but they are concerned about the environment, join Friends of the Earth, sign petitions, have food allergies and have often managed to downshift – deliberately earning less for a better lifestyle, increasingly outside London. It is thanks to the Crunchies that the fastest-growing areas in the UK over the past generation have been the Muesli Belt (a term coined by Martin Stott), the counties that circle London beyond the Home Counties, in a huge circle from Dorset to Norfolk.[48]

Mike Savage and his colleagues are conducting a widespread survey through the BBC about modern class, and he and his colleagues normally now determine class in rather different terms, dividing people according to what aspects of culture they enjoy, into professional classes (hardly ever watch TV), the intermediate class (which would be the professional class except that it shares a much lower life expectancy with the working classes), and the working class (watches four times as much TV as the professional class, but never goes to musicals).[49]

This nomenclature slightly muddies the water, because 29 per cent of all three classes still go to the pub once a week. It also omits the emergence of the new class, the international One Per Cent that is hoovering up the money from the middle classes (I am self-employed, which should make me officially 'intermediate class').[50] Then the house prices began to rise, until the point where that keynote of middle-class life – the partner at home doing the housework – became unaffordable, just when housewifing became unacceptable to many women. But through each twist of policy, they adapted.

In short, the middle classes cling on. Reports of their demise are premature and, although the blow may not have been fatal yet, we still need to search for the weapon used to fell them. They cling on also in a variety of forms and versions, highly eclectic and quite impossible to define. The middle classes are like elephants: you know one when you see one.

The key question is whether there is anything any more which holds these disparate identities together. Patrick Hutber's thrift may have disappeared. Even the sense of deferred gratification which used to define the middle classes is not quite as secure as it was.

The famous experiment by Walter Mischel in the 1960s offered four-year-olds one marshmallow now or two in twenty minutes and found that those who waited went on to enormously outperform the others in the US scholastic aptitude tests. For a moment this seemed to be a justification for all those middle-class efforts at saving for education, a way to glimpse the essence of middle-class life actually there under the microscope. But the revelation that those who are not able to resist the instant marshmallow are often children of single parents, where the father is absent, rather undermined it as a middle-class definition. It isn't that the instant marshmallow children are psychologically different; they are just more worried about the future. They have learned to grab their chance while they have it.

Even so, there is still something here about a distinctive middle-class approach to thinking ahead and their obsession with education – not always as an ideal but as a way of defining themselves against the other. So many people I talked to about this book began their replies to me: 'I don't want to sound snobbish, but . . .' As if the very act of defining themselves as middle-class was somehow aggressive and disapproving. As if the heart of middle-class identity, even now, stems from a fear of fecklessness, disorder and ignorance. No wonder people sound apologetic, and no wonder the middle classes feel so embattled – defending themselves against the encroaching tide at the same time as battling with each other for the scarce resource, the edge in education.

'The middle class family has become both citadel and hothouse,' wrote Professor Cindi Katz, describing the American documentary *Race to Nowhere* by the San Francisco lawyer and mother-of-three Vicki Abeles, inspired by the suicide of a local teenager and describing the panic attacks of middle-class children pushed beyond the limit by their competitive parents. She describes the American middle classes 'cultivating perfectly commodified children for niche marketing in a future that feels increasingly precarious'.[51]

Cindi Katz urges an 'unplugging' to rescue children for a proper childhood, but she doesn't see how. 'It seems almost impossible to unplug while others are plugging away (taking advanced placement classes, studying in high achievement school tracks, attending sports clinics, and the prize is university admission).'

This desperate panic is part of the same 'squeeze' phenomenon. It is considerably less intense than it is in the USA, but it is happening in the UK too. We have all seen the poor middle-class battery hens in their uniforms, weighed down by satchels of homework and the cares of the world.

Perhaps this begins to explain the embarrassment about claiming middle-class status, the implied disapproval – the failure to celebrate its best values, the inverted snobbery directed at suburban values in so much British culture, even the ad breaks. 'Never has a section of society so enthusiastically co-operated in its own euthanasia,' wrote Patrick Hutber back in 1976.[52] Still so today, perhaps even more so.

I don't quite understand this. It is true that the English middle classes can demonstrate a debilitating snobbery and a boneheaded dullness – their failure to understand the changing world about them is at the heart of their current problems. But they also represent enduring values from generation to generation, which I inherited from my parents and grandparents and am proud to have done – about learning and tolerance, a determination to make things happen, about courage and leadership and, yes, even creativity. I have a feeling this double-headed set of values goes to the heart of the problem, as the middle classes maintain their principles in the face of constant self-criticism, in case they are espousing the wrong ones. Are they approving of scholarship or criticizing people who refuse to learn?

The problem is that saying that they are middle-class seems to be admitting to a whole shedload of prejudices, snobberies and pursed-lipped disapprovals. Some of this is clearly caricatured – most middle-class people these days are among the most tolerant people in the world, not just in the UK – but some of it is undoubtedly real. The middle classes may be unfailingly polite in public, but there is definitely an undercurrent of grouchiness, which might explain the apology. It is the impression they give themselves that they are somehow the thin red line that prevents the nation being overwhelmed by fecklessness, brutishness or a branded nightmare of violent computer games, dominated by Tesco, McDonald's or Virgin.

I have to be honest about myself here. I have looked unflinchingly in the mirror and it is true: I also harbour this quite unjustified disapproval. Of how people dress, how they shop, how they spit on the pavement or scream at their children. So, if there has to be a hint of an apology about being middle-class it is because of this fear at the heart of it, that we all know about but do not articulate – that drives us in our financial decisions, or our choice of schools and places to live, in what we buy, how we dress and how we behave.

But let's not go overboard here. Even those who apologized to me about sounding middle-class are among the most open-minded people I know. There is an extraordinary inverted snobbery in British culture about this, which is far tougher on the fantasies of the middle classes than on anyone else, and it has turned the middle classes in on themselves. It is hard to see any portrayal of middle-class families on TV in the UK where there is no hideous secret under the carpet or in the closet. I don't think I've ever seen a happy middle-class family portrayed on *Casualty* without it turning out that the father is a child molester or the mother a secret addict (though sometimes it is the other way around).

None of this suggests that the pursed lips are justified, or that other classes are any less loving. You only have to watch the mixture of classes and races struggling to teach their children to swim in my local swimming pool on Saturday mornings to realize that. I certainly don't suggest that there are no neglectful middle-class parents either. It is all very sensitive.

It may always have been a bit like this. When the English middle classes emerged as we might recognize them now, in the 1820s, it was a process driven by geography. The middle classes were those who were geographically separated from their workplace. But they had also discovered the joys of political economy and took it up with a moral fervour. 'Political economy', said the Reverend Thomas Chalmers, the great Victorian exponent of charity, 'is but one grand exemplification of the alliance, which the God of righteousness hath established, between prudence and moral principle on the one hand, and physical comfort on the other.'[53] There it is again – that same duality: values, but bound up with unforgivable smugness.

For those early middle classes, the way that money worked, and its apparent moral behaviour – rewarding hard work – brought economics almost to the level of religious truth. It drove the boom in self-help and self-education and it carved out both the drive and the fears of the middle classes in the future. It made the great middle-class ideal – what the sociologist Ray Pahl called 'the dogs bounding round the lawn, the children with their ponies, a gentle balanced life' – seem almost a moral one. The more embattled that ideal becomes, and the more embarrassed they are about it, the more the middle classes seem to cling to it.

Behind all the clichés, this is in many ways the life so many people want – independent, peaceful, leisured, safe, where they can create the home and the life around them, stay healthy, and pass some of those values of imagination and independence on to their children. It is precisely this ideal, and the best values that lie behind it, that is now in danger.

The thrift has gone. I no longer go into my friends' houses and find that their fridge or stove is older than I am, and sometimes older than their parents. But the Crunchies give a bit of a clue. The middle classes, whoever they are, are absolutely committed to health, independence and education and whatever will promote it, even if they interpret the path to that ideal – working harder or working less – in very different ways.

It still requires sacrifice, saving and planning ahead. It still means deferred gratification. It still means the middle classes turn out independent-minded, intelligent children quite capable of understanding the world, even if sometimes they don't. But it also explains that embattled sense that goes beyond economics. This is a cultural struggle for survival as well as an economic one. As Paul Ray said about the American 'cultural creatives': they demand authenticity, but they tend to believe their tastes and beliefs are shared by themselves and a few friends – and beyond that, the wasteland.[54]

The terrible truth is that the key to this health and independence is education, that the opportunities and advantages it can give are more and more scarce and competitive, and that they require investment in bricks and mortar.

Christopher Stockwell used a trust fund set up years before the Lloyd's Scandal broke, which he had intended for his children, to buy another house. He also managed to claw back some of his businesses, but he says it has taken him two decades. He says that making the house habitable, and creating a garden in the field next door, was what kept him sane during the desperate years. When I met him there, the whole story was finally coming to its end in the European courts. The legacy of the scandal that engulfed Lloyd's of London is that there are now only a few hundred Names left. Their place has been taken by institutional investors who are better able to look after themselves.

It was Stockwell who suggested the parallel with events around the 2008 banking collapse. I had previously seen no further than the 'lie' of unlimited liability and its terrible human consequences. But there are other parallels with the moment when the financial system tottered.

For one thing, the whole weight of government action was thrown behind preserving the status quo, at all costs. We have come to believe that governments govern on behalf of the middle classes. That clearly isn't so any more. In their terror that the whole system would unravel, Western governments outdid themselves in their desperation to protect the guilty. The Lloyd's Scandal showed that they would, and if the middle classes must suffer to preserve the system, they were a necessary sacrifice.

The scandal showed something else as well. If willing and naive investors were required to fill the yawning financial gap that threatened the Lloyd's insurance market, then they would be recruited. Like First World War generals, they herded the little investors over the top – into the path of the machine guns.

Ever since they discovered political economy in the 1820s, the English middle classes have felt secure in their financial knowledge. They might not have enough money – yet – but they trusted the system that would allow them to invest it safely and sensibly. The problem at the root of their serious decline, and present crisis, is that something has happened, decisions have been taken over the past generation, that have turned that position upside down.

We now have to find out how and why.

Middle Classes in Figures

Percentage of UK population declaring themselves to be middle-class: 43 per cent (though other surveys have taken this up to 70 per cent).[55]

The New Middle-Class-Values Dictionary

INDEPENDENCE: Perhaps the old middle classes valued independence too, as long as people used it to reach the correct conclusions. Not so now: the middle classes believe passionately in their own independence and admire it in other people. In fact, the desire for independence is now central to the middle classes; not necessarily independence from employers, but from landlords and tyrannical bosses, and the long, desperate uphill struggle towards financial independence. It leads them to invest terrifyingly in property just as it leads others to disinvest and downshift. They also admire independence of mind – in moderation, of course . . .

Dispatches from the Frontline

Brown & Green café, Crystal Palace station, Friday 10.30 a.m.
Gipsy Kings waft out of the digital player behind the counter, over the luxurious sound of sizzling bacon. This is an English scene,

with all the luxury of a late breakfast when everyone else is at work, but with a Latin American edge.

The middle-class newcomers to Crystal Palace, high on the hill above south London, are generally pretty oblivious to the culture they are displacing – which is anyway on the exhausted side. Since the original Crystal Palace building, designed by Joseph Paxton, burned down so spectacularly in 1936, nothing much has changed around here except for the closure one by one of the public toilets and the slow march of gentrification, as confident and as doubt-free as the Plantation of Ulster.

So there has been a flurry of excitement locally about the opening of this café, run by the televisual Laura and Jess who have made such a success of the café in the next station down the line. Even so, there are not so many people here at our odd collection of rescued 1960s tables, with the red Formica tops and strange tapering legs, hallmarks of an alien civilization.

The usual herds of buggies that clutter up middle-class cafés in the mornings these days are conspicuous by their absence. Instead there is a whole collection of black cocker spaniels, with their owners. One of them turns out to be called Peggotty, a distinctively middle-class literary reference (*David Copperfield*).

There is also a mixture of class symbols in this café, with its tomatoes being chopped behind the counter and the carrot cakes sweltering above it. The blackboard advertises porridge with seeds, honey and yoghurt. I am drinking green tea as if it were going out of fashion. The walls have been whitewashed. Aluminium sauce-pans hang from the ceiling (do they ever use them?). On the black-board above me are the lines from *The Sound of Music* about climbing every mountain (we know from Mike Savage's research (see page 44) that the working classes never go to musicals, so this is as clear a sign that we are in middle-class territory as anything else).

Yet dotted around are also the traditional symbols of working-class café life – rusty old signal lamps, third-hand furniture, and here in front of me a tomato-shaped plastic dispenser for ketchup, straight from the 1960s. It is as if the symbolism of working-class culture in another age is a reliable sign that this is not *nouvelle cuisine* and the helpings will be encouragingly and comfortably generous.

Crystal Palace station, with its vast echoing staircases, was built to handle the crowd for FA Cup finals (100,000 people in 1900), which were played here until the advent of Wembley Stadium. The huge Victorian windows of this reclaimed station were the very centre of working-class culture in south London. Yet here we are in 2012, eating our scrambled egg on rye.

'No, she's not pushy,' says Peggotty's owner behind me. 'She's shy and retiring. Just like me.'

2

The first clue: the staggering house-price escalator

'Every summer we can rent a cottage in the Isle of Wight,
If it's not too dear.
We shall scrimp and save . . .'
Paul McCartney, 'When I'm Sixty-Four', December 1966

Spring 1979. No Internet. No mobile phones. No cash machines in the wall. No personal computers (or very few). Only three television channels. Orange street lights. Pirate radio stations. Electric fires. Flared trousers (occasionally). The Central Electricity Generating Board, British Rail, the Department of Health and Social Security and other huge bureaucracies running our lives. Grunwick. The National Front and the Anti-Nazi League. Tom Robinson and 'Glad to be Gay'. Works to rule. Closed shops. Angela Rippon, Morecambe & Wise and Tinker, Tailor, Soldier, Spy on the TV. Brian Redhead and Jimmy Young on the radio. Prince Charles still unmarried. James Callaghan in his last few months, and his last few sessions of beer and sandwiches, at 10 Downing Street. Patrick Hutber's The Decline and Fall of the Middle Class on the bookstalls.[1]

It was my middle year at university, shivering in a room with no central heating. I had long hair and dreamed of student revolts that – as it turned out – had long since disappeared. This was the generation caught between the certainties of the hippies and the certainties of the yuppies which the novelist A. S. Byatt writes about so sensitively (and I appreciate it because I was one of them). I had no idea at the time, nor for many years afterwards, what I wanted to do with my life, and couldn't imagine anyone ever employing me – let alone paying me enough money to buy a house.

We were already talking about house prices in those days, in training for a thousand middle-class dinner parties to come, but actually – compared with what came later – the average price of a home in the UK was very low: £18,000 (now worth about £74,500 at today's values).[2] Despite that, there had already been a round of major house-price inflation during the so-called Barber Boom of the early 1970s. There was another flurry in 1977–8 when controls on lending mortgages were briefly loosened because of fears about the house builders. It was enough to get the tongues wagging.

This was not quite the 1930s, the heyday of middle-class house buying, when a new semi-detached cost just over £500, available with a down payment of £50, and when mortgages cost about 10 per cent of a middle-class income and were paid off within sixteen years. But looking back, 1979 was actually the beginning of the extraordinary process which – over the next three decades – has goaded the rise in prices so brutally that it has ended the house-owning dream for many people, and which now, more than anything else, threatens the very existence of the middle classes.

There is always an argument about why house prices rise, and why those prices accelerate. Politicians like to say that it is a shortage of homes, and there certainly is a shortage and it doesn't help. But if it was only about housing shortage, you would expect massive price rises in the late 1940s, whereas – after a burst after the war – house prices stayed completely steady from 1949 to 1954. In our own day, planning permission has already been given for 400,000 unbuilt homes in the UK, yet prices still rise, as they do in places like Spain, where there is little or no planning restraint.

Politicians get muddled about this because building houses sounds like a tangible thing they feel confident about tackling (though they usually don't), whereas they don't feel confident about mortgage supply at all. Yet that is the other side of the process: inflation is about too much money chasing too few goods, and the main reason for the extraordinary rise is that there has been too much money in property, both from speculation and from far too much mortgage lending.

Sometimes this came from people's rising incomes, which translated into rising home loans. Sometimes, more recently, it was bonuses and buy-to-let investors. But most of the time, it has been a catastrophic failure to control the amount of money available to lend, and which has fed into all the other trends to create a tumbling cascade of money, with its own upward pressure on incomes and debt until the acceleration now seems quite unbreakable. It was a roller coaster that terrified and thrilled the middle classes, as they saw the value of their homes rise so inexorably, but which ended – as we have seen – in undermining the very basis for their continued existence.

So what happened? As so often, there is no smoking gun, no deliberate policy, but a series of decisions – taken for very good reasons and often in other areas of policy – by a close-knit group of people. Back in 1979, as they prepared for the historic election that swept Margaret Thatcher to power, there *was* an institution that was designed partly to prevent house-price inflation. It was called the 'Corset', which tripped off the tongue a little easier than its other name: the Special Supplementary Deposits Scheme. It worked by penalizing banks when they lent too much, and – although it was not always effective at limiting the money they lent – it did keep bankers out of the mortgage market.

So travel back with me to the moment of the first clue in this book, the autumn and winter of 1978, as it turned into 1979, when a small group of economists and radical thinkers was meeting regularly at the home of Sir Geoffrey and Elspeth Howe next to Vauxhall Park, in the elegant Georgian terraces of Fentiman Road. Elspeth was then deputy chair of the Equal Opportunities Commission. Sir Geoffrey was a former Solicitor General and had good reason to believe that he would be appointed as Chancellor of the Exchequer in the new Conservative government, if Mrs Thatcher could lead them to victory.

These were people who had bought into the intellectual argument for free markets, which emerged from divisions inside American liberalism in the 1940s, and was identified with the controversial economist Milton Friedman. In Howe's sitting room week by week were the economic journalist Nigel Lawson, a future Chancellor himself, and Sir Keith Joseph, the former health minister who had performed a kind of *mea culpa* for his role in the sins of the last Conservative government under Edward Heath, and was now an agonized intellectual figurehead for the new dispensation. There were also a number of other young advisers and thinkers, prominent among whom was the future banker Adam Ridley.

It was a heady and exciting time as they met, through the events known to modern history as the 'Winter of Discontent', when the trade unions rebelled against their government's incomes policy and rubbish piled up in the streets. Inflation was running at 10 per cent and rising. But Howe's group were not just fairly certain they would win, they had the confidence of a big idea behind them – that inflation could be squeezed out of the system by reducing the amount of money in the economy.

Their other idea was in some ways the very opposite. It was that ending all the detailed controls on banking – most of all the restrictions on money leaving the country which had begun at the outbreak of war in 1939 – would provide a kind of discipline to Britain's unruly economy. As many as 750 civil servants policed the exchange control system at the Treasury and Bank of England.

Everyone's passport in those days noted the money they were taking out of the UK on holiday on a page at the back. This radical group believed the whole system must go.

Ridley and the other policymakers were aware that the controls had tightened through the decade, and especially when the government had been forced to borrow money from the IMF in 1976. 'The essential concern was that a sophisticated financial system finds ways of outflanking most controls within a few years,' he says now, 'and from that point on the complications and distortions cause more damage and loss than any of the uncertain benefits which they may have initially brought.'

The problem was that these were highly uncertain times. John Hoskyn, then the head of the Prime Minister's policy unit, described running the British economy as 'fighting for the controls of an aeroplane that can no longer fly'.[3] The price of oil was soaring and pushing the economy, yet again, into recession. Nobody on the Conservative side wanted to frighten the markets or the electorate by revealing their plans too publicly. It certainly wasn't in the Conservative manifesto for the election, which had been ready the previous year when they thought the election would take place. Lawson risked using his column in *Financial Weekly* during the election campaign to talk about relaxing exchange controls. Howe was 'apprehensive but fundamentally sympathetic', at least according to Lawson.[4]

Looking back at the May 1979 election with the benefit of hindsight, it is extraordinary how united the middle classes were – perhaps it was the last election to be fought strictly on class lines. I remember watching the documentary series about the public school Radley College later that year, and seeing their entire staff room gather to watch the results, united in their assumption that they were all cheering the Conservatives on to victory.

They did indeed win – by forty-three seats. Margaret Thatcher quoted St Francis of Assisi on the steps of 10 Downing Street.

Howe was duly appointed as Chancellor with Lawson as his deputy (Patrick Hutber had already taken over from him as City Editor of the *Sunday Telegraph*). Ridley became their special adviser. The revolution had begun.

I bought a house in the early winter at the end of 1986, just over six years after the events I have just described, when interest rates stood at 11 per cent. It was a struggle, even with help from my stepfather, but then I wasn't earning very much either. I remember the strange, adult excitement of the key going into a front door of my own place, even if was a little damp and dilapidated. I remember the excitement (yes, and the expense) of doing it up myself, and the misery when the flat roof leaked down the staircase and I had no idea how I could afford to mend it.

The following eighteen months were almost the eye of the house-price storm, as money cascaded into the mortgage market and house prices began to rise, slowly at first and then catastrophically. I benefited from that rise, and there certainly was a feeling of delicious self-congratulation by the middle classes, then and later, that our assets – though we may not have owned them outright – had risen so much in value.

Pinpointing the abolition of the Corset is not straightforward, but its demise was a direct result of the revolution wrought by Howe, Lawson and their colleagues. Of course house prices rise for many reasons, and it is hard to believe that the Corset would have prevented the flood of foreign financial institutions, mainly American, that poured their money into the UK housing market. The fact that fewer homes were built in 2009 than in any year since 1924 doesn't help. Often prices rose because the middle classes compulsively *wanted* them to do so. They loved it. It made them feel rich, right up to the point where it ruined them. The Corset may have been impossible to sustain, but its demise marked the end of mortgage rationing. Mortgage debt didn't rise at all in the Corset years of the 1970s. From 1979 to 1987 it grew at 10 per cent a year. The real problem was not so much the demise of the Corset. It was the failure to replace it with any policy that could possibly hold down house prices as the Niagara of mortgage money roared through the national economy.

Howe wrote in his memoirs that he was only ever lobbied once by his government driver, and then it was about house prices – during the cabinet battle over mortgage-interest tax relief (set at £25,000). That amount 'would have bought me a small country estate when I first joined the car service', said the driver.[5] House prices had begin to thrill, and the decisions to loosen lending after the 1987 Stock Market Crash accelerated the process. So did the housing-boom years under Tony Blair and Gordon Brown.

Now, you need double the average national income to buy a two-bedroom flat in Tower Hamlets in the poverty-stricken East End of London. As I write, average house prices in London are around £408,000, over fifteen times the average income. Anyone buying a house in the capital for the first time will need to cobble together a deposit of £100,000 and still have a salary of over £87,500 to get the mortgage.[6] No wonder there are 800,000 people in London waiting for affordable or social housing.

I am acutely aware now that my 1986 purchase (£45,500, which I eventually sold for £225,000 two decades later) was also a kind of lifeline. If I had bought ten years later, certainly twenty years later, I would now be paying ruinous monthly mortgage interest payments which would seriously restrict my choice of what I want to do in my mid-fifties. I would be forced to concentrate on the handful of jobs that would allow me to earn enough to service my mortgage, assuming I could find one.

Of course, there is a range of experimental shared ownership schemes on the market – part rent, part mortgage. These make buying a home just a little easier, though they are few and far between. Ironically, these are very similar to the Homebuy schemes of the early 1970s, which were used as evidence back then that the domestic mortgage market was too restricted. Now it isn't restricted at all – if you have a deposit – and we are back to square one.

The Conservatives having won the election in 1979, Howe moved into a second-floor office of the Treasury, which was carpeted throughout, under the Treasury's exemplary and parsimonious regime, in red lino. There was a plaque above his desk explaining that the Air Council had met there throughout the war. There is some irony in knowing that Howe's decisions were taken in the very room where they had planned the carpet bombing of German industrial cities four decades before.

Howe was a peculiar mixture too. His bank-manager spectacles and quiet speaking style gave him the appearance of caution. His long-term Labour opponent Denis Healey nearly ruined Howe's career, during a Commons spat, by describing himself as having been 'savaged by a dead sheep'. This belied the reality. In fact, Howe was a serious radical, according to the political columnist Edward Pearce. 'If you listened to Sir Geoffrey for his oratory, you would hang yourself,' he wrote. 'The man is absinthe masquerading as barley water. Like the good lawyer he is, Sir Geoffrey uses tedium like cuttlefish ink to obscure the news.'[7] Lawson, the new Chief Secretary to the Treasury, was rotund and frighteningly confident. Together, they made hay of the old guard at the Treasury. The permanent secretary Sir Douglas Wass was sidelined and new advisers were brought in.

The key problem, as the Bank of England governor Gordon Richardson explained within days of the election, was how to bring down the value of the pound. The unspoken assumption was that doing so in the wrong way threatened a disastrous run on the currency, but Richardson's remarks seemed to the revolutionaries like the green light to lift exchange controls. Howe, Lawson and

Ridley met at the Conservative Party conference in October and decided there was no middle way. They would go ahead and stop controlling who could take money out of the country.

All they had to do was persuade Margaret Thatcher. Again, later reputations are not a very good guide for understanding the time. These were the days before 'Thatcherism'. The trio of revolutionaries were still not quite certain of her support for economic deregulation. They knew that, when Edward Heath was leader, she had opposed the sale of council houses and anything else which risked raising mortgage rates. What they did know for sure was that, whatever happened, she was on the side of the middle class. The Conservative manifesto had promised 'to support family life, by helping people to become homeowners'. There had certainly been nothing about deregulating the mortgage market. Only weeks after the election, she was writing notes to Howe: 'I am very worried about the reports in today's press that mortgage rates may have to go up within days. This must NOT happen. If necessary, there must be a temporary subsidy.'[8]

The very last thing Howe and Lawson wanted was a subsidy, temporary or otherwise. They had set their faces against any such thing. There was a gap between the Prime Minister's absolute commitment to middle-class homeowners, and their convictions about economic change, which is directly relevant to house prices today. Political mythology suggests that it was Lawson who persuaded Thatcher that a 'property-owning democracy' required people to go into debt – which definitely meant changes to the mortgage market. Maybe that conversation happened at the same party conference. No one is saying.[9] What we do know is that she was persuaded.

What the revolutionaries didn't do was talk to the cabinet. 'Do you know,' Howe told a dinner party a few weeks later, 'there hasn't been a single economic discussion in the cabinet since this government came in.'[10]

That wasn't strictly true, but it was quite right that the cabinet was never consulted about the end of exchange controls. They were informed. The critical moment came about mid-morning on 25 October 1979, when Howe explained to the cabinet what he was about to announce. Mrs Thatcher was apologetic, recognizing that 'some other members of the cabinet might have liked to have an opportunity of expressing their views before a decision was taken'.

Only one voice was raised against. The then Environment Secretary Michael Heseltine warned that people might respond by taking their money out of the country to buy villas in France. But, again, we only have Lawson's word for this.[11]

Howe and Lawson had calculated that, despite the worst fears of their critics, there would be no catastrophic outflow of funds, nor a collapse in the value of the pound – for the same reason that the economy was in crisis. Because of North Sea Oil, the pound was now a petro-currency. So they took a deep breath and hoped for the best. The announcement was made and, to their surprise, the pound kept on rising. It carried on doing so until Britain's exports were unaffordable abroad and UK manufacturing industry staggered, and – hopelessly outdated, under-invested and beset by insane labour relations – all but gave up the ghost. But that, as Kipling might say, is another story.

The decision to abolish exchange controls was a defining moment for the rest of the planet, which rapidly followed suit. It cleared the way for the modern world, where national spending decisions are kept in check by the vigilance of global money markets which can, and do, bankrupt nations overnight. The huge bureaucracies of exchange control were certainly hard to justify, but then so are some of the results of their disappearance. As much as $4 trillion a day now churns through the world financial system, most of it foreign-exchange speculation. It is a terrifying, uncontrollable and largely unpredicted force in modern affairs.

But Howe had also made a brave and imaginative decision. He and Lawson wanted financial discipline and some encouragement for British companies to invest abroad, and they got it. Those involved in the decision to end exchange controls made a special tie to commemorate it, which said 'EC 1939/1979'. Lawson wore the tie later to deliver his budget speeches when he was Chancellor himself. 'It was the only economic decision of my life that caused me to lose a night's sleep,' wrote Howe later, 'but it was right.'[12]

What makes the exchange-controls decision important here is that it made the controls on bank lending impossible to sustain. Sooner or later, overseas banks or offshore branches of UK banks would start bypassing the Corset. Sooner or later, the Bank of England feared, they would start lending money for mortgages and push up the price of houses.[13]

So it proved. Fast-forward nearly three decades, and there was Sebastian Cresswell-Turner writing sadly in *The Times* about the discovery that he could no longer afford the life his parents had. 'The poor aren't the only ones who are getting poorer,' he wrote, describing the effects of twenty-seven years of accelerating house prices. 'Whole swathes of the professional classes are too':

An unmarried and badly paid knowledge worker, I live in a rented room in Hammersmith and have no hope of ever buying a home anywhere. Indeed, when I return to the agreeable parts of central London that I know so well from earlier periods of my life, I realise that I am looking at the attractive stucco houses in just the same way that a tramp looks through the restaurant window at a group of people enjoying a carefree meal. I am effectively an exile in the city where I was born.[14]

When Howe became Chancellor, and despite the two blips during the 1970s, house prices were being kept low by another strange institution that the Corset made possible. This was the building societies' 'Cartel'. Because the banks were kept out of lending people mortgages, the building societies were allowed to get together and keep interest rates much lower than they were in the mainstream lending market. They were only allowed to lend out money that people had deposited with them. Because of this, mortgages often had to be rationed. There was a waiting list, sometimes for months. It was inconvenient, and it is hard to imagine mortgages being rationed these days, but to some extent it worked.

The Cartel was presided over by a joint committee of building societies, regulators and ministers, whose task was to set an interest rate low enough to keep the house builders building, but high enough to stop house prices rising. The first step in its demise was when Lawson, as Chief Secretary to the Treasury, refused to provide new guidelines for an interest rate. He said afterwards that he didn't realize he had to. Without the interest-rate guidelines, there was no point in a Joint Advisory Committee.

'It was the first step in what was to become a far-reaching programme of financial deregulation, with consequences – some of them wholly unforeseen – which were to have a major impact on the course of the economy and the conduct of policy,' said Lawson later.[15]

The joint committee limped on until 1984. Once again, it all depended on the Corset and – now that exchange controls had gone – the Corset could not stand. For months, the stockbroker Gordon Pepper had been saying so. The new ministers set great store by Pepper and copied his speeches to each other. Peer into the cabinet papers of the day, now they are publicly available, and you find Pepper's speeches everywhere.

The pressure was also on from the Labour opposition. Denis Healey rose in the House of Commons, only three weeks since exchange controls were lifted, taunting Howe about giving people the 'unhappiest Christmas ever'.[16]

'How long will he and his colleagues allow the nation's economic prospects to be ruined by a bunch of bumbling doctrinaires?' Healey went on. The Labour benches roared their approval behind him. Then the killer blow.

'Why on earth has he kept the Corset still in place when it is well known throughout the banking community its worth is useless now that he has abolished exchange control?'

Even the Wilson Committee, Harold Wilson's final act in frontline politics, and packed with trade unionists, recommended that it should go. So did Lord Young of Dartington, the author of the 1945 Labour manifesto, who urged its abolition in a letter to *The Times*.

But there was another consideration. The new cabinet was determined to expand the homeowning classes by selling council houses to their tenants. It was a bold and populist move, designed also to tackle the patronizing record of the big cities in designing and managing council housing – but implemented disastrously (the money earned from the sale just sat there, and wasn't used to build new low-cost housing). For tenants to buy their own homes, even at discount rates, the means to borrow the money had to be available to them.

There was really no contest, and Howe gave the Corset six months and confirmed the deadline in his budget speech in March 1980, an event that was threatened by the loss of the famous battered red budget box at the Treasury. The box turned up at the last minute and Howe rose to deliver what the Labour leader Michael Foot called a 'no hope budget'.

'The Governor and I have agreed . . .' he said. The Labour MPs opposite roared with laughter. For a moment, it sounded as if this was a peculiar and deferential way of referring to Margaret Thatcher.

Howe kept his cool. 'I am referring not to any foreign or outlandish figure but to the Governor of the Bank of England. We have agreed that the supplementary special deposit scheme – generally known as the Corset – should not be extended beyond mid-June, when the present guideline ends. One of the effects of the Corset has been to encourage the development of credit channels just outside the banking system . . .'

This is certainly true. Once exchange controls had gone, there really was no way under the system as it was then to prevent money from abroad flooding into the UK property market. It certainly did, which is some explanation why 900,000 more households are renting in the UK than they were in 2005.[17] It also explains why Britain now lies behind Romania and Bulgaria for its percentage of homeowners, and why only half of London's homes are now owner-occupied.[18] It explains a little why London is rapidly shifting from property-owning democracy to a city of supplicants to the whims of landlords and rental agents.

There are many people who might welcome that kind of shift, towards a society less obsessed with owning our own homes. But renting is really no escape from high house prices, because they feed straight into high rents, and a third of all mortgages in 2006 were for buy-to-let homes. The cost of servicing a mortgage provides a kind of basic floor for rents too, which is why so many people in successful jobs remain trapped in flatshares, sharing the bathroom, well into their thirties and probably beyond. The newspaper columnist Owen Jones complained on Twitter about London rents (£1,000 a month for a two-bedroom house in inner London). Hundreds of people responded with their own horror stories – a 35 per cent rent hike imposed after Christmas, a couple who had to abandon their 'tiny flat' in Zone 3 after their monthly rent went up from £720 to £950.

A recent report by the National Housing Federation predicts that average London rents will rise by 50 per cent, to over £2,000 a month, within ten years, that the average London home will rise to £688,000 by then too.[19] Nobody believes that average wages will match that rate.

It is easy to blame the landlords for this, and there is certainly greed and opportunism involved, but the real difficulty is that the level of rents depends on the level of mortgage repayments. That is what landlords need to charge to pay the mortgage. It isn't enough to condemn our 'addiction' to property ownership (actually, I don't have a problem with people owning the place where they live), but the costs of private renting are actually driven by high house prices in just the same way that mortgages are.

So when it comes to imagining how our children will house themselves, it isn't enough just to abandon home ownership. Private renting will make them just as dependent on high house prices, without the independence that ownership brings – miserably dependent on the whims of landlords, forced to move constantly, without the local roots that their own children – anyone's children – need. If independence is the new hallmark ideal of the middle classes, it is hard to see how it can continue except for the few – the only children who inherit, the children of those in financial services, the heirs and successors of the One Per Cent.

Were we dreaming when we allowed our hearts to leap at the signs in the estate agent's window? When we cashed in the rise in house values with loans to fuel the consumer boom? When we got so into the habit of using loans to fund holidays and buy cars that outstanding household loans have tripled in the last decade (or worse, when we used the extra money as collateral to become Lloyd's Names)? How did we get sucked into the phenomenon of the Emperor's New House Prices, when we dared not criticize their inexorable rise for fear they might fall again?

Certainly the whole phenomenon took the Treasury by surprise. None of their econometric models showed how rising housing wealth fed into consumer loans and debt. Nor did house prices behave in the same way uniformly across Europe (in Germany, they have barely moved for a generation). We knew all that, but we still cheered. It took an intelligent commentator like Martin Wolf of the *Financial Times* to break the log-jam. 'It is mad to applaud ever rising prices,' he wrote in 2008.[20] And so it is.

It is also easy to blame the revolutionaries in the Thatcher government in 1979 and 1980. The decision to end exchange controls made the demise of the Corset and Cartel inevitable too, and you might argue that the cosy world of the building societies in those days – refusing to lend in some neighbourhoods or to single women – sealed their fate. But the real blame has to go to the middle-class cheerleaders of rising house prices. It was their nest egg, their early retirement guarantee, as unprecedented wealth flowed from their parents through to them. They did not stop to wonder – and I was the same – whether it might stop flowing, and what it would do to their children's lives if it did.

The debate was complicated right from the start by a rapid rewriting of history. Some months after these fateful decisions, Lawson was boasting to Swiss bankers about the huge success of the end of exchange controls ('highly successful in every material respect') and getting rid of the Corset too:

> With the wisdom of hindsight a strong case can be made for the proposition that we should have followed our original instinct and announced its abolition immediately on taking office, a year previously: a thermometer which gives a false reading, however flattering, is no use to anyone.[21]

History was already being rewritten to make the decision an obvious one, whereas it had actually been far more difficult than that. As we have seen, once the Corset had gone, there was nothing to prevent the banks dashing into the mortgage market and pushing up house prices as a result. Horribly burned by the Latin America debt crisis, they were desperate to lend money somewhere. The UK housing market looked like a good bet, especially for American lenders borrowing money on the wholesale markets. All that now held them back was the building societies' Cartel.

The first sign of trouble for the Cartel came within days of the 1980 Budget speech. It became clear that NatWest was setting up a home loans unit to start as soon as the Corset was dead. Lloyds Bank was also dipping its toe in the mortgage market with the intention of 'picking up the top end of the market', according to their domestic banking manager.[22]

Lawson laid into the building society chiefs in an address to their conference at the Bournemouth Winter Gardens, but they were not keen to struggle against the world's most powerful financial institutions. 'I don't think a return to the jungle is in the national interest,' said Building Societies Association chairman Leonard Williams.[23] For two years, he led the building societies into battle with the banks – aware, to start with, that the banks were tending to pick up custom initially from the people the building societies turned down as bad risks. But in the long run, it was an unequal battle. The days of mortgage rationing were over.

The crunch came in October 1983. All the senior managers of the building societies were in Melbourne at a big international conference when the Abbey National took the opportunity to break the arrangement to limit interest rates. 'The Cartel is an arrangement to stifle competition,' chief executive Clive Thornton told the press. 'We want none of it.'[24]

When building society interest rates started to rise up to market levels, wholesale funds were available to the banks on the wholesale markets – but not to the building societies. They had to wait for new legislation in 1986 (see the next chapter) that allowed them to bypass their own depositors and raise money in that way – eventually the cause of disaster for Northern Rock and HBOS a quarter of a century later.

The year 1986 was also the year that the former *Times* editor Simon Jenkins said he heard a director of Halifax Building Society, as it was then, say: 'God help us if the bankers get their hands on our mortgages or if our brokers get their hands on their deposits.'[25] Both events did take place in the fullness of time, as we shall see.

Lawson talked about the end of the Cartel, but feared the short-term consequences of killing it. 'I accept my prominent part in this though I was by no means alone,' he wrote in 1992.[26] In his autobiography, which he was writing the previous year, he described the explosion of mortgage lending that followed as 'unprecedented and unforeseen', saying that the late 1980s – with the huge explosion in house prices which he presided over as Chancellor – were a 'once and for all occurrence'.[27] As we have found to our cost more recently, that wasn't so.

But by then, the world had changed. Within months of the decision to end the Corset, the whole tenor of the debate had shifted. We know now that the idea that somehow all prices reflected something real was a fundamental mistake which still infects many – especially in banks, where they still bolster their balance sheets with property values, only to have those values slip through their fingers. We might know that now, but by then it flew in the face of the new spirit of the times to point it out.

Hidden in the archives of the Bank of England is a revealing note. It is a memo from the governor (still Richardson) in May 1980, weeks before the Corset was finally loosened, and describes meeting a City grandee who asked him why nothing had been put in place to replace it.[28] The deputy governor has added his own note on the file describing the hapless grandee. 'Were he a Tory MP he would I fear rightly qualify for a certain adjective in rather wide current use.'

The adjective he referred to was 'wet', Mrs Thatcher's new

designation for her opponents in the cabinet. 'Rather sad, I think,' said the governor.

Nothing has replaced the Corset, and Thatcherism – heralded by the new and vigorously enforced consensus implied by this note – would countenance no such defences. House prices would find their proper level, whatever they happened to be, and the acceleration upwards had barely begun. The consequences have been profound.

If Surbiton holds a special place in the affections of the British middle classes – and I'm far from certain about that – it is because it was the fictional home of Tom and Barbara Good, the quintessentially middle-class downshifting couple who hit the TV screens in 1975 in The Good Life, the blueprint for a new middle-class craving for independence.

The Good Life was actually filmed in middle-class, semi-detached Northwood rather than semi-detached Surbiton, but a quick walk from the art deco railway station in Surbiton still makes it a kind of middle-class Ground Zero. There are the leafy suburban streets, the little slices of middle-class life, divided by wooden fences as far as the eye can see, the lawnmowers and electric drills getting dusty in their huts through underuse, and their silver cars in the garage, or on a concreted-over front garden (I can't see the Goods concreting over their front garden, but let's not go there).

It is also clear that things have changed since The Good Life. The curtains don't twitch. There is hardly anyone at home behind the reclaimed front doors with their stickers for the National Childbirth Trust in the windows. The people who get off the train from Clapham Junction with me still carry shopping bags from Peter Jones, as they always did. Yes, the slightly faded advertisements for the Surrey Comet still grace the newsagent stands. Yes, I am nearly run over by a delivery van from Ocado. But there are also men on the platform bawling into their mobile phones in Polish, and there is one man dignified and resplendent in the white robes of an imam. What would Margot Leadbetter have said?

Things are different for lunch too. I'm not at all sure that the menu in the Surbiton Brasserie (if it existed in 1975) would have offered 'lemon chicken with pine nuts'. Still less my jacket potato with Mediterranean vegetables and mozzarella. But what really strike me are the conversations among the mainly women clientele around me.

'What is his role exactly?' asks the lady on my right. 'Is he one of the finance guys?'

'It doesn't make sense,' says the lady on my left. 'It's just something HR came up with. Just to get brand-holders in the same room.'

They may be eating, but these are emphatically not 'ladies who lunch', and once again I realize the pressure of the mortgage market. This isn't like it was when Margot spent her days with the local amateur dramatic groups, or battling with Mrs Dooms-Paterson and Dollie Mountshaft in the Music Society. These are working women, either because they choose to be or because they must work because their mortgage depends on joint salaries. The average house price in Surbiton, judging by the nearby estate agent, is around £600,000 for a three-bedroom semi.

There is even an argument that the mass appearance of middle-class women on the jobs market is one of the factors pushing up house prices over the last three decades. They earned money, which meant that bigger loans were available, so the house prices rose to meet them. That is how it works. Inflation is too much money chasing too few goods, and what we have seen since the deregulation of the mortgage markets is ever more reasons to lend more, so that the house prices rise to take account of it, and so the cycle goes on – in retrospect a terrifying rack for the middle classes.

Terrifying especially if women didn't want to work, because that freedom is now beyond them. Once lenders had began to calculate the upper limit in multiples of joint salaries, there was another escalation of house prices. It is part of the far bigger vicious circle that is caused by people desperately stretching to afford the home they want, and which is outpacing their income as they watch – a spiral that keeps on spinning: smaller houses, bigger loans, more salaries, higher prices, smaller houses and so on.

One twist to this cycle we have so far managed to escape in the UK is lengthening the repayment terms. We have not yet been given the pleasure of Japanese-style Grandparent Mortgages, which extend the mortgage period so that the next two generations have to pay it off. It was no coincidence that, after Grandparent Mortgages emerged in Japan, Tokyo property prices rose to be the most expensive in the world. The losers got to buy small tubes they could live in. As yet, we have been spared all that.

Nor have we had subprime lending on quite the same scale as the USA's, with loans packaged to their lower-paid 'middle classes' in such a way that they could never be paid off. But we have some elements of that. Interest-only mortgages – a hefty segment of the UK market – are also mortgages which will never be paid off without a change in financial circumstances. Given that the last few years have seen interest rates at a historic low, this is bound to mean trouble in the future when they rise again, as they almost certainly will.

The British version of the vicious spiral has been lending against ever-greater multiples of salaries, which also feed into the cycle of higher prices. Until 1988, the limit was usually twice the salaries of the people buying. Loans of four times joint salaries were unheard of, but over the past decade loans for four times joint salaries came to outnumber those of twice joint salaries.

Here is the strange reverse alchemy of the house-price spiral. Victorian economists calculated that the average English peasant in 1495 needed to work for fifteen weeks to earn the money they needed to survive for the year, supported as they were by access to the common land. In 1564, it was forty weeks.[29] Now, when GDP tells us we are incomparably richer, it is extremely difficult to buy a house in southern England and live a reasonable life without both partners working flat-out all year long. Even when both partners work, it is often simply not possible (certainly for twenty-first-century peasants, of course).

This aspect of the spiral has had some peculiar effects. When the 2001 census unexpectedly revealed that half the UK population now lives within half an hour of where they were born – not exactly globalization – it did cause some scratching of heads among policy-makers. The real reason was that only working couples can now afford to buy homes. That means they need to live near their parents or in-laws to provide childcare during the day. Those who can't rely on parents for whatever reason are thrown on the mercies of an expensive, understaffed childcare sector that often eats away most of the second household salary.

Hence the sad sight of exhausted mothers wheeling home exhausted toddlers in the dark at the end of a long day at the nursery, long after bedtime, finally picked up after another long day at the office.

The Blair government helped in 1998 by introducing Sure Start centres (124 of which have since closed down). But what they gave with one hand, they took away with the other, all but outlawing informal childcare – you can look after children for neighbours but they are not allowed pay you, even in biscuits – and by regulating the co-operative nurseries out of existence. This was important. Mutual nurseries are how the middle classes afford childcare in North America and Scandinavia, keeping costs right down in return for helping to run the nursery once or twice a month.

There are certainly some brilliant nurseries out there. There are also many less than brilliant ones. The columnist Lucy Mangan described herself as 'aghast at apathetic children – one group in a nursery in a basement flat with no garden and virtually no natural light – or at childminders who reach for the paperwork to sign the child up without ever reaching for or engaging with the child'.[30]

The other aspect of the spiral which stands out in the UK is the phenomenon of the Incredible Shrinking Homes. This isn't rocket science. You only have to look at the generous gardens of the semi-detached houses of the 1930s to see that something has gone wrong – all that space for hens and vegetable patches if need be, compared with the pinched and mean pocket handkerchiefs of turf and concrete in modern estates.

The famous Parker Morris space standards of the 1960s are now long gone, though the UK is the only European country not to set a minimum floor space, apparently unaware that the house-price spiral was almost bound them to make them smaller. New homes in Denmark are 80 per cent bigger than their equivalents in the UK. The design agency CABE lays the blame on the idea that houses are an investment – a financial commodity rather than homes. This 'works against quality standards in house building', they say.[31]

The Royal Institute of British Architects (RIBA) have tried to translate that lost space into more human terms. If the average new home in England is only 92 per cent of the recommended minimum size, as they say it is, this amounts to eight square metres missing for a three-bedroom house.[32] That is the size of a single bedroom, the space for a new arrival to the family, the space for children to have a room of their own, or for a spare room for a guest to stay overnight. It is the space that could take the kitchen out of the sitting room and the sounds and smells that go with it.

The RIBA dubbed these new homes 'shoebox houses', and the BBC interviewed two sisters who had just moved into a new three-bedroom house in Devon.[33] The largest double bedroom was 11 foot 2 inches by 8 foot 2 inches, just enough space for a double bed as long as nobody tries to squeeze into it. They had to give their book collection away to the local charity shops: 'We are just on top of each other the whole time. We find we are arguing much more than we used to – simply because there's not the space to get away from one another.' Nearly half of those who replied to the RIBA survey of new home buyers in 2009 said that they had so little space that they were unable to entertain visitors.

The one beneficial aspect of this is that new houses are getting taller to compensate, which gives a little space to escape for children and adults alike. What are not taller are the doorways – they are a fifth lower since the 1920s, even though on average we are 3 per cent taller.[34]

Then there is the phenomenon of the Incredible Shrinking Plots. This is partly because builders get a premium for making homes 'detached', even if the space between them is only a metre wide, which is why noise complaints about neighbours have been rising over the years. Whatever the reason, housing densities have increased from twenty-three homes per hectare a decade ago to over forty, and much more when they are built on land which has been developed before. This was deliberate government policy by the Blair government, fuelled by a misplaced idea that high densities were more sustainable than medium densities, an idea peddled by an alliance between environmentalists and architects like Lord Rogers.

Actually, there is no real difference in energy use between housing densities except at the extremes of high and low. Very densely populated cities like New York or Tokyo are not known for their low energy use. Really sustainable cities are going to need more space, not less, so that people can generate energy and treat their waste on-site, or grow some of their own vegetables (rather than truck them all in and out) and process waste materials as resources for new enterprises. Sustainable living needs space for harvesting rainwater too. But high land values, thanks to high property prices, are pushing up densities instead – and making ever more exclusive the middle-class craving for homes and gardens. Housing at forty-five plus homes to a hectare more or less rules out gardens, though 80 per cent of people say that is what they want.[35]

These shrinkages are a problem for children as much as adults. I know when I am staying somewhere smaller with my own children, it often crosses my mind to wonder – as they crash so irritatingly into the furniture and break small ornaments (and sometimes large ornaments) – whether perhaps they are somewhere on the autistic spectrum after all. I have no doubt that, because we can only afford smaller homes than we actually need, the rise in autism and Asperger's Syndrome is also partly related to rising house prices. I have always collected peculiar statistics, and wondered why autism rose in Illinois by 62,000 per cent in the ten years to 2003. Perhaps this explains some of it, because the great US housing bubble began its tumultuous ascent around 1994.

Of course these shrinking homes also impact on our relationships, given that as many as 40 per cent of UK marriages now end in the divorce courts. Too much sharing of bedrooms with children or with double beds that take up the whole room can't be good for us – and this drives the price spiral too. One estimate suggested back in 2000 that divorces would meant another 3.8 million households needing homes in the next fifteen years. House prices are that much higher as a result – money which should have been spent on family life, but has gone instead into unnecessary property.

That has knock-on effects too. Children of divorced parents are more likely to get into trouble, perform badly in school, get stress-related illness and get divorced themselves. When the 'Aga saga' novelist Joanna Trollope researched her book about divorce, *Other People's Children*, she said she had never come across so much hidden pain. 'I regard it as a personal holocaust when the parents separate,' wrote the Tavistock Clinic psychiatrist Sebastian Kramer.

David Birkbeck of the CABE project Building for Life says that 'people who live in three- or four-storey houses have a more successful family life'.[36] Just as good fences make good neighbours, good staircases make easier relationships. Quite right, but can the next middle-class generation afford them?

Harry is a successful entertainment lawyer, living with his wife and two very small children in a two-bedroom flat in Tufnell Park, an up-and-coming neighbourhood of north London with a little way more to come. He is middle-class almost by definition (he is a lawyer), but he was also a public school scholarship boy and an Oxford graduate, and one who hasn't always played it safe. He spent three years – ultimately not successful – running his own small film production company. Now he has an annual salary of around £100,000. By any definition, he ought to be comfortably off.

Why not? Well, two reasons. One is that Harry isn't your average lawyer. He is one of six children, partly educated at home until his father died when he was six. He read from the age of three and played the piano from the age of four. Despite a successful few years in a law firm, he really wanted to try his hand at something more creative. 'I thought: is this it?' he says now. It wasn't it: for one successful year and two rather unsuccessful ones, he became a film producer.

By the end of the period, he was forced to sell his small flat and lived for six months largely off credit cards, before realizing he would have to go back to the law. Then he had to endure a series of interviews by rather snooty senior lawyers who could barely understand his varied life. 'It was a frustrating period, coming back to the blandness of it,' he says. 'I thought: "I've walked on the moon and you're still on the earth."' Then he landed his current job, loved it and never looked back. But that entrepreneurial period in between has taken its toll and still does so.

The second reason Harry feels less well off than he should is simply the price of houses in London. Tufnell Park is far from being the most desirable corner of London, and he has managed to find his way through the forest of red tape to extend his flat there ('adding square footage will add more value than it costs to buy new'), but now he feels trapped in it. The flat is worth somewhere over £450,000 and his mortgage is for £380,000, which costs him about £1,000 a month in mortgage payments (as much as £300,000 of the mortgage is interest only, which means that something has to change if he is ever going to repay it).

He still has £20,000 debt on his credit cards, and he has had to buy a people carrier to fit the new family in. He still feels heavily in debt. There are many like him, especially in London, where the cost of childcare can eat up the whole of a second salary.

'Maybe some of that is my fault,' he says. 'I don't think I've been particularly frivolous, but I earn a hundred grand and it's difficult. I'm not exactly struggling, but I'm not well off at all – and the cost of childcare is unbelievable. Here I am, at forty odd, a relatively successful lawyer, and I'm living in a two-bedroom flat in an OK area and only just managing it.'

Harry is far from being alone, and – looking enviously at the generation above – it is hard for him, and those like him, to imagine himself in their happy situation, with generous state pensions, big houses bought at low prices, plus more inherited from their own parents (his parents bought their house in 1968 for £4,000).

This is all too obvious in Harry's street. On one side of his first-floor flat is a former nurse, now in her sixties, who bought the whole house thirty-five years ago. On the other side are two retired teachers. In both cases, they are living in large houses worth at least £1.5 million each. 'The whole road is like that,' he says. 'Every alternate house is owned by bankers, doctors and lawyers who bought when prices were top-notch, and in between those who are never going to be in that position.

'My immediate worry is how the hell to get my kids through school. I can't even dream they would have the same schooling as I got. What is sort of frustrating is that I played by the rules. I did everything right and I haven't been rewarded.' He laughs at himself for a moment. 'When I gave it a go in 2000 and it didn't quite work out, I was badly penalized. I'm still counting the cost of those few years and it seems very harsh.'

If you couldn't decide whether you could be born rich or poor, then in which period of history would you choose to be born? he asks. I say 1960; he says 1950. Something has gone wrong since then. Then he says something dramatic, and I note it down and underline it.

'Basically, we are all slaves,' he says. 'There isn't really a class divide now. The real divide is between people who own stuff and people that don't, and owning stuff gives you such an advantage. I see it every day in my work, how the people who have stuff abuse the people that don't.'

There is something important here. When mortgages for the semi-detached homes of Metroland in the 1930s could be paid off in fifteen years, and the house cost £500, then that was a reasonable debt to take on. When an inadequate flat for a family now costs a sum so vast that it constrains our lives, our dreams and our careers, that may not be slavery, but it is a quarter of a century of indentured servitude. It means we can't decide to be what we always wanted to be. We need to keep our noses clean, get a job in financial services, and stick to it – and obey.

For centuries, those who managed empires – the Romans, the Conquistadores, the British in India – knew that you could exact obedience from the population simply by imposing a debt. Then they would be forced to work, and to obey, just to pay it off.

Whatever else it might have done, the fateful decision to let the mortgage market rip forces us all to swallow our dreams and do as we are told.

Harry's story was echoed by the *Daily Telegraph* columnist William Leith when he described a man realizing that 'the middle class was no longer a safe place to be':

> 'To buy a house,' he told me, 'you can't do it if you just make a middling income. No – these days, you have to be rich. Or have rich parents. Or maybe steal some money.' And none of these things applied to him. 'I'm always going to be at the mercy of landlords,' he said. He makes nearly twice the average wage.[37]

So it is worthwhile to think a little about what this does to the lives of those who can afford it – *just*. It means that the chance for downshifting, for earning a little less for a better life, is going to be beyond them – and beyond the next generation of middle classes.

'Downshifting' is a word coined in the 1990s, based on a prediction by the futurist Faith Popcorn in 1991 that there would be a mass exit from the rat race which she called 'cashing out' – and which she defined as 'work at something you want to do, where you want to do it'.[38] By the end of the decade, one survey found that 28 per cent of people were deliberately earning less in order to have a better life. It was this phenomenon that drove the exodus of the 'Crunchy' middle classes towards the ring of counties around London from Dorset to Norfolk, once dubbed the 'Muesli Belt', still among the fastest-growing areas of the UK.[39]

Here is the question. Is that conscious decision to shape your life differently, and get out of the rat race, going to be possible for the next generation, or even those in the housing market now? Will my children be able to decide to work at something they love, and earn less as a result? Will they have that kind of choice when they are my age but still struggling to replay a mortgage of £1.2 million, broadly what average prices will be if the next thirty years are anything like the last? That weight of debt will determine their career choice, whatever they most want to do.

The values I was brought up with set great store by my ability to choose, to be whatever I felt compelled to be, and to provide myself with the qualifications I needed to be as independent as possible. That was what being middle-class meant, for many of us, at its best. But here again is the terrible lottery of age. Because I am fifty-four as I write this, and I bought a house in 1986, I can afford to write books, which is rarely the most lucrative way of making a living. But my mortgage is relatively low, so I can shape my life to earn a little less.

'Basically, we are all slaves,' says Harry, contemplating his £380,000 mortgage. 'But to whom and why?'

This is particularly crazy when you think that the houses have long since been built and paid for. They may need some repair but they are complete, the builder pocketed his cheque generations back, but we insist on using our homes like a giant pyramid scheme because it might fund our pensions in the long run. We vest our property with this fantastical aura, a Ponzi scheme that our lives now depend on.

So there lies the great threat to the middle-class life of independence: shrinking houses, shrinking leisure, shrinking green space, shrinking chance to do what you want to with your life, and all because – in order to repeat the middle-class life we were brought up with – we have to sign ourselves into indentured servitude to our mortgage provider. That may be many things, but it certainly isn't independence.

Of course, things might change. There might be a major policy intervention as there was in 1979, or a housing catastrophe as in 1991, that will bring the price of homes crashing down. But that would have serious consequences too, trapping people with outrageous loans which amount to more than their homes are worth, threatening banks and pension funds (including mine), and all the other investors with worthless property portfolios.

Will we benefit from these hugely inflated prices because we inherit the profits from our parents? Yes, sometimes, but when it comes to passing the benefits on to our children, all too often the equity in our homes is going to be swallowed up replacing our non-existent pensions or paying for our long-term residential care as we linger on into our nineties. Or replacing some of the health-care that a dwindling NHS used to give us, whatever our incomes.

Will prices be dragged down because there are so few new entrants on the housing ladder? I don't think so – not now that property has become a speculative investment. In the USA, inves-tors get on planes and buy up whole new housing developments. In the UK, we barely notice the international investors who do the same, or the bankers who use their bonus to buy a couple of flats every year. Chinese and Asian buyers are currently keeping London house prices going up, and London drags the rest in its wake like a long, winding goods train. House prices have set themselves free from average earnings like a child letting go a gas balloon. It may pop, but it probably won't just drift down again.

Of course there will be a downward pressure on house prices in the long run, if people can no longer afford to rent. But in practice we have waited for a generation for the downward shift to happen, and if it does, it is only for a few months, and then back goes the line to soar upwards again. By far the most likely future is that the equilibrium is maintained, with the investors at the controls of the engine – steaming through and scattering the remains of the middle classes to the winds.

Our children will be faced with a life of renting. Not such a terrible fate, perhaps, but their pension costs will be higher as a result, because they will carry on paying rent into old age when they would have paid off mortgages before. They will be constrained by the whims of landlords and the lists of breakages totted up by estate agents at the end of the lease. If the defining feature of the new middle class is their craving for independence, it is hard to see how they can have it.

We have lived through a peculiar period when the mere visit to an estate agent meant confronting our dreams for our own future lives and realizing we couldn't afford them. That period is drawing to a close. Visiting estate agents with the intention of buying is set to become a preserve of the very rich.

Middle Classes in Figures

Cost of a suburban semi if it had kept its value since 1930: about
£24,900.

The New Middle-Class-Values Dictionary

CONFIDENCE: Confidence has always been a middle-class value,
but now it seems to have overtaken other values of days gone by,
like thrift. Once upon a time, the middle classes avoided debt.
Now they have replaced their commitment to being careful with
money with confidence that they can manage it – and a tolerance
of debt that has allowed them to surf the house-price explosion.
Confidence is a defining characteristic in other ways too: the
middle classes believe they understand the world, and know their
way around it, and can finesse the little problems that beset us all
in a competitive world. When they find the education system
impossible, they reach first, not for the placards and barricades,
but for a quiet word in the proper ear. Confidence is both their
great weapon against fate but also, potentially, their undoing.

Dispatches from the Frontline

National Trust café, Mottisfont Abbey, Hampshire, Saturday, 3 p.m.
The lady opposite me, sitting at the rustic table, is wearing white

gloves and I'm waiting to see how she eats her scone and jam. Despite this, it is clear that the clientele here are not the cut-glass, upper-crust types you might expect, who jostle to the till in National Trust cafés across the nation, but mainly older couples having a special afternoon out. You feel they have saved up for it. I watch them under the willow-pattern plates along the wall, staring sadly past each other as they contemplate their tea. They seem to have little to say.

One of them breaks the silence. 'I don't remember it being self-service before.' They had hoped for something a little more, shall we say, personalized.

Perhaps that is hardly surprising, since we have colonized the servants' quarters of this stately home. The abbey was stolen from the monks by Henry VIII and his henchmen, and now the basement has been stolen from the servants, and is decked out with dried flowers along the old Aga stove, together with a brushed stone floor, beige paint, 1930s wirelesses and tasteful bowls of cutlery. There is a strange 1950s fridge. Why does the English middle class have this extraordinary penchant for twentieth-century servant chic?

But I have struck lucky, because I find myself talking about the politicians' word 'aspiration', which is supposed to define the middle classes. I'm not at all sure about this, and neither is my friend.

'I don't know what aspiration means any more,' she says. 'My father grew up in an agricultural workers' cottage. I went to Oxford. That was aspiration. My parents had a sense of rising prosperity. They had foreign holidays and they bought their own home. But I don't believe my child will have better opportunities than I did. I don't want his life to be about earning large sums of money.'

She talked about growing up on a modest housing estate in Watford, and then the key point: 'I have two friends who are hospital consultants, and they can't afford a home in the estate I grew up in. It's a very ordinary estate.'

Hospital consultants are doing very nicely, thank you. The conversation makes me nervous. It seems to imply that prospects for my own children are worse than I thought.

On the wall next door, opposite the array of Victoria sponges, is a huge black metal contraption above the Tudor fireplace. There are heavy wheels and pulleys and black chains holding it together. 'It's a Victorian spit,' says the girl behind the counter in a quiet moment. 'They never use it. It's just for decoration.'

3

The second clue: the strange case of the disappearing banks

'Fifteen years ago, a half-dozen houses stuck here and there.
There's the old cemetery, squirrels, buttercups, daisies. Dozens of
the prettiest little homes you ever saw. Ninety per cent owned by
suckers who used to pay rent to you.'

Estate agent tells the landlord what a building society
can do, in *It's a Wonderful Life*, Frank Capra et al., 1946

Martins; Glyn, Mills & Co.; Williams, Deacon's; Cunliffe, Brooks & Co.; Nichols, Baker & Crane; William & John Biggerstaffe; Knaresborough & Claro; Dingley, Pearse & Co.; Shilson, Coode & Co.; J. W. Pease; United Counties; Woods & Co.; Molineux, Whitfield & Co.; Woodhall, Hebden & Co.; Goslings & Sharpe; Gurney's; David Morris & Sons . . .

Ring any bells? Those are some of the names of English banking, and it sounds almost like a list on a war memorial. They are gone. Perhaps not completely forgotten, but swallowed up long since by the great banking houses, one by one, and those in their turn swallowed again. I say not forgotten because I once met a lady in Birmingham who still treasured her account book for the Birmingham Municipal Bank, founded by Neville Chamberlain in 1919. It grew to have more than sixty branches across the city before it succumbed to the Trustee Savings Bank in 1976, in turn swallowed up by Lloyds to become Lloyds TSB, and so on and so inexorably on.

All of them were emphatically middle-class institutions, founded with the middle-class values of economy and common sense running through them like a stick of rock, their names engraved on great brass plaques down the high streets of England. They have proved not quite as sturdy as they were believed to be. Their absence also represents a peculiar difference from the high streets of other wealthy countries, across the continent as well as in North America. They have a multiplicity of small banks; we don't.

I spent the winter a couple of years ago in the town of Great Barrington, Massachusetts, where they had eleven small banks to serve a population of 7,500. The equivalent-sized UK town, even in the wealthy south-east, has nothing like that. Heathfield in East Sussex has four; Steyning in West Sussex has two. Romsey in Hampshire, twice the size, has five – and all national chains, unlike those in Great Barrington, which are overwhelmingly local.

The issue of why this matters is what this chapter is all about, and the story of how we lost our grassroots banks is a strange one, going back a long way. It might not have mattered at all, given that we developed instead a diverse and varied network of building societies, dedicated to thrift and property ownership, two key feature of the middle-class life. But would you believe it, these were also bundled into oblivion during the 1990s, in a bizarre and hysterical series of incidents, and the arid banking desert, dominated by a handful of international megabanks – with no roots anywhere except in the 'market' – is all we have left.

This double loss – first the little banks and then the big building societies – is one of the most peculiar aspects of the history of the middle classes in England. The first phase brought about the demise of those lending institutions with a genuine interest in local economic success, which made the huge growth of the Victorian middle classes possible. They financed the newspapers, breweries, farms and small factories that underpinned the towns and cities of the nation, and the burgeoning middle classes that managed them. Then they disappeared in an extraordinary flurry of acquisitions over five decades: six-sevenths of British banks disappeared during the half-century to 1920.[1]

The full implications of the second phase are not yet clear, and there are still building societies left behind from the wreckage. But the demutualization of Britain's huge mutuals, in a flurry of greed – feasting on the combined reserves built up by careful and responsible generations gone by – was the very opposite of thrift. The days of the early 1980s, when two-thirds of all UK adults saved with building societies and a third of all children, have gone for good.

Now the middle classes have to do without these supportive institutions, and have had to put their trust in the small group of mega-banks, whose attention is somewhere else entirely. And even if the demise of so many financial institutions over the century did not matter back then to the average middle-class family, it matters very much now. The way out of the predicament – a renewed commitment to enterprise – demands institutions exactly like this, and they barely exist any more.

Bank managers have always had a mixed press in England, and there is no doubt that the English – in contrast to the Scots, for example – are the most conservative nation on earth when it comes to money. Some years ago, I was assured by the Washington correspondent of one of the Fleet Street papers (it was Fleet Street in those days) that all money is based on gold, which hasn't been true of the pound since 1931. Admittedly, he was from the Sun, but you understand the point.

The leading figure in the TV series *Dad's Army*, Captain Mainwaring, seemed to epitomize the type – solid, dull, sensible, extremely conservative, a true believer in the reality of money and the consequences of debt, and a glorious buffoon anywhere except on a spreadsheet. Mainwaring managed Swallow Bank, a fictional creation, but there remains a sense among the English middle classes that Mainwaring still sits at his desk and all's right with the world, when the truth is he has long since been replaced by risk software operated from regional office. It is part of the fearsome middle-class naivety about the way the globe is these days.

The story of the demise of Swallow Bank and most of those like it goes back to the end of the nineteenth century, and the culprit – at least as much as anyone else – was Barclays, then known as Barclay, Bevan, Tritton, Ransom, Bouverie and Co., or in the City of London as the 'long firm'. In 1896 they persuaded nine smaller banks to join them, mainly in the East and North, in a major enterprise to secure Barclays for the future. Even then, it held a quarter of all the deposits in the private banking sector, and it had a unique approach to local management. The boards of the banks they took over stayed in existence. 'Local management will remain in the same hands as heretofore,' they said, 'the private character of the Banks being thus preserved.'[2] It was a very English kind of bank.

This was a period when the middle classes were flocking to open bank accounts, just as the local banks which had served their forefathers disappeared month by month into the jaws of the City. By the outbreak of the First World War, Barclays had doubled their branches, mainly by the most frenetic merger activity, starting straight away with the Newcastle bank Woods & Co. Their biggest takeover was the Consolidated Bank of Cornwall in 1905, itself a recent merger of family banks. The most dramatic was the purchase of United Counties Bank, giving Barclays a major presence across the Midlands.

By 1918, even the government was worried about this merger mania, and appointed a committee of inquiry which urged it to legislate at once. Being the British government, it never quite got round to the task, and agreed to drop the idea of anti-trust legislation – which was bitterly opposed by the banks – on condition that there would be no more mergers between the big ones. Desperate to get under the wire, Barclay's just had time to snap up the massive 601 branches of the London, Provincial and Western Bank. By 1920, they employed 11,000 clerks in 1,783 branches. There were now five big banks left standing: Midland, Westminster, Lloyds, Barclays and National Provincial.

It was already the most concentrated banking infrastructure in the world, and deeply conservative. Left-handed people were banned from its staff, at least in Barclays. Women were dismissed when they got married. Board minutes were still written by hand. In Barclays, ledger clerks were issued with special ink designed to clog any new fountain pens, which the banking oligarchy disapproved of. In Manchester, banks were still transferring cash across the city using the last horse-drawn cab as late as 1940. The Gurney family, now part of the Barclays empire too, still took their hounds into the bank with them in Norwich.

The Big Five oligarchy was preferred by the Bank of England governor Montagu Norman, who dominated British banking between the wars, with his flowing cloak and his strange private life (he was a pioneering patient of the psychoanalyst Carl Jung, who believed he was mad). Norman thought that big concentrated banks were more likely to survive the upheaval of the Great Depression than small banks. This may have been right: there is no doubt that Britain avoided the banking disasters that overtook the USA in 1933.

It was a middle-class world which became a caricature of itself. The arch-conservatism of English money led to widespread welcome of the disastrous decision to join the Gold Standard in 1925. The banks also failed miserably to understand the technical challenges of the new industries, unlike our continental competitors, and have made little progress in this direction since. A strange dreamlike fantasy has infected English banking ever since:

what began as snobbery about trade continued as ignorance about industry, to culminate in disdain for anything except speculation. The big British banks have never really regarded the fledgling enterprise economy, and the new technologies behind it, as their concern.

The Big Five stayed in place until the 1970s when, fearful of the new American giants, Barclays launched a whole new round of banking mergers by snapping up the last of the independents, the ancient Liverpool-based Martin's Bank, with over 700 branches. Barclays cleverly secured a deal with the Bank of England whereby they were allowed to buy Martin's if Westminster Bank was also allowed to take over National Provincial (creating NatWest) and none of it would even be referred to the Monopolies and Mergers Commission. The Big Four remained in place until the demutualization of the building societies in the 1990s.

But the Big Four, and their even more highly consolidated successors, were not interested in local economies. Their eyes were glued elsewhere, where the big profits are. They had no particular interest in the economic success of any locality where they happened to have branches, and for the entrepreneurial middle classes who wanted to make things happen for themselves and their communities, the disappearance of small financial institutions from the UK, and small banks especially, was a disaster.

Of course, there are huge banks also in the USA. But in the USA, their place was taken not only by hundreds of small local banks – half the money saved in the USA is kept in small banks – but also by a growing sector of sizeable credit unions and community development banks known as Community Development Finance Institutions (CDFIs), which are actually financed by the big banks under American law. Families who don't want to bank with the megalosaurs of banking – Citibank, Bank of America – do have a real local choice.

The same kind of choices exist in continental Europe with the small agricultural banks of France, the *caja de ahorras* of Spain, the *Landesbanks* and *Sparkassen* of Germany and the cantonal banks of Switzerland, even the popular postbank BancoPosta in Italy. In the USA, small banks represent less than 11 per cent of banking assets, but they make 40 per cent of loans to small business.[3] All these other countries still have some kind of local financial institutions that are interested in customers, prepared to back local business and support homeownership – on the side of the middle classes in a way that the big banks are not. We have no such support on the high street.

Which brings us to the building societies, and it is time to continue the story we left off during the last chapter, when we abandoned the building societies without the means to control rising house prices. The chain leading to disaster goes back to the peculiar position in which the building societies found themselves after the revolution by Howe and Lawson, the end of exchange controls, the end of the Corset to keep house prices low, and the slow but inevitable unravelling of the Cartel which allowed them to operate in that protected environment. There they were in 1983, at the height of their popularity and financial muscle, but facing nose-to-nose competition from the big banks.

The idea that the building societies were predominantly middle-class institutions might need some argument. We tend to think of them as emerging from the friendly societies that helped poor people struggle out of industrial poverty, and they certainly did. But the first purpose-built building society began in Birmingham in 1775, to help the lower middle classes buy a roof over their heads. Helping the middle classes buy homes and providing a safe place for the working classes to save allowed them to become a mainstay of both, enabling the boundaries of class to stay permeable, reflecting and encouraging those eminently middle-class values of thrift and restraint. In the early 1980s, building society losses on their mortgage accounts were one two hundredth of those of the banks.[4]

The middle classes wanted low-cost home loans and they wanted a safe place to keep their savings, which would give them a comfortable rate of return and the security that their money would never be gambled away on the international markets. Here was the *raison d'être* of the building societies. Every sizeable town had one (more than 2,200 in the UK by 1900). It was true that there were fewer than a thousand by 1940, but they had ten times the assets.[5] They were underpinning the huge increase in home ownership and, at the same time, underpinning the middle classes and their careful but comfortable way of life.

So what went wrong? How did we lose most of our building societies in little more than a decade, and lose the underpinning infrastructure, the pit props that kept the institutions the middle classes needed – and not just the middle classes either? The answer lies back in that moment of uncertainty in the mid-1980s when the world seemed suddenly more dangerous for the building societies. What followed was a frenetic campaign to give them the weapons they needed to compete, but one small mistake – one Achilles heel in the whole enterprise – brought about the extraordinary explosion that has become known as 'demutualization', a strange public drama involving merchant bankers, carpetbaggers, butlers and some titanic electoral struggles among some of the biggest ranks of customers of any banks anywhere in the world.

It was a tragic error which meant that their successful race to stay in the market led to an explosion of greed – with terrible consequences, not just for the middle classes, but for the UK economy.

Mark Boléat is one of those economists and policymakers who everyone acknowledges are extremely clever. He is now effectively leader of the City of London Corporation, but he led the Building

Societies Association through the revolutionary 1980s, having joined the organization almost straight from university in 1974. He was already linked to the band of Conservative radicals around Geoffrey Howe and Keith Joseph as they prepared for power in the 1970s, and shared their view that mortgage queues – the result of the Corset which kept interest rates low – were really no longer acceptable. It was a bit like allocating mortgages as they did bread in Soviet Russia.

Before the election which brought the Thatcher government to power, he co-wrote a Conservative policy pamphlet with Nigel Lawson called *Towards Freedom in Housing* – but did so anonymously because he knew the building society grandees would be furious. Half a decade later, the world had changed and Boléat was deputy director-general, responsible for managing the Cartel – which meant phoning round the general managers of the member societies and telling them what their interest rates should be.

As we saw in chapter 2, the Corset unravelled because banks could get round it by borrowing on international markets – and the Cartel slowly went the same way, largely unlamented, despite its critical role in middle-class lifestyles. Boléat watched as the months went by and the building societies' share of the mortgage market plummeted from nearly 90 per cent, and went rapidly downhill to less than half.

It was a cosy world they were defending. Any building society that wanted to step out of line had to give twenty-eight days' notice. General managers took no decisions about prices or products – they were only allowed to provide savings accounts and mortgages. They could open new branches, and did so with such enthusiasm through the 1970s – at the rate of nearly eight a week – that they were accused of threatening the viability of high streets. A strange irony, given what was about to happen.

This was the world of the so-called 3-6-3: offer 3 per cent on savings, 6 per cent on mortgages, and be on the golf course by three in the afternoon. Except that by the summer of 1984, with the Los Angeles Olympics in the background, the advice system on interest rates fell apart, just as interest rates shot up to over 12 per cent. Boléat relished the new dispensation which gave building societies the freedom to set what rates they wanted. 'I used to say the world will not end,' he says now. 'Chief executives would call up and say, how do I set the mortgage rates? I would say: "Be a chief executive – take a decision!"'

It was a thrilling time to be in mortgages. The sale of council houses to their tenants, which Boléat had advocated along with Lawson, represented a kind of apotheosis of the middle-class ideal, despite the difficulties about replacing them later. It was bold and it was intended to be a major shift in the balance of power in the direction of people who wanted the independence of their own home. We forget now the terrible record of post-war public housing design under local authority control in the 1960s and 70s: impersonal, concrete, miserable, featureless, No Ball Games, and all the rest.

Either way, the building societies were going to have to fight if they were to survive in the new world, with Citibank and the other American giants breathing down their necks. Yet they didn't even have the power to clear their own cheques, let alone offer a range of other housing-related services. Something Had To Be Done, and Boléat set about doing it. Lawson, now Chancellor of the Exchequer, confirms that his officials had been trying to get the government to legislate on building societies for years, but that he had been 'unwilling to go whole hog'.[6] Now Whole Hog was suddenly on the agenda. Through the early months of 1985, Boléat was in and out of the Treasury helping them draft the new legislation. When it was unveiled later in the year, the Building Societies Bill – passed as the Building Societies Act of 1986 – gave building societies most of the powers they wanted.

Not quite all: the Treasury drew the line at letting them take the place of solicitors in the sale of homes – a pity, because most of us would like to shake the conveyancers up a bit – but they got most of the rest. Building societies would be able to clear cheques, run estate agencies, issue credit cards, organize overdrafts, build homes and run houses for rent, and much more besides. (It wasn't until the final week of John Major's government in 1997, and also thanks to Boléat, that they were given a general power to do whatever they wanted.)

Much more controversially, if they didn't have enough depositors' money for the mortgages people wanted, they would be allowed to raise 40 per cent of their mortgage finance on the international markets (raised by the Blair government to 50 per cent). It was overusing this power that would eventually bring down Northern Rock in 2008.

As the new law came up for its first reading in the House of Commons, the building societies' share of the UK mortgage market dipped below 50 per cent. Would the legislation be in time to provide any kind of opposition to the rampaging banks? Boléat dampened expectations. 'In fact,' he said in a speech once the bill had passed through the House of Commons, 'the building society legislation will be the cause of comparatively little.'[7]

As it turned out, Boléat was wrong. Something else was going on.

Everyone in the industry knew that Abbey National, the second-biggest society, wanted to become a bank, to escape what they saw as the limitations of building society regulations. That was why they had appointed an outsider, the former Gillette UK chief executive Peter Birch, to lead them in 1983 – a man with little knowledge or interest in the strange traditions of the building-society sector. He objected to the term 'surplus' rather than 'profit': 'surpluses are for choirboys,' he said, wielding the corporate axe.[8] Abbey persuaded the Treasury to give them a means of converting. Building societies were mutual organizations – owned by their customers – and turning them into banks would mean somehow converting members into shareholders. Halifax had 10 million members. Nothing comparable had ever been contemplated on that scale before, and here lay the root of the nightmare that loomed ahead.

As it happened, the Treasury was not too keen on building societies. They had all their eggs in the housing basket. They looked unsafe. Treasury officials were only too happy for them all to become banks, if necessary. But Boléat and his colleagues hardly wanted to lose all their members, and certainly not on a whim, so the new law was packed with safeguards when it came to voting. If Abbey National wanted to become a bank, they would have to persuade as many as 750,000 of their 8 million members to agree to give up their ownership rights.

But here was the rub. What if the building-society managers used their reserves – built up little by little over generations – to bribe the members into voting yes? The team writing the new law was only too aware of this risk, so they made sure that only 4 per cent of reserves could be used to compensate the members. The drafting team even realized what might happen if that kind of bribery became possible – everyone would rush to open accounts. So they included a provision in the new law that members would need to have had accounts for two years before they became eligible for any kind of payout. That should have been that.

The debate took place in a restless House of Commons at the end of the year, with MPs anxious to get away for Christmas. Most of them were overwhelmingly in favour, but a handful warned of trouble ahead. One of them was the popular Liberal MP for Truro, David Penhaligon, who pinpointed precisely the flaw in the bill:

> With some limitations, details of which I find difficult to interpret, the large building societies would be able to offer a bonus to the depositors in the small building societies to obtain their votes.

Some years ago, Parliament outlawed the practice of offering financial inducements to obtain votes. I have honest doubts about this measure, but I shall listen to the detailed arguments before I condemn it absolutely . . . We should never forget that the societies' real job is to help people to buy homes. We should never forget that people expect building societies to be cautious, conservative, and even dull. There is nothing but honour in the course that has been followed for the past 150 years. Smart dealing should be left to the whiz kids. The societies do not need that type of business, and they should not be looking for the type of director or general manager who will urge it on them.

It was the last Commons speech he ever made. Three days later, in the early hours of the morning, he was killed in a car accident on his way to talk to constituents sorting the Christmas post.

Penhaligon was far-sighted on two counts – first to pinpoint the obscure wording of the safeguards against paying a 'bonus', and second because 'the type of director' he warned against was precisely the kind of person the biggest building societies were now desperate to recruit. One anonymous building society manager remembered it like this:

When the Building Society Act came in in 1986, as of 1987 the word 'profitability' existed for the first time . . . as opposed to surplus of income over expenditure, stick it in the reserves. So people said 'Oooh, profitability', and that took them down the appropriate commercial road. 'Well, if we're a business and now it is expected to make profits and maintain capital ratios, we've got to have people from plc worlds that are used to doing that type of thing' . . . So then: 'Oh crumbs, we are competing with these; we are not just lunch clubs any more' . . . We used to have lunch with each other . . . sharing all kinds of confidences. That doesn't happen any more. Life is tough; we are one wolf pack against another wolf pack.[9]

At the head of the pack, Abbey National's board was extremely worried. How on earth would they get their members to vote in big enough numbers to satisfy the requirements of the new law? Only a handful of them ever voted at AGMs – why would they vote now? Certainly not 750,000 of them. Nor did they really understand the wording about the two-year rule.

It occurred to the board that this obscurity was actually rather an opportunity. So they took the brand-new regulator, the Building Societies Commission, to court to challenge it – and they won. Even the judge described it as an obscure and complex piece of legislation and he found in their favour. It also became clear that, although they might not be able to ransack the reserves, they could pay members in shares in the new company. Abbey National managers were nervous that the government would act to fill the loophole, but Nigel Lawson did not stir. 'The legislation was faulty,' says Boléat. 'It intended to limit the payment to members but it referred only to cash payments. There was no limit on payment by shares.'

Abbey National had a million borrowers and 7 million individual accounts. All were now potentially the lucky owners of shares worth about £190 – if they voted yes to abandon their ownership rights. It was a huge undertaking. Eight million voters made this an election bigger than many countries'. The share giveaway would be to a population bigger than Norway's. Professor John Kay, an influential financial critic, wrote shortly afterwards about the paradox which faced the Abbey members campaigning against: 'They were fighting to preserve a degree of accountability to the membership which the management of the Society patently did not feel. For incumbent management, the contrary views of some of their members were not matters to be weighed in the balance and taken account of in formulation of policy. They were a nuisance to be dealt with by the costly use of public relations advisers and legal processes.'[10]

This was only one of the eye-openers about the whole affair – just how little mutual ownership had come to mean. Members got a rather dull letter once a year urging them to vote for a dull-looking slate of candidates recommended by the board, and that was it. Were there any benefits of ownership? If there were, most people seemed to have forgotten them. It is easy to blame people's greed for what happened next, but we must remember how empty mutualism had become in practice.

The machinery pressed on. Deloitte Haskins and Sells were recruited to count the votes ready for a special general meeting at the Wembley Stadium complex in April 1989. Abbey chairman Sir Campbell Adamson was increasingly seen in the media. But even as the ballot papers were being prepared, senior Abbey officials were getting nervous again. One of them went to see Mark Boléat at the Building Societies Association, where he was now director-general, to ask his advice. The idea that converting to a bank would mean better customer service was barely cutting any ice. Why would it? Nor were the arguments about needing to raise more capital on the financial markets. They needed some better reasons for conversion.

The real reason, as Boléat says now, was 'because PLCs are important and make lots more money', whereas building societies were 'tin-pot, stuffy'. 'That was Abbey's motive,' he says now. 'Frankly, it was the motive of most of the others that, simply by being quoted as a bank, they were much more important. Part of it was also the persuasive charm of the investment bankers – "We might be looking for a director or advisor in a year or so, and your experience of demutualization would be really helpful to us."'

When 11 April dawned, and the crowds expected at Wembley did not show up, Adamson and his colleagues must have expected the worst. Only about a thousand of the 8 million arrived (the event cost Abbey National £700 a head), except that by then they had some inkling of the vote they were about to announce. It was a massive vote of confidence in demutualization. As many as 3.2 million Abbey National members voted and 90 per cent had chosen to take the money. Not one of the rebels was elected to the board. Clearly, £190 in shares was a powerful argument in itself.

Even so, it was in many ways a sad end for a historic institution, the product of a 1944 merger between two pioneering organizations: the Abbey Road Building Society based at Sherlock Holmes's fictional address in Baker Street, and the National Building Society, formed back in 1849 by the two campaigning Liberal MPs Richard Cobden and John Bright. In one stride, Abbey National became the nation's fifth-biggest bank.

A week later, the popular postbank Girobank, set up by Tony Benn inside the Post Office in 1968, was sold at a knock-down price to the Alliance & Leicester Building Society for £130 million. It was a sign of the times.

The real storm was yet to come. The legislation settled down. Boléat set up the Council of Mortgage Lenders to keep Abbey National in the fold, and began pushing for other reforms. At the same time, a young stockbroker called Tony Greenham was working his way up Barclays BZW, the British candidate for global domination of the financial markets, and was to take a frontline seat in the coming drama as part of the team which was going to demutualize the Woolwich.

Barclays BZW was a strange animal, a massively ambitious merger between a stockbroker and a stockjobber, and an uneasy mix with the fusty old bank that was Barclays. It was said that Barclays' chairman Andrew Buxton used to go out into the street outside his headquarters in the City of London and send away all the taxis waiting to take the brokers to lunch in the West End.[11] It was this outfit that was given the task of selling the Woolwich, and Tony Greenham accepted the argument in favour. 'The theory was that the building societies would become dynamic new banks and be able to raise the capital they needed to expand,' he says now. 'They would be able to pay proper rates for top executives, who would all be geniuses, of course. In a way, it seemed quite exciting because there were lots of new banks appearing on the scene which, given the complacency of the existing ones, seemed quite a good idea.'

The qualms came as he helped write the prospectus for the sale of shares, eulogizing Woolwich's history and heritage:

> At the time, I couldn't quite understand how you could sell all this heritage for what for most people was about a hundred quid. I expressed my disquiet and talked about 'carpetbaggers' when many of my colleagues were opening accounts wherever they could, and one of my colleagues was quite cross about it. He said: 'If you're not doing it, you shouldn't be working in this job, because that's what we do – we make money and seek profits.' It was a mystery to him. I thought, this heritage is being flogged off in a moment, and people are going to get the cumulative scrapings of people who dragged themselves out of poverty by saving.

The process was the same as it had been for Abbey National. You created a limited company, and you asked people to trade in their ownership rights for shares in the new company. It was intended as a good way to spread shareholder democracy, but in practice most people sold on their shares straight away and they were auctioned off in the first few days of trading. Barclays was waiting in the wings and – at the right time – they swooped and snapped up the new Woolwich bank. They also closed my local branch, which I have never quite forgiven them for.

'In retrospect, it was an act of vandalism,' says Tony Greenham. 'We lost a quite distinctive mutual financial institution, which was part of the British fabric. If only we could get it back, but we can't.

The clue was in the names – "Woolwich", "Halifax". These were local institutions, which went national and were sold off.'

Here was the problem. It made sense to convert some of these institutions into banks if that was what the members genuinely wanted, but in practice they cared very little either way. Yet there was something about the sturdy values of the mutual sector, and the way in which they supported the middle classes, which should have rung alarm bells. The values of the middle classes had been underpinned by this sense of thrift about money. Something was wrong.

After the Abbey National shares flotation, everything went quiet in the building-society world. Society boards discussed what they might do, but the truth was that the economy was in too dodgy a state to encourage anyone to issue shares in anything much. The housing market was also just recovering from its most destructive period of hyperinflation.

This was one of the strangest episodes in the history of home ownership. In those days, you used to be able to get tax relief on your mortgage repayments for the first £30,000 of the mortgage. If your partner had bought the house with you, then you got double the tax relief. It was one of the strange ways in which poorer people's taxes were recycled to encourage middle-class home-owners, and, as house prices rose inexorably, Chancellor Nigel Lawson announced in the 1988 budget that this benefit – known as 'double MIRAS' – was going to end for new purchases.

The trouble was, in those early days of IT, the Inland Revenue said it would take six months to change their computers, so Lawson delayed. For six incredible months, people dashed to take advantage of tax relief as a couple. If house prices were rocketing before, it was nothing to what happened next – if you could find someone to buy a house with. Prices rose at an incredible rate of nearly a third in one year. Boléat used to tell a joke about cocktail parties at estate agencies. You could go along at 7 p.m. without a house, or a mortgage or a partner. By 10 p.m., the estate agent had fixed you up with all three.

Two years on from that heady summer of panicky house prices, with Abbey National now firmly in the banking sector, everything looked very different. Nigel Lawson had resigned, Margaret Thatcher was on her way out, the economy was in recession and mortgage interest rates were shooting up. They had doubled by 1991, and many of those people who had bought in all the excitement of 1988 were sitting on property they couldn't sell – because it was worth less than the mortgage. Worse, they still had the shotgun relationships taken on to claw the last chance of double MIRAS.

Boléat's deputy Adrian Coles, soon to take over from him, had a new version of the estate-agent joke – that people had mortgages they couldn't afford, houses they couldn't sell and partners they couldn't stand.

But fast-forward a few years, to 1994, and there was a new prime minister, the economy had begun to pick up again, and demutualization seeped back on to the financial pages. April that year was a tumultuous month: the Rwandan genocide began, the multiple murder Fred West was arrested, and Nelson Mandela was elected South African president. Late in the evening of 20 April, Adrian Coles got a call tipping him off that the following morning Lloyds Bank would pay £1.8 billion for the Cheltenham & Gloucester Building Society and its million members.

That took him aback in itself – a demutualization followed by an acquisition – but what really shocked him was the scale of the bid. If the C&G managed to sell itself to Lloyds, every member and borrower would get a massive sum in recompense, probably around £2,000. The High Court would have to rule on the proposal, but if it went ahead it was clear that almost anything was possible. Any bank could buy almost any building society simply by paying its members. Hostile takeovers were possible. The building society network might not survive at all.

'I realized that it would blow the sector apart,' said Coles. 'Most of the customers of Cheltenham & Gloucester had less than that in their accounts. Most of them didn't realize they were owners of it, and – in return for giving up membership, when we were so poor at explaining what mutuality was – they would get all this money. It was a real no-brainer.'

Two weeks later, Northern Rock said that it would merge with the Heart of England Building Society. Something was going on, and the Cheltenham & Gloucester announcement changed everything. Even the giant Halifax decided it would have to rethink its decision not to convert. What if there was a hostile bid? Could they ever withstand it? Were their own reserves too much of a temptation to corporate raiders? Could building societies survive at all? A year of agonizing and rethinking followed, and the *Observer* was reporting: 'The great and good of the building society industry will sit down together on Thursday to consider whether the organisations they lead are bound for extinction.'[12]

In the months that followed the C&G announcement, as Coles took over the reins at the Building Societies Association, it began to look as though he would have no members left. One by one, the announcements came. Bristol & West sold itself to the Bank of Ireland. National & Provincial sold itself to Abbey National. Leeds merged with Halifax. Alliance & Leicester, Halifax and Northern Rock turned themselves into banks. This was also the point where the Woolwich changed its status, assisted by Tony Greenham's team at Barclays BZW.

By the end of 1997, a staggering £36 billion in cash and shares was put into the hands of building-society members, providing a huge boost to consumer spending, which fed into the sense of feel-good in the early months of the Blair government which came to power in May that year. Time after time, Coles and his colleagues came away from the Treasury convinced that they would act to close the loophole – but they never did. Gordon Brown arrived as Chancellor that year, but he never acted either. Not a bit of it. Brown's adviser Ed Balls regarded the idea of regulated small-scale banking as an anachronism. The word 'Jurassic' was used.

There was also a completely different culture taking over. Banking people were employed by the new banks and the remaining building societies. Fees for board members and salaries were going through the roof. In the short time during and after takeover by Barclays, a quarter of the senior managers of the Woolwich left because they didn't like the new culture.

That same year, the comedy duo known as the Two Johns – John Bird and John Fortune – staged a fake interview with a building-society chairman converting to a bank, and it struck a chord. 'Building societies are relics from the past,' said John Fortune at his most oleaginous. 'Look at the words, like "mutual", "friendly", "beneficial", "society", "building", just examples which are completely ludicrous in the environment of modern business.'

Conversion, he said, meant that they needed 'no longer be concerned about the feeble ambitions to own some pathetic semi in Willesden'.

The trouble was that, although many of the public – most of them customers and members of building societies – could understand that criticism, a payout was a payout. The term 'carpetbagger' was first coined to describe those profiteering in the defeated southern states after the American Civil War. Now it was exhumed to describe the millions of people who began opening new building-society accounts in the hope of striking it lucky.

It was clear to Coles and his colleagues that, if building societies were to survive at all, they had somehow to rediscover the virtues of mutuality – of ownership by customers – and to sell them. Otherwise they might as well all become banks. And it was at this point – as many commentators were saying that building societies were finished – that he took a very brave decision. The Council of Mortgage Lenders clearly had to be hived off on its own, and Coles had the opportunity to be director-general of either. Courageously, he chose the embattled Building Societies Association.

'Some people said it was a brave decision at the time, because it looked as though the whole mutual sector was about to convert,' he says now. 'But I thought it was morally the right thing to do.'

But of course there were actually benefits of being a mutual, though these had somehow been forgotten during the recent debates. It meant you didn't have to pay dividends to shareholders. You could plough the profits back into the business, or give them back to customers. You could certainly provide a better service, and a more local service – closer to customers. It was also becoming clear what takeover by the big banks meant. One in five bank branches in the UK closed during the 1990s. Northern Rock lost half of its branches in five years. The Halifax lost a third. Abbey National lost a quarter. Woolwich disappeared altogether.

So the following years finally saw some success for the mutual lobby. Skipton, Portman and Chelsea all managed to resist attempts by carpetbaggers to force a vote, but the bitterest battle was being fought out around the remaining giant building society, the Nationwide.

'We were very lucky in the quality of the carpetbaggers, who gave us a mild dose of what might happen if they won,' says Coles now. Sure enough, the self-appointed carpetbagger spokesman was a butler who had been employed by Prince Charles, called Michael Hardern. Ironically, he had been among those campaigning against the odds to prevent Abbey National becoming a bank, but he shifted to the dark side in defeat and stood for election to the Nationwide board. Among his stranger proposals was the idea that they should invite the Spice Girls onto the board with him.

He lost but, in defeat, he launched the real battle. He put down a motion for the next AGM to force Nationwide to convert into a bank. Nationwide chief executive Brian Davies was under no legal obligation to put the vote to the members, but there needed to be some kind of resolution to the endless argument, so – very bravely – he did so. It was to be a damned near thing.

Reports in the press suggested the payouts for converting to a bank might be as high as £1,500. At the height of the storm, as many as 125,000 people every week were queuing up at Nationwide branches hoping to cash in. But this was to be the line in the sand, and Nationwide's managers fought back, winning the vote by a slim margin of 37,000, less than 1 per cent of the membership. Adrian Coles and his colleagues drew a huge sigh of relief.

'I would have left the BSA if the vote had been lost,' he says now. 'But it was very narrowly won, then we really had to do some thinking about what a building society was, and what it stands for, and how do we stop hundreds of thousands of people opening accounts to get free money and vote the organizations out of existence.'

The vote under its belt, Nationwide's managers took on the carpetbaggers directly. They closed their books to new accounts and, when they opened up again in November 1998, new account holders had to sign an undertaking that any benefits they might earn in the future would be assigned to the Nationwide Foundation, their own charity. It effectively prevented carpetbaggers, and Nationwide members remain bound by that agreement now. Nationwide is now bigger than all the other remaining building societies together – the biggest in the world.

'Nationwide was never under threat again after it won that vote,' says Coles. 'It was a huge moment of cheer.'

Bradford & Bingley was the last demutualization, in 2000. One of their senior executives, John Wrigglesworth, blamed panic attacks by investors. 'It has been a self-fulfilling, cataclysmic spiral into the abyss,' he said.[13] The Irish plumber Stephen Major who led the Bradford & Bingley campaign warned that Nationwide was next, but it wasn't – Nationwide was now beyond reach. The poor wording in the Building Societies Act had come close to destroying a century and a half of tradition – but it had also wrecked a whole sector which had supported the middle-class way of life for most of that period, providing people with their first rung on the housing ladder and a safe place to keep their money.

Even so, it is too easy to blame the new law. 'The Act was not what I intended but what government and Parliament intended,' says Boléat now. 'Most legislation has unintended consequences. But there was nothing intrinsically wrong in members receiving compensation for losing their membership rights and in the level of compensation being set by the market, as opposed to legislation. The Act was just one factor influencing behaviour. It would have been possible to find a method of conversion even with the old legislation.'

That must be correct. The problem was not so much legislation. A new attitude was abroad, and largely at odds with traditional middle-class values, as if nothing mattered but the profit opportunity, and it was this that finally drove Tony Greenham out of banking.

By the time the storm was over, Barclays BZW had also disappeared. It was sold to the thrusting American bank Credit Suisse First Boston, which was desperate to expand in Europe. Greenham found himself working with the technology banking division led by Frank Quattrone, the controversial American banker who had taken Amazon, Cisco and Netscape public and who ended up with the blame for some of the excesses of the dot.com boom which was even now gathering strength. It was a completely different culture from Barclays BZW, says Greenham:

> Having come from a very English firm, it was a massive culture change. It was all about the transaction, not the relationship.

Nobody cared about the integrity. My understanding of being a corporate stockbroker was that it was all about reputation, my-word-is-my-bond and so on. It was our job to bring companies to market and to make sure the numbers stacked up, do the due diligence. All that was absolutely thrown out of the window during the dot.com boom. If you were seen to want to defend any traditional practices, you were labelled out of date, out of touch, not getting it. My former BZW colleagues and I continued to wear suits even as everyone else was desperately following the dot.com crowd by dressing down. I think this was a sort of protest at what we saw as a general attempt to erode standards – standards of integrity, and the standard of quality and suitability of the businesses whose shares we were offering to the public. I guess we thought that if we couldn't defend these standards, at least we could dress professionally.

Quattrone was then earning about $120 million a year. He later went on trial in New York for interfering with a government investigation, though charges were dropped after three high-profile court battles, but by then Tony Greenham had moved on. Sitting in a hotel room in Australia at the height of the boom, he caught himself wondering how long he had to work there to earn enough money to leave.

'I really wasn't enjoying it,' he says. 'I thought it was having a bad effect on my personality, because you naturally tended to fall into macho behaviour patterns just to fit in. It wasn't collaborative at all. I thought, this is crazy. Am I just going to do this for three or four years? But then it's easy to decide you're not influenced by money when you've got quite a lot of it.'

His father died the following year, and he left to join an Internet start-up. His colleagues made fun of him at the bank for not owning a fancy car. They didn't understand why he didn't drive around in a Porsche, though he could have afforded one. In fact, he was saving money to leave, but leaving the gravy train is not at all easy – because the vast divisions that have opened up, even inside the middle classes, are now painfully apparent when you are on the wrong side of them:

> I have to say at this stage now, at the age of forty-two, that it is quite tricky knowing that if I had stayed in banking, I would be a multi-millionaire – that's quite a sacrifice to make on principle. Now I'm working in the charity sector, and having missed out on the London property boom, I have a real problem being able to afford to buy somewhere for my family to live in south-east England. There are vast disparities in wealth now. We were all equal at university, but five years later some people are earning six-figure salaries while new teachers are on £20,000. I felt uncomfortable about this when I was a banker and I think the situation has only got worse.

Why have some of them got ten or twenty times the income? 'It isn't as if they are any cleverer. Certainly not because they are creating any more real wealth,' says Greenham. 'Of course those on the big-ticket salaries always delude themselves that they must be getting paid that much because they are worth it, not because the financial sector has turned into a vehicle for extracting value from the rest of the economy, which I would say is the real reason.'

More than a decade since he left the City, Tony Greenham is now one of the most effective and articulate campaigners for small, local banks in the UK, based at the New Economics Foundation. His regular lecture involves two graphs showing the frenetic line of the big banks in the German and Swiss markets since 2008, and the straight, sturdy and reliable line of their small banks. He points out that the UK graph looks much the same, but there is no line for the small banks – because there are no small banks.

The building societies could never really take the place that small banks have in business lending. But they did provide some elements of that same stability, and the middle classes – any middle classes – really depend on stability.

As the carpetbagger storm reached its height, the Building Societies Association annual report for 1996 made a fatal prediction:

> One of the most fascinating experiments in British commercial life is about to begin with direct competition between mutual and stock based institutions in some of the key personal financial markets. The next five years will show which of the two approaches adopted by those institutions currently called building societies proves successful.[14]

That statement was bravado on the part of Adrian Coles as he watched his sector being dismembered in the enthusiasm to escape to the freedom of the banking sector. A little more than a decade later, things looked completely different – not so much because of any overwhelming success for the remaining mutuals, but because of the disastrous performance of the new banks.

As always, it was Abbey National that paved the way, buying crazily into rolling-stock companies, leasing planes and lending money to the fraudulent and doomed energy company Enron, not to mention the two other most outrageous corporate collapses in 2001, Tyco and Worldcom (the disgraced CEO of the US conglomerate Tyco, Dennis Kozlowski, had a penchant for $6,000 shower curtains and $15,000 umbrella stands).

As the century turned, the management of Abbey fulfilled all the predictions of the Two Johns, first telling customers to close accounts they believed were unprofitable and then charging them £5 for paying bills in their branches. 'I am very angry with Abbey National,' said Michelle Fell from Newcastle-under-Lyme. 'My parents do not deserve this shoddy treatment. I rang and lodged a complaint, but was told there was nothing they could do.'[15]

Abbey National tried to start afresh by changing their name to 'Abbey', but it wasn't enough. In 2004, they sold out to the Spanish bank Santander.

But there was a sign of something else too. The new gung-ho managers of the demutualized banks turned out to be suffering from what is a peculiarly middle-class disease – a disastrous ignorance of the world as it really is. Unable to look ahead, they gorged themselves on cheap finance from the money markets, on buy-to-let mortgages and the UK equivalent of subprime mortgages, lending to people who could never afford to pay them back.

The banking crisis of 2008 made it all horribly clear. Northern Rock faced a run on the bank. Halifax brought down their HBOS partners Bank of Scotland thanks to their dreadful property portfolio and had to be handed over to Lloyds. Bradford & Bingley went the same way. Alliance & Leicester followed on exactly the same path and also ended up as part of Santander. Lloyds tried to close all the Cheltenham & Gloucester branches which they had bought so expensively in 1995, finally offloading them on the Co-operative Bank. The surviving fifty-eight building societies were barely touched by the crisis.

'It has been utterly, unbelievably, astonishing,' Coles told the BBC. 'Seeing the swift disappearance of the former societies in the firestorm, which I don't claim to have predicted, has also been astonishing.'[16]

Looking back to the 1990s, the demutualization process now looked like a 'catastrophe', according to the *Independent*'s economic commentator Hamish McRae.[17] None of the demutualized building societies now exist, except – like a speechless Little Red Riding Hood – trapped in the belly of some vast international bank. They were all either taken over or went bust.

Gordon Brown's successor as Chancellor, Alistair Darling,

wrote the obituary of the former building societies, after the experience of being in the eye of the storm – having taken a call from the RBS chairman in October 2008 warning that his bank could only survive for a couple more hours. This is how he explained the Halifax Bank of Scotland (HBOS) debacle: 'It sold mortgages aggressively, offering amazing deals, to the point that it was not making any money out of them . . . The bank had tried to compensate for that by making commercial loans, especially on property, which were to result in colossal losses.'[18]

What went wrong? Why did the middle classes turn their backs on the institutions that supported them? And why did the building-society leaders ever dare give Abbey National the chance to become a bank in the first place?

'The feeling was, if they really wanted to be a bank, then they shouldn't really be allowed to be a building society,' says Adrian Coles now. 'We felt at the time that we were protecting the building-society brand from being tarnished by banking.'

The problem was that, at the same time, they were measuring their progress in exactly the same terms that the banks were. The truth was that they had already questioned the brand when they failed to see the importance of those other aspects of what building societies were doing – loyalty to places, to customers, to thrift itself (not a value much admired in modern banking). 'We were using all the banks' measures,' says Coles. 'We totally absorbed, mistakenly now in my view, the market Thatcherite ideals.'

Nationwide is now a mammoth institution with 15 million members, bigger than either Halifax or Abbey in their heyday, but the remaining building societies are relatively small and dedicated to local causes. Their recruitment is done on attitude and personality. Their customer service is impeccable.

'Will the customers notice the difference?' John Bird asked in his 1997 lampoon of an interview with a converting building-society chief.

'I think they will notice a difference. We will treat them like shit,' said John Fortune. And so it proved.

The idea that the building societies were a 'movement' always horrified Mark Boléat, the architect of the 1986 Act, partly because it sounded so socialist, partly because it reminded him of bowels. He wrote a book called *The Building Society Industry* just to make sure.[19] But there is now a distinction. The movement continues, but the sector remains a shadow of its former self.

Boléat argues that nothing much has changed, because the sector was never actually dedicated to getting people housed. 'Rather it was dedicated either to growth or an easy life,' he says now. 'There was very little thinking on how to get people on the housing ladder and very little understanding even of how the housing market worked. I doubt if life would have been very different if none of the building societies had demutualized. There is no evidence at all that people save less because the building society sector has shrunk. There are still building societies. If the public want to use building societies for their savings and mortgages, it is easy for them to do so.'

But it is more difficult now. The new demutualized banks were at the forefront of supporting the middle-class lifestyle with debt, and for a long time it seemed to work. Then it didn't.

The building societies began as financial institutions, patrolling the borders of the middle classes, with the intention of lifting people inside. But they became so much more than that: they were the core institutions that encouraged the middle-class values of thrift and saving. On the other hand, the middle classes didn't want to queue for mortgages, Soviet style. They did not value their membership of these mutual institutions which had stopped valuing the same idea themselves. It was the middle classes who created the building societies and the middle classes who came close to destroying them, and I share some of the guilt. I took my

£190 of shares from my mortgage with Abbey National, and the fact that I never managed to get around to carpetbagging stemmed more from laziness than principle.

I admit it. But the middle classes require institutions to support them, and particularly financial institutions, and in Britain – almost uniquely in the developed world – these now barely exist. If the middle classes retreat to the public sector, or they aspire to be Masters of the Universe in the One Per cent, perhaps this doesn't matter. But the middle classes are also the entrepreneurial classes, and will have to be even more so in the future. They are the ones who make things happen – with charities, local business, innovation and enterprise. They see things differently and can make it happen. Not uniquely, but enough to matter.

That requires financial institutions which are on their side. Which do not devolve all their decisions to risk software. Which build up local knowledge and experience to make effective loans. Which provide the support and encouragement for saving and the rewards for doing so. This infrastructure has not completely gone, but much of it has.

Its destruction was the result of continuing suspicion in government circles about mutuality and building societies, and a love affair with the new world of high finance which the middle classes largely shared. Plus a belief, which now turns out to be fantastical, that if you leave everything to the market the optimal benefits will emerge. It may do, but these are optimal benefits for the corporate leaders rather than anyone else, and their interests no longer align with those of the majority of the middle classes. What has been so destructive here is the big fantasy that money is as effective as any other money, however it is earned.

Government initiatives to funnel resources to small business, like 'credit easing' or the Enterprise Finance Guarantee (EFG), now have to go through the remaining infrastructure, but – as we have seen – that is no longer on anyone's side but its own. Horror stories followed the EFG in 2009. Banks used the money to pay off existing overdrafts, leaving too little to keep the client company afloat, or simply failed to deliver promised injections of money.[20]

Perhaps the real solution is to have the guts to act like the woodcutter in the tale of Little Red Riding Hood. Round up the big bad wolves of banking, slit open their stomachs, and let the institutions we need come back out again into the light – the Woolwich (inside Barclays), Bristol & West (inside Bank of Ireland), Halifax (inside Lloyds), Girobank (Santander), Williams & Glyn's (Royal Bank of Scotland), Martin's (Barclays), Birmingham Municipal Savings Bank (Lloyds). And so on and so on.

It's a Wonderful Life is sometimes listed among the hundred best films ever made. Despite its hard-nosed brand of sentimentality, it is certainly a favourite one, with its strange tale of George Bailey, the reluctant manager of a small-town building society, and his spiritual crisis in the face of a trumped-up charge of fraud. Not to mention Clarence the angel, who is not to everyone's taste. But then director Frank Capra – who employed Dorothy Parker to help him with the script – was originally attracted to the story as an antidote to atheism.

In the event, the initial reception at the Globe Theater in New York City in December 1946 was rather flat. But the people it really enraged were J. Edgar Hoover's FBI. One agent wrote a report the following year that the film 'represented rather obvious attempts to discredit bankers'. This was, he claimed, 'a common trick used by communists'.[21] But the message that lingers, despite the fears of the FBI, is about small-town America. We watch the town through Bailey's eyes throughout the boom and depression years and the Second World War as, time after time, he never quite manages to leave.

The difference Bailey makes is by providing the means by which people can escape from Mr Potter's slums, own their own home, and lead a middle-class life. Without the Building and Loan, Bedford Falls becomes Pottersville, a brash and brutal casino-ridden hole. We are intended to believe that Bailey as an individual is what makes the difference, but it might equally be Bailey's tenacious yet reluctant determination to keep the local building society going.

You can see why the FBI was nervous about it. *It's a Wonderful Life* makes a distinction between the civilized, middle-class life of home ownership, respectability and trust – enabled by a small piece of mutual financial infrastructure – and the relatively classless world of turbo-capitalism where it all falls apart. We have been told for the last generation at least that money is money and, within the law, it makes no difference where or how you earn it. In many ways, the middle classes have been the cheerleaders for that attitude to life and economics. But Pottersville is the counter-example. The middle classes don't live there: it is a place dominated by a handful of owners, many desperate punters and the underclass outside.

I went to Pottersville once, or its equivalent. I wandered into the small town of Black Hawk, Colorado, one of those struggling small towns in the Rocky Mountains, 8,000 feet above sea level, which were supposed to be 'rescued' by becoming casino towns. 'Population: 350' it said at the foot of the hill, but the legalization of gambling in Colorado in 1991 changed that overnight, and changed everything else too. Go there now and you find yourself directed by men in dark glasses at the tiny crossroads in the town centre, and almost every building from the Silver Hawk Saloon to the end of the town is devoted to gambling – Doc Holliday's Casino, Bonanza Casino, Crook's Palace, Bronco Billy's.

You can go there virtually as well, at www.blackhawkcolorado. com, to see what gambling does to a local economy. 'We might point out that if you visit Black Hawk, leave your children at home,' says the website. 'Black Hawk is not a friendly place to people under the age of 21.' Almost every economic activity apart from gambling has been driven out. Thanks to the legalization of gambling, nothing else is viable there. Which is why the town manager of Central City next door, which has all but merged with Black Hawk, now says anyone thinking of opening their community to gambling 'needs to have their head examined'.

Black Hawk is Pottersville. It is a testament to the memory of the idea that wealth will trickle down through the community. It is also a town which has long since lost the critical inoculating factor against this kind of moral and social decay. It has no little banks. So, taken together, Bedford Falls, Pottersville and the corrupted town of Black Hawk make me suspect there is a lesson here for the middle classes. To live a civilized, independent life, with institutions that support you in your desire to save, and which help you buy a home of your own, you need human-scale banks and you especially need building societies.

Middle Classes in Figures

Proportion of small-business loan requests turned down by the
   UK banks (2012): 42.4 per cent.[22]

The New Middle-Class-Values Dictionary

MODERATION: This might once have centred on pronunciation
and respectability, but it is now an emphasis on restraint – at least
when the middle classes are outside or in public view. Other classes
may rage and swear in public, but the middle classes want their
violence and intimidation kept firmly behind closed doors, and
preferably done via respectable solicitors.

Dispatches from the Frontline

National Theatre foyer, South Bank, London, Wednesday, 7.15 p.m.
The play is called *Damned by Despair*, but there is nothing remotely
despairing about the audience all around me on the ground floor
of the National Theatre, with the lighted bar behind me, the cafeteria on my right – if 'cafeteria' is the right word for somewhere
that serves Black Forest Gateau quite like that. It is a place alive
with anticipation.

The weather outside is chilly and people are wearing duffel
coats, overcoats, fur coats and the occasional woolly hat. There

are rather a lot of beards too, but I believe that is style and not to keep the warmth in – though who knows, it might be. They sip their red wine and tea, their faces bright with excitement – or is it the satisfaction of successfully meeting up at the right place and at the right time, and with the right people? Life isn't like that nearly often enough.

The bell rings insistently and they troop slowly and obediently, carrying their Italian scarves, past the ice cream and programme vendors, to queue for their seats. A few hang back and open their computers. The bookshop staff relax, as well they might (years ago, my son insisted that I ask them if they had any books about Thomas the Tank Engine and I haven't dared show my face in there again).

It is hard to see evidence here of middle-class decline. Quite the reverse. The ticket prices start at £12, so this is an eminently affordable night out. But there is something strange: this hideous concrete building, so reminiscent of the kind of neo-brutalist housing 'prisons' built for the poor in the 1970s, is subsidized theatre. Even the £12 tickets are backed by Travelex. Private-sector West End ticket prices will set you back considerably more. So, why is this audience so overwhelmingly middle-class?

London's South Bank is the biggest arts complex in Europe, and it is certainly more crowded and more eclectic than it was ten years ago. I know the council estates of Elephant & Castle, just down the road – from where you could walk on overhead walkways all the way to Peckham – have now been pulled down or gentrified. But even so, it hardly explains the way that white, middle-class audiences dominate here to the extent that they do.

So here is the real question. Is this the fault of the middle classes for being exclusive, and for hugging to themselves some of the most important products that England creates for the world? Or is it something to do with the prevailing culture?

4

The third clue: the corrosive explosion of finance

*'On Wall Street he and a few others – how many? – three
hundred, four hundred, five hundred? – had become precisely that
. . . Masters of the Universe.'*

Tom Wolfe, The Bonfire of the Vanities, 1987

One of the peculiarities of the financial world over the past two decades or more, which has drawn even more of the middle classes into its grip, has been the recruitment of physicists and mathematicians into the exclusive world of trading and electronic markets – the growing belief that there were patterns to be recognized in the markets if only you could see them. One of the British pioneers of that idea has been Paul Woolley, a tall, donnish, slightly crumpled figure who became one of the leading experts in the world on applying mathematical principles to the financial markets.

Now, decades on, Woolley runs his own think tank in London and Toulouse dedicated to explaining why the financial markets have been so disastrous to the economy of the world, and especially in the UK, where they have developed almost more than anywhere else. He has grown deeply sceptical of their ability to allocate resources effectively – which is the job description of financial services, and the idea which has driven their extraordinary growth during the past generation.

The financial markets took on a new lease of life in London

after the policy shifts brought in by Howe and Lawson and their fellow revolutionaries. They were welcomed by the middle classes, embraced as part of their fightback. In practice, it was this mistake above all which is probably most responsible for the plight of the middle classes today.

Woolley's great advantage – also his great disadvantage, perhaps, because it made him restless – was that the role of trader, hard-headed and obsessive, was at war within the Woolley soul with the role of academic. He was endlessly intrigued with the big questions, untiringly fascinated and delighted with the peculiarities and quirks of the market, because of what they proved, as much as what they might earn.

He had an unusual route into finance. He joined a firm of stockbrokers in Birmingham straight from school in 1959, and, instead of a quick taster before university, he found himself put in charge of the statistical department at the tender age of nineteen. 'I had an absolutely amazing time,' he says now. 'In those days there was a ban on brokers having their names associated with research notes. I could go off to companies, write up reports, agonize about things like whether the market was efficient, decades before this became fashionable. Incredible fun.'

When the ban on names was lifted some years later, one of his research notes was written up in the press on the first day. 'I was almost knighted on the battlefield,' he says. But instead of pursuing his career as a partner, he horrified his parents by throwing it all up and going to university. From there he was offered a lectureship, taught students about the efficiency of markets, spent some years at the IMF in Washington, and eventually met the prescient investor Jeremy Grantham – which is how he ended up at Grantham's Boston company GMO.

These were the days when the economic doctrine known as the Efficient Market Hypothesis was taking hold. Promulgated by the Chicago economist Eugene Fama and his colleagues in 1970, it suggested that market prices were always right. They took all the available information and computed the correct price. The Hypothesis lay behind the extraordinary growth in financial trading since then, and it remains the justification for the vast rewards of the traders. They are paid so well, or so they say, because they are efficiently producing accurate prices.

But there was a peculiar contradiction about the Efficient Market Hypothesis: it meant that there could not be any price anomalies for traders to exploit for a bargain. Yet clearly that was what traders thought they were doing. This was the issue that Woolley worried away at, fascinated by mathematical patterns in the way the markets behaved. He and Grantham worked together at GMO, on US equities, looking for mathematical patterns which they could use to beat the market, creating what turned out to be one of the first active 'quant' funds. What the quants were doing – and Woolley was one of the first people in finance to recruit mathematicians and physicists – was to look for these patterns behind the market prices that, according to the Hypothesis, should not be there.

What he found was that the price of stocks tend to overshoot. They carry on going up beyond what ought to be the top of the market, just as momentum tends to take them down further than they should go at the bottom. Here was a potential key to unlock the puzzle, and it was the central flaw to the Efficient Market Hypothesis on which everything else was based. It also provides a small part of the explanation for everything else that has gone wrong with the City of London, set out so graphically by the governor of the Bank of England, Mervyn King, in 2011.

Governors of the Bank of England are not usually in the habit of giving interviews. They are remote and powerful figures, because they have to be: their merest whim can move the markets, create millionaires and paupers. They also need to keep their power in reserve and retain their moral influence over the banking sector, such as it is, with a nod and a wink. It used to be said that the banks were ruled by the eyebrows of the governor.

So when, in 2011, Governor Mervyn King gave an interview to the *Daily Telegraph*, it was no ordinary event. It meant he had something to impart which he felt extremely strongly about. For a whole generation, King and his predecessors had been distant, godlike figures, presiding with benign pride over the rumbustious cacophony of the speculative markets, dispensing the occasional reproof and the occasional blessing. Three decades after Howe, Lawson and their colleagues changed the financial architecture of the world, after a generation when the middle classes had smiled on the financial markets, King was in a very different frame of mind:

> If it's possible [for financial services firms] to make money out of gullible or unsuspecting customers, particularly institutional customers, [they think] that is perfectly acceptable . . . Why do banks in general want to pay bonuses? It's because they live in a 'too big to fail' world in which the state will bail them out on the downside profits.

Had any Bank of England governor ever attacked the values of the City of London before? The City's historian David Kynaston suggests not, and it was the long list of failings which were listed in his speech that was so dramatic. Too much emphasis on making money out of customers, too little genuine trading, too much destruction of good companies in pursuit of short-term profit, not to mention the rising clamour of the casino in the background.

Mervyn King's intervention may not have had the effect he wanted, but something important had changed. It was as if this was belated recognition that Pandora's Box had been opened and the devils had been unleashed. The monster that the financial sector had created so unexpectedly had not just left the banking system reeling, propped up by governments around the world, but – more fundamentally perhaps – it had also left those traditional middle-class values of thrift and hard work, just rewards for application and respectability, in tatters. What King didn't say was why the corruption of the financial industry mattered so much. Perhaps it was taken for granted that, if these increasingly powerful institutions were devoted to fleecing their customers, that was a bad thing in itself. Perhaps the unspoken assumption went further – that the City was shifting from helping the national economy to actively subverting it. But there is something else as well, which stays unsaid: a note of disappointment, even betrayal.

Because, for the British middle classes, unleashing the success of the City – and the sheer power of finance – was the secret ingredient that was supposed to buttress them for the future. It was a middle-class project to restore national pride. And the fear is not just that it failed – that is only too clear – but that it actually had the reverse effect. It undermined the middle classes just when it was supposed to rebuild them. It replaced them at the top of the economic pyramid with a new elite class. It sidelined and disempowered them and, as we shall see, it had to do so to avoid the inflationary effects of the Niagara of money pouring into London's financial district. It ridiculed their moral sense and their sense of responsibility.

Unleashing the City – the knock-on effects of the event known as Big Bang – may have systematically destroyed the very values of the middle class it was supposed to support, leaving their future in doubt.

The idea that the Efficient Market Hypothesis was wrong was not exactly new when Paul Woolley began to worry away at it. The billionaire financier George Soros pointed out that markets don't actually have full information. There was also the idea, known as the Grossman–Stiglitz Paradox: that if all the relevant information was reflected in market prices, then no single agent would have enough incentive to get the information which prices are based on. There are also behaviourist critiques which point to the madness of crowds.

Woolley wasn't satisfied with any of these explanations. The problem wasn't that people were behaving strangely. They were actually behaving as rationally as they could, but the system still didn't work. Even so, the way that markets overshot at the top gave him the clue he needed. In fact, as he was to discover to his cost, as trading gets faster and increasingly automated, it takes huge energy and grit to jam the brakes on.

The full force of the markets when they get it wrong was what gave Woolley the impetus to really think through what was going on. He had joined Barings Bank in London after his period at GMO, but found, as he put it, that 'they weren't really very interested in ideas'. Instead he went back to GMO and set up a London office for them. 'Over the next eighteen years, we hired nuclear physicists and Ph.D.s,' he says. 'We were like a little research lab in a university as much as anything. We weren't particularly good at marketing, but that was fine.'

There was a hiccup in the recession of 1992, when he resisted the momentum of the market into consumer durables, but the real test was to come nearly a decade later. This was the dot.com boom, and it was the same crisis that drove Tony Greenham out of the financial sector in the last chapter. The boom took shape as the anonymous Web bulletin boards hyped pointless dot.com projects and fed what became a frenzy, and the value of completely unproven Internet start-ups soared. Technological development was supposed to remake the economy completely. Nothing would ever be the same again, and the doubters were ridiculed in the press. For a moment, they had many people believing that a website like @Home was suddenly worth the same as Lockheed Martin, or the Internet share-trader E*Trade was worth the same as the giant American Airlines. Tiny AOL even took over the giant media empire Time Warner – one of the most disastrous mergers of all time. 'We have one general response to the word "valuation" these days: "Bull market",' said Morgan Stanley's Mary Meeker, the so-called Queen of the Net. 'We believe we have entered a new valuation zone.'

What were Woolley and his colleagues going to do in the face of this insanity? If they followed the momentum, they knew they would lose money when the spell broke. But in the meantime, *unless* they followed the rest, then their customers would demand to know why not. It was the ultimate test of the Efficient Market Hypothesis. What Woolley could not know was how long the boom would last, and, as it was clear they were underperforming the market, the clients began to complain. Then they began to withdraw their money. After two years, the value of their fund was 25 per cent below their competitors. The board meetings were especially difficult, but Woolley gritted his teeth and stuck to his guns. He knew the dot.coms were disastrously overvalued and was determined to act accordingly, however difficult it became.

'For two or three years, I expected every phone call to be somebody firing us,' he says. By the time the boom hit its peak in March 2000, their customers had removed £100 million from their fund, about 40 per cent. By then they had lost 10 per cent of their value in ten weeks.

'Another year and we would have lost 60 per cent,' he says. 'It wasn't pleasant. It felt like being on a little ship trying to round the Horn, through the waves and storm in our faces. It was awful actually. Another year and our backs would have been to the wall. We knew we were right. I sometimes wondered if there had really been a paradigm change, but no paradigm change could account for what was happening.'

Then suddenly, on 10 March 2000, the spell broke, the dot.com values began to fall, with increasing speed, and Woolley's fund at

GMO outperformed the market by three times more than they had underperformed. The money came flooding back.

There were no apologies from the customers, and no congratulations that he had been right, but he hardly cared. He was now interested in why this should have happened. 'All through this, the academics were still teaching the efficiency of markets,' he says. 'Yet here was something so extreme, such obvious mispricing. Now, twelve years on, it's just the same. I thought: this is fascinating!'

The financial sector wasn't always like that in London, and to find out what changed we have to go back a few decades. A generation ago, the ultimate middle-class occupation of stockbroking was hardly the thrusting, overpaid, 'big swinging dick' profession that it became. It was rather a dusty business, deeply respectable, and – if not always quite honourable – it was at least intended to be gentlemanly.

As I write now, stockbrokers are going through a period, which may be permanent, when the rewards have tailed off and there is worried talk about the outlook being 'worse than the Seventies'. But in between, it become a lordly yet classless business, magnificent in its disdain for ordinary life, the very linchpin of the new Masters of the Universe in finance, and the epicentre of the earthquake that has paradoxically undermined the status and security of the middle classes.

It does seem an extraordinary shift in fortunes, and in many ways it was a by-product of the very British success story that put London back at the centre of the world financial system. Yet the author of the Big Bang reforms that caused it, Nicholas Goodison, was still able to describe the headquarters of his first stockbroker as 'a grotty old office in the City covered in dust'.[1]

Goodison was tall, patrician and deeply cultured. He was a member of his father's and grandfather's firm Quilter Goodison (his father had urged him not to go into the City because there was no future there). He was the central figure in the explosion of London as a financial centre in 1986, but the story goes back to the final months of the Labour government led by James Callaghan.

Callaghan and his colleagues had watched while Wall Street deregulated their stock exchange in 1975. They began to look more closely at the bizarre restrictions and conservatism of their own broking sector, and found that it was creaking. It refused to admit women. It operated an indefensible closed shop, and much else besides. Fair-trading legislation only covered things you bought in those days, stuff that came by mail order or which you carried home from the shops. But the following year, the future Labour deputy leader and historian Roy Hattersley, then Minister for Prices and Consumer Protection, issued a new regulation that extended the Fair Trading Act to cover services. It was called a Restrictive Trade Practice (Services) Order. It was to have huge implications.

Very reluctantly, the London Stock Exchange handed over its rulebook to the Office of Fair Trading (OFT), and waited for the explosion.

The man whose responsibility it would be to explode was the prominent OFT director-general, the lawyer Sir Gordon Borrie. Borrie was a former Labour candidate who had morphed into an impressive socialist grandee. He cut an impressive figure, resplendent in Italian suits made by his tailor in Stratford-upon-Avon. He was also said to collect books of matches from restaurants. The Times compared him to a fox terrier, 'small, fussy and persistent'. They also called him 'the most powerful faceless bureaucrat we have'.[2]

The City of London in those days was a peculiar place, well past its prime, still a hotchpotch of semi-medieval peculiarities, of which the man in the pink tailcoat who greets you at the door of the Bank of England to this day is one of the few survivals. It had its own aristocracy in the British merchant banks, Barings, Morgan Grenfell, Samuel Montagu. Even Barclays – still then the biggest bank in the world – was run by hereditary scions of the founding families. But the world of stockbroking was particularly genteel, rigorously divided between the brokers who dealt with the clients and the more classless jobbers who actually made the trades on the exchange.

The brokers traditionally resented the jobbers for charging too much money. Jobbers resented the stockbrokers for their relaxed life. It was a traditional division, like the farmers and the cowboys, though it was also designed to avoid the kind of conflicts of interest that have since made the financial sector such a byword for semi-legal corruption, but in those days sweeping away artificial divisions looked like modernization. Yet what really put the Stock Exchange in the sights of the OFT was their fixed charges. Exchange members fixed minimum commission prices. Borrie considered all this for a year and, in 1978, he acted. He referred the Stock Exchange to the Restrictive Practices Court. The case was due to be heard years ahead, in 1983.

When Goodison was appointed chairman of the Exchange in 1980, the looming court case was the biggest threat he faced. He was only too aware that London was losing out to Wall Street and the offshore eurobond market, and the court case meant he could hold no discussions in public about the need for reform, in case anything he said was used as evidence in court. He asked Borrie to meet him for tea and told him that the court case was getting in the way of modernization. Would he drop it?

Borrie stood firm. Why should the City get privileges that were not available to the other companies he was pursuing? All Goodison could do was quietly to persuade his own members that they had to accept some kind of change – at least ending the practice of fixing commission prices to avoid competition. Quietly and behind the scenes, he warned that the Stock Exchange could eventually empty. They could not force the world's traders to use it.

The late 1970s had been a period when it was fashionable to

debate the decline of Britain. This was the spark which had driven the Thatcher government to break open the mortgage market, not to mention the end of exchange controls. Something had to be done.

The Bank of England was nervous about the idea of breaking down the traditional divisions between different kinds of job – jobbers and brokers – but even they were coming round to the idea of reform. One of their directors, David Walker (now Barclay's chairman), commissioned a report known as the Bank's 'Blue Skies Plan' and began to invite himself to lunch with the great stockbroker firms to talk about it. He became known affectionately as 'Walker the Talker'. 'By the end of March 1983, I noticed some willingness to entertain the notion of change,' he said. The great glacier was beginning to thaw.[3]

It was getting late. Borrie's court case had been delayed, but what really worried the Bank was that the British jobbers – known as 'market makers' in the reformed world – were struggling to make a profit. If some kind of deregulation had to come, and it clearly did, the American firms would bulldoze them. And if deregulation didn't come, then another European financial centre would emerge – probably in Frankfurt. It was a nightmare dilemma.

This was paradoxically a glimmer of hope for Goodison, who could use these fears to shift his most conservative members. Then, if there was any evidence of willingness to change, he could offer reform in return for dropping the court case. The government's attention was now elsewhere, because the election was looming that would crown Margaret Thatcher's government with the fruits of her Falklands victory. But Goodison was ready, and two weeks after the vote, and the triumphant re-election of the Conservative Party, he made his move.

The new Trade Secretary was Cecil Parkinson, who had been in the Falklands war cabinet and had been there to provide a 'manly arm' for the prime minister in difficult moments.[4] He was also, as Goodison probably knew, deeply sceptical of the whole business of stockbroking. He was the son of a railwayman, and when he audited a number of stockbroking companies in the 1960s he had been horrified by their snobbish and autocratic ways. Now Goodison took the opportunity to send him a handwritten note asking him to lift the court case. If he didn't, Goodison warned, he could not 'guarantee the integrity' of the market.[5]

Parkinson talked to Nigel Lawson, now Chancellor of the Exchequer, and together they managed to persuade Mrs Thatcher and her deputy William Whitelaw. Very cleverly, Goodison had sown enough seeds in the minds of the politicians to make them believe some kind of deal was their own idea. On 29 June, they told Borrie that he must drop the case. He was predictably furious. Then, two days later, Parkinson put the idea to Goodison.

'I had been working on this for three years,' said Goodison later. 'But I still think he was surprised that I agreed so quickly.'[6]

Working in secret, and despite a leak to the *Guardian*, the two sides began to hammer out an agreement. Only three weeks later, the Stock Exchange council met in emergency session one Thursday morning. The representatives of the great names of English stockbroking, all of them now gone – Rowe & Pitman, Greenwell's, Pinchin Denny, Dunkley Marshall – crowded into the room before lunch. Goodison told them that their minimum commissions would have to go as the price for getting the Exchange off the hook. Would they agree?

It was not a tough debate. The stockbrokers gargled with phrases like 'hard bargain' and 'high-handed deal', but they capitulated. Minimum commissions would end in three years' time. The question of ending the distinction between brokers and jobbers hung in the balance.

Parkinson had problems of his own by then. A scandal had erupted around him when it became clear that he had tried to disown an illegitimate daughter, born to his secretary. One of his final tasks as the scandal mounted was to persuade the cabinet. At the last moment, Whitelaw wobbled. 'Are we doing the right thing?' he asked. But it was too late. The die was now cast. The City would reform itself by breaking down barriers. They would allow foreign companies to own up to 29 per cent of the members of the Stock Exchange, as a preliminary to letting them own 100 per cent. This was to be the basis for the explosion of finance now known as Big Bang.

Not everyone was impressed. 'Sir Gordon Borrie . . . has every reason to resent the way that a government committed to free markets and untrammelled competition has systematically abandoned its own guardian of competition policy,' said the *Daily Telegraph*.[7] One stockbroker, David Hopkinson, the chairman of M&G, glimpsed the future and the problems that lay ahead:

> I cannot see how the small investor is going to benefit at all from the government proposals and, indeed, nobody seems to have given much thought to what happens when large financial conglomerates like Merrill Lynch start to use their petty cash in order to force out of business all but the largest British firms of brokers. In addition, is it really desirable to encourage large financial conglomerates in this country with the banks, merchant banks, finance houses and stockbrokers all teaming up to exercise power which must be achieved at the expense of the small institutions and the smaller men?

'Talk about the Gadarene swine,' said Hopkinson later, rather mixing his metaphors. 'They were all galloping for all they were worth.'[8] He also stuck his head above the parapet in a television documentary and said what so many of the others in the City dared not say. He was amazed by the letters of support. 'Quite a lot of ashamed people, that they weren't standing up and being counted,' he said. 'A lot of ashamed people.'

Hopkinson was at least partly right, and the first trickles appeared that autumn of what would become a towering cascade of money which would end – just as he predicted – in the disappearance of all those British names in broking, ushering in a corrosive and inflationary world of vast salaries and bonuses, and of Chinese walls inside institutions that in practice barely existed. Big Bang may have been inevitable, and some elements of it were a complete success, but the results have been extreme, and especially for the middle classes.

The traumatic experience of the dot.com boom fed into Paul Woolley's growing frustration with the City, so when he retired in 2006 he was determined to step up his investigation into what was wrong. 'The fees were disgusting. The size of the market was obscene and ridiculous,' he says. 'They probably thought I was becoming a pinko so, rather than begging me to stay, they were quite happy to see me go. My colleagues probably thought I was focusing too much on the inefficiencies of the market and not enough on private gains to be had.'

But after a lifetime in investment, he could afford to do something about it. He decided to fund two academic research centres. He was also determined that he was going to call them the 'Centre for the Study of Capital Market Dysfunctionality'.

This proved to be a problem. The Efficient Market Hypothesis ruled the academic world. To call a centre something like that flew in the face of conventional economic thinking. Maybe it also showed disrespect to the markets themselves. There was a hint of heresy about it, even blasphemy. York University said no to his largesse. So did Imperial College London. 'They just didn't get it,' he says.

It was now 2007, the first whiff of what would become the subprime mortgage crisis was wafting into the news, and this time the London School of Economics said yes. His centre is now based there, next to the huge LSE Library, and at Toulouse University in France. The twin centres cost him £4 million and Mervyn King, the Bank of England governor, came to the launch party.

The basis of the new theory that Woolley and his colleagues have been constructing is that people rarely invest directly in the markets themselves, but do so through agents and fund managers, who have rather different objectives from their customers (and also by far the best slice of the profits). What actually happens is that, if the fund managers perform in line with the market, they are rewarded for doing so. But if they think differently, more long-term or more presciently, and – like Woolley during the dot.com boom – are temporarily below the level of the short-term traders, then their clients will sack them and take their money elsewhere. Then the momentum of the market is increased, and even more money is released to follow the market trend. The business of firing investors just accelerates the process.

For Woolley, everything follows on from that. Despite conventional wisdom, the markets are not actually efficient after all. The prices are not accurate. The traders are not fairly recompensed as efficient organizers, sorting resources to their most productive uses. They are staggeringly overpaid *rentiers* presiding over what he calls a 'wobbling blancmange of mispricing'. And every time they sort, whether the bet wins or loses – and the fee structure encourages them to trade faster and faster – they carve another slice for themselves.

Woolley realized that, if markets were dysfunctional, it actually increased demand for services, and because the investors were so inefficient at providing the returns people might expect, they had to invest more often and more frenetically. If the vast sums poured into various kinds of derivative instruments were doing the job effectively, then there would hardly need to be such a vast market for derivatives out there. (A simple definition is perhaps impossible, but according to the *Financial Times* Lexicon: a derivative is a financial instrument whose value is based on the performance of underlying assets such as stocks, bonds, currency exchange rates, real estate; the main categories of derivatives are futures, options and swaps. In a simpler age, a 'future' contract to buy wheat in three months' time at a certain price would protect a trader from a price hike caused by crop failure.) In short, the huge scale of the financial sector was a testimony to its failure, as it sucked in the resources that ought to have been providing the rest of us with productive, lucrative activity.

Either way, the speculative tail was now wagging the productive dog, and as that speculative engine began to suck in more and more resources from the middle-class world, it seemed for a while that it was beneficial to them. They did not realize that it was also slowly hollowing out their culture and their futures. Banking assets were worth about half of UK GDP when I was in school (1970). Now they are worth six times UK GDP. Even the biggest four UK banks are worth three times UK GDP, as financial services and financial trading slowly push out the productive economy like the cuckoo in the nest.

As it annexes more and more of the economy, the City also gathers increasing proportions of the profits to recycle into pay and bonuses, inflating prices for those of us without access to an annual bonus that can buy a small house, and creating the new class of Übermenschen, the Masters of the Universe, who have broken out of the conventional class system but weigh heavily on the rest. 'Where do people think all that taxpayers' money went?' asked a banking contributor to a fascinating BBC2 documentary about Portland Road in Notting Hill.[9] 'It went into bankers' housing.'

The issue of executive pay, and especially chief executive pay, has now been with us for a decade. It began to be a matter of public concern across the Atlantic when Disney's CEO Michael Eisner was paid a package worth $575 million in 1998 – about 25,070 times the average Disney worker's pay, and far more than that if you count the low wages paid in factories in Honduras or Bangladesh that make Disney shirts and bags. In 1980, people in finance still earned broadly the same as other industries. Even after Big Bang, the chief executives of the biggest UK banks earned seven times average household income. Now it is 230 times.[10]

The banker John Pierpont Morgan, founder of JP Morgan, used to say that nobody at the top of a company should earn more than twenty times those at the bottom (a bottom-to-top ratio of 1:20). That was widely understood by many companies for most of the twentieth century. The Royal Navy, which was sensitive about its own equitable culture, especially after the embarrassment of the Invergordon Mutiny against pay cuts in 1931, had for many years a ratio of lowest to highest of 1:8.

But we have forgotten these guidelines, and the resulting divisions have been particularly corrosive to the middle classes. Those who work their way up to be a Royal Navy captain, or a local solicitor or head teacher, or a range of other professionals which provided the backbone to the middle class, are not just priced out of the old benefits of middle-class life – from homes to private education – they are also undermined by the sheer scale of the pay packets of those in the financial elite. It doesn't matter how much they earn, there will still be someone out there who will make their efforts, their expertise and their salary look puny. And even in the tough times, the doyens of 'plutonomy' in the UK Rich List keep getting richer.

The City old guard is still able to see the injustice, and they dispute whether these were really rewards for extraordinary brilliance. 'It was a bull market,' says Brian Winterflood, who describes himself as 'the Last Jobber', and has become a kind of spokesman for the Old City. 'None of those blokes were clever. All these bankers will tell you they're worth it – but why would they be worth 140 times the lowest-paid salaries? Absolute nonsense. It's greed for greed's sake. They have been screwing the balls off everybody and stuffing it down their throats – and the divide gets wider and wider.'

It is a sentiment that is heard on both sides of the Atlantic. 'So let me just say that I remain completely unpersuaded that traders, bankers, and private equity investors who have made fortunes over the last ten years deserve to be unconstrained, unregulated, and untaxed because they did it all themselves,' wrote the notorious Wall Street blogger known as the Epicurean Dealmaker. 'Go pull the other one, sweetheart. I've worked in finance for more than two decades. You can't fool me.'[11]

But using his new theory of market behaviour, Paul Woolley is even tougher. 'Why on earth should finance be the biggest and most highly paid industry when it is just a utility, like sewage or gas?' he asked the New Yorker in 2010.[12] 'It is like a cancer that is growing to infinite size until it takes over an entire body.'

This is the charge against Big Bang as far as the middle classes are concerned. That by modernizing the City in the wrong way, moulding it in the image of the dysfunctional American markets, we have drained middle-class life of its dignity and purpose, and we have plunged into an illusory and inflationary world which now caters increasingly for the needs and protection of the new class of Übermenschen who take the lion's share of the rewards.

'This is the death of prosperity,' says Woolley. 'I think capitalism is being driven over a cliff, and the funny thing is that the people who are driving it are meant to be custodians of capital, and they've got the wrong instruction book. The finance sector is capturing the better brains, capturing the resources, causing the UK to essentially lose its industrial power and strength because we are so effective at finance. The largest global industry now produces nothing except instability and crises. A healthy economy should deliver five or six per cent in equity markets, but our pension funds are closing, there is no money in the pension pot, and the finance sector is bleeding us dry, and they are doing it in the name of efficiency. All the tools they are using are predicated on a dud theory. They are doing the precise opposite of what they should be doing.'

The self-styled Last Jobber, Brian Winterflood, now has a successful company, Winterflood Securities, which is one of the most respected institutions in the City. It carries on the old City tradition of 'dual capacity', operating just as a trader, buying and selling stocks and bonds. Winterflood himself was born in East Ham and was advised to go into the City by his Latin master. He began his career in 1953 as a messenger for the stockbrokers Greener Dreyfus & Co.

Those were the days when share trading happened face to face and when lunch could take three hours. It was also a gentlemanly world. Too much so in some ways, and he found himself frustrated by the sheer snobbery of the stockbroker companies, their rigid hierarchies and their miserable deference. 'It was very much them and us,' he says now. So, after National Service, he jumped the fence to the jobbers Bisgood Bishop, where the spirit was much more equal, and all the partners worked on the trading floor alongside everyone else.

Jobbers bought and sold stock. It was a job that required huge mental dexterity as you constantly recalculated share prices, and Winterflood took to it at once, rising over the next quarter of a century to be chief executive in the company. It was hardly an easy time in the City. The market was so quiet in 1974 that some stockbrokers wondered whether they should buy weekly season tickets into work. Winterflood filled his attic with food and buried krugerrands in his garden in case civilization unravelled. He supplemented his income running an antiques stall in the New King's Road.

Bisgood Bishop has disappeared now, along with all the others. It was swallowed up by County NatWest that first autumn in 1983 when it was clear that the old world was passing away. Now, another three decades later, Winterflood Securities is as close as you can get to the old jobbers, and without the conflicts of interest that beset so many of the new investment banking leviathans. 'Our strength is that we have no axe to grind,' he says. 'We are "Honest Joe" in the stock market, and that's a huge, huge strength.'

Winterfloods was also one of the last companies to leave the trading floor of the old Stock Exchange, but this does not mean that they have somehow turned their backs on the modern world. Quite the reverse. Their trading floor has nearly 200 traders, each watching the changing prices flicker by on six screens in front of them. As many as 94 per cent of their trades – 'bargains' he calls them, in the old style – are now automated, where computers make trades within nanoseconds against agreed criteria continually fed into them by the trading managers. But their independent status means that they can keep trading in the uncertain times.

Back in 1983, as autumn turned to winter, it was clear that something momentous was happening to the City which had little to do with fixed commissions. Speaking at a London conference that October, the leading banker Jacob Rothschild predicted that the finance houses of the world would merge with the banks to produce what he called 'the ultimate, all-powerful many-headed financial conglomerate'.[13]

Within weeks, his prediction, and David Hopkinson's worst fears, were coming true. The giant American bank Citicorp snapped up a 29.9 per cent stake (still the maximum they were allowed) in the London brokers Vickers da Costa. Warburg's bought the same stake in the jobbers Ackroyd and Smithers. The mining group Charter Consolidated took a stake in the brokers Rowe & Pitman. Midland's merchant bank Samuel Montagu bought into Greenwell's. Barclay's flung money at both a broker, de Zoete & Bevan, and a jobber, Wedd Durlacher, to produce the all-singing, all-dancing Barclays BZW. It set up its headquarters in an old multi-storey car park and drove straight into trouble.

One by one, the century-old names of British brokers and jobbers disappeared. 'A small circle of merchant bankers persuaded the government that their interest in going into market-making and stockbroking was consistent with the national interest,' said one anonymous stockbroker in March 1984. 'But that's open to question.'[14]

That same month, the compromise Restrictive Practices (Stock Exchange) Act 1984 became law, giving them immunity from competition rules and setting the exchange free to govern itself, and on the very same day – as if to prompt the zeitgeist – the FTSE 30-Share Index hit a new high. It was exuberant. It was successful in its own terms, but it was also a worrying sign of what was to come. Nor were the existing brokers and jobbers very pleased. Goodison spoke on the floor of the Stock Exchange later that month, explaining that they must accept outsiders. He was received with a stony silence. His Quilter Goodison colleague Paul Killik promised that 'the brokers will fight to keep the human element in trading. After all, you cannot look a screen in the eye, can you?'[15]

But they didn't fight. How could they? The real stuff of Big Bang, the electronic trading screens, in the form of SEAC (Stock Exchange Automated Quotations), was agreed that July. Barclays led the field, testing the new terminals out in the public, installing five of them in branches in London's Piccadilly, Edinburgh, Cambridge, Eastbourne and St Helier in Jersey. It was another sign of the times: Jersey was rapidly emerging as the nearly respectable end of offshore banking.

The old guard remained unhappy. One broker complained that their new owners 'treat us like dirt'.[16] The problem was that the merchant banks which had flooded into broking and jobbing were unfamiliar with the culture they had bought, sometimes even reluctant to be there. Brian Winterflood, leading the old Bisgood Bishop team at County NatWest, was particularly frustrated. He describes his life then as 'hell'.

'It was the only eighteen months of my career that I didn't enjoy,' he says. 'It was big business as opposed to small business. It was tiered control. It was red tape. It was a matter of: "This is our business now and we will tell you how to run it."'

It was frustrating for both sides. Finally, he was summoned to what he calls a 'Star Chamber' of the senior directors and kept waiting outside. It was a humiliating gesture, and when it was over he was told that he must either toe the line, get the sack or retire. It was clearly time to go, and Winterflood negotiated a severance package, only to be warned that the money would not come through if he spoke to the press. 'They found me guilty,' he says, 'and they told me to please leave the premises. They gave me a black bag for my possessions. I couldn't even say goodbye to my staff.'

Despite the manner of his departure, many of his staff joined him in the new venture that still bears his name today. But something of the same mismatch between the two worlds was apparent in the growing rage of the old brokers. One anonymous stockbroker was quoted in The Times during the long summer of the miners' strike. 'Screw them [the Bank of England] and screw the government,' he said. 'The miners can do it, so why can't we? I haven't worked twenty years to roll over and die like some unwanted sheep dog.'[17]

But the zeitgeist seemed to be heading in the opposite direction, as the middle classes discovered high finance, and also found that they loved it. The sale of shares in British Telecom at the end of 1984 was five times oversubscribed, and there were frenetic scenes on the Stock Exchange trading floor. Takeover fever was mounting as the junk-bond revolution, emerging from a finance company in California called Drexel Burnham Lambert, began to load unrepayable debt onto the balance sheets of target companies in order to wrench them from their current management. The exchanges were beginning to boom. The FTSE 100 was launched at 1000 points in 1984. The weekend before Big Bang, it was already on 1577. Lawson fuelled the fire by halving stamp duty on share transactions.

It was the start of the bonanza, in the days we thought we would all benefit from it. Japanese banks like Nikko and Yamaichi, flush with cash from the Tokyo property boom, were arriving in London seeking whom they might devour. American banks like Salomon Brothers, which had made more money in 1982 than all the member firms of the London Stock Exchange put together, were setting up in London to offer mortgages – and in the process fuelling the London house-price explosion. So was Chase Manhattan.

City salaries were also doubling and redoubling. One twenty-eight-year-old analyst on a salary of £35,000 was snapped up by an American bank on a salary of £130,000, but this was only the beginning. Basic salaries in the City doubled in two years. Middle-class England tut-tutted, but failed to see the significance. Even Norman Tebbit, who had taken over the trade portfolio from Parkinson after his resignation, called pay levels 'ridiculous and extremely embarrassing'.[18] This was the period when the novelist Tom Wolfe published his bestselling novel *The Bonfire of the Vanities*, where his hero Sherman McCoy – one of the 'Masters of the Universe' in Wall Street – was unable to explain to his son what he did for a living.

The three-year run-up to Big Bang in London rid the City once and for all of its old aristocratic snobbery and deference. The new City was classless, even egalitarian, in its relentless pursuit of profit, but the extraordinary salaries were a sign that perhaps it might not stay classless – a small clue that a ferocious new class was emerging. 'People became rocket scientists and earned vast sums,' says Brian Winterflood now. 'They shouldn't have made that sort of money. What upset the banking community more than anything was all these blokes in banks, who worked their way up to become managers – all of a sudden, they were on half of what these monkeys were on. It was absolutely terrible. Upset so many people. Just disgraceful behaviour, money grabbing money. And that sort of sickness has endured actually.'

So, as the countdown moved towards the inevitable moment of Big Bang, there was increasing opposition from the sidelines. By April 1984, as the historic names of City stockbroking were disappearing in broad daylight, Goodison's detailed proposals came under fire from inside and outside. They were 'a perfect horror', according to the city editor of the *Sunday Times*, Peter Shearlock. 'It would tear down a viable and tolerably honest structure and replace it with a market that fails to meet the basic requirements of customers.'[19]

Shearlock added, almost as an afterthought, that 'the potential conflicts involved are horrendous'. But with the benefit of hindsight, this was by far the most important point. We know now that the culture of massive bonuses was going to encourage traders to take huge bets, gambling with their customers' money, betting against their own clients, in ways that would have been quite impossible in the old structures. Ending fixed commissions and electronic trading must have been inevitable, but ending the tradition of divisions between different trading functions was not inevitable at all.

For those who could peer dimly into the future, the signs were already there. One study published in the week of Big Bang showed that, even before the deregulation, insider trading seemed to be endemic. The great sceptic David Hopkinson, due to retire in the month of Big Bang in October 1986, sent Goodison a public warning letter at the end of that summer, with only months to go.

'I hope that the big battalions will behave responsibly,' he replied.[20]

It was a forlorn hope. With just weeks to go, the new Bank of England governor Robin Leigh-Pemberton used his Mansion House speech to call rather pathetically for 'a degree of restraint'.[21] Leigh-Pemberton's own solution was that 'the most convincing of Chinese walls must be erected between . . . functions'.[22] But then, as the old, politically incorrect City used to say: 'Chinese walls have chinks in them.' It was anyway far too late already.

On the afternoon of 24 October 1986, the floor of the Stock Exchange was resplendent with banners, fluorescent aerosol sprays and a pantomime horse. The trading floor closed at 3.20 p.m. to sing 'Auld Lang Syne'. On Monday morning, the computer screens went live and the new world had begun.

Three decades on, the mistakes of Big Bang have grown painfully clear. Conflicts of interest are endemic. The new culture that those years ushered in on both sides of the Atlantic, so alien from the traditional values of the English middle classes – and which had so alarmed Tony Greenham at Credit Suisse First Boston – created its own momentum, its own class and its own purpose. That is why it has been so difficult to reform. The former IMF chief economist Simon Johnson sees parallels to the way the governments in the developing world resist reform after their crises, and the way our own banking industry is resisting reform here:

There's a deeper and more disturbing similarity: elite business interests – financiers in the case of the US – played a central role in creating the crisis, making ever larger gambles, with the implicit backing of their government, until the inevitable collapse. More alarming, they are now using their influence to prevent precisely the sort of reforms that are needed.[23]

The financial lobby employs 700 people in Brussels alone, costing up to £300 million, making the case against reform. In the USA, the scale of their influence is even bigger, particularly given the extraordinary intermingling between Goldman Sachs alumni and the Obama administration. There is even evidence that the more banks spend on lobbying, the worse their lending record is.[24]

But the real problem, where it also impacts on the future of the middle classes, is the failure of finance to do the job it is designed to do. Part of this critique of the City is familiar, even traditional. The City has borrowed some of the most disastrous snobbery of the middle classes about manufacturing. They have never understood it and never really provided for its needs, as the equivalent institutions in Germany or Japan have done. Even the Industrial Revolution had to be financed from elsewhere (James Watt got his investment from Birmingham). Back in 1930, the Macmillan Committee introduced the idea of the 'Macmillan Gap', with their famous statement that 'the relations between British banks and industry have never been so close as those between German and American banks and industry'.[25]

Now, led by the American investment banks, they are even further away from a useful role – the former Financial Services Agency chairman Adair Turner called them 'socially useless'. JP Morgan now earns only 15 per cent of its revenue raising money for companies or advising them on deals. For Goldman Sachs, it is just 13 per cent.

This is the heart of the process known as 'financialization', and the main reason why Citicorp's secret reports hailed a new era of 'plutonomy' (see chapter 1). It means that the financial sector has used its ingenuity to manufacture an endless series of financial bubbles which burst because those who created them start to sell again – only to buy their deflated assets back when the market reaches the bottom. Last time the global economy was pushed into depression by the disastrous 1929 bubble bursting, the government bailout went into the productive economy in the New Deal. This time, it went into the financial economy, propping up the failed banks and creating money in the form of quantitative easing which boosted bank reserves, and was then recycled into more exorbitant bonuses. It was testament to what had been created in the financial districts, something beyond arrogance or insolence.

The result is a kind of economic stagnation for everyone else. The middle classes, buttressed by modern capitalism, have been deluded into cheering on the very forces that have caused their disintegration. But largely unnoticed and unremarked, traditional capitalism has been disappearing too. It is no longer about financing enterprise and production, but struggling to recreate the conditions of the last bubble, and to hold down wages in order to boost corporate share prices.

'The very size of the finance sector is testament to its malfunction, not its efficiency,' says Paul Woolley. 'If you looked at the world through the dysfunctional window, you realize that almost everything is reversed. If markets are inefficient, you don't want to promote high turnover in mispriced stock because it aggravates the mispricing. I realized that the whole thing was a sad sick joke.'

Far from retired, Paul Woolley now shuns the financial markets as he battles to find strategies to persuade them to change course. Instead he collects Victorian adventure stories. They are a kind of investment and they are also good to read.

Michael Lewis is one of the most successful business writers in the world. Educated at the LSE, he joined the bond-trading department of the doomed Wall Street investment bank Salomon Brothers just before Big Bang. His book about the experience, *Liar's Poker*, was a huge success, and it described graphically how the new world of Big Bang was corroding the values of the middle classes:

> My father's generation grew up with certain beliefs. One of those beliefs is that the amount of money one earns is a rough guide to one's contribution to the welfare and prosperity of society. It took watching his son being paid 225 grand at the age of twenty-seven, after two years on the job, to shake his faith in money.[26]

Lewis was cutting his financial teeth in London and Wall Street at the height of the junk-bond boom. Bonds are simply agreements to pay a specific sum on a specific date in return for a loan. Junk bonds are those that are rated riskier than investment grade; the risk is that the issuer won't pay. The upside is that junk bonds have a higher yield, and they allowed companies that couldn't get conventional backing to launch themselves. The downside was that some of them were extremely risky. 'The securities involve a high degree of risk,' said the front page of one junk-bond prospectus two days after the 1987 Crash, 'and accordingly, investors may lose their entire investment.'

A quarter of a century on, the Collateralized Debt Obligations (CDOs), the complex instruments that bundled up good mortgage debt with unrepayable subprime debt, were deliberately packaged to be obscure so that the credit-rating agencies could not value them, and they could then be sold to less sophisticated investors. Michael Lewis interviewed the handful of people who had seen what was coming, and whose bets against the subprime bonds flew in the face of market momentum – just as Paul Woolley had done during the dot.com boom. The result was his book *The Big Short*, which allowed him to revisit the era of Big Bang and his first book.

> What I never imagined was that the future reader might look back on any of this, or on my own peculiar experience, and say 'how

quaint'. How *innocent*. Not for a moment did I think that the financial 1980s would last for two decades longer, or that the difference
in degree between Wall Street and ordinary economic life would
swell to a difference in kind. That a single bond trader might be
paid $47 million a year and feel cheated . . .[27]

The great subprime unravelling, and the global banking crisis
that followed, demonstrates something relevant here. Those
responsible for a disaster that cost the UK taxpayer everything
they had earned in taxes from the City for the past decade had
moved into a never-never world where they could not be expected
to make sacrifices themselves. In the USA, Merrill Lynch CEO
Stanley O'Neal admitted that he had allowed his bank to become
overexposed to the subprime market and walked away with a severance package of $162 million, before his bank was rescued by Bank
of America. In the UK, angry Aviva shareholders forced the resignation of their overpaid chief executive, but failed to prevent the
semi-nationalized bank Lloyds from offering its chief executive,
Antonio Horta-Osorio, a £2.4 million bonus for his 2011 performance, even though the bank was still losing money.

Recent developments of financial markets represent an even
more devastating threat to the middle classes, who rely on a degree
of stability. Warren Buffett called derivatives 'financial weapons
of mass destruction', and they are part of the financial 'nuclear'
threat, along with the unregulated 'dark pools' of trading which
are now thought to include about a third of the world's markets,
most of it hidden. The New York Stock Exchange now accounts
for just 39 per cent of share trading in the USA. A larger proportion goes quietly through a warehouse in a nondescript business
park just off the New Jersey Turnpike. One of these, Direct Edge,
handles over 10,000 trades a second. The unlikely capital of stock
market trading in the USA is Kansas City, but the Nasdaq index
currently holds the record time for one of these trades, in

98-millionths of a second. Similar processes are undoubtedly happening here but – because of our bizarre monetary conservatism – nobody talks about it.

The new exchanges are catering mostly to a new market, the high-frequency traders who can use algorithms to change orders and strategies within seconds, using computer programs to speed-read news reports and Twitter messages, interpret them automatically and apply them to shift trading patterns. It is the logical extension of what Paul Woolley was pioneering decades ago.

Derivatives are not useless. They can help companies smooth out the bumpy cost of key inputs like fuel, or soften the impact of bad harvests. But most derivatives are sophisticated forms of gambling. Credit Default Swaps, which were instrumental in the bank crash of 2008, are usually used to bet that a bond will default. By the time of the crisis, there were $60 trillion in outstanding swaps, four times the GDP of the USA, and no real economic value had been created at all. Worse, many of them were bets taken out by banks against their own clients. Banks do not usually consider it to be their responsibility to inform you if they are also betting against you elsewhere, which is one of the more squalid by-products of Big Bang.

The German bank IKB bought lots of CDOs. One Wall Street investor tipped off the *Financial Times* that IKB was seen as a 'patsy', because they knew they didn't understand them. When IKB bankers turned up at conferences, there was always a pack of traders following them.[28] It was hardly illegal, but somehow the Wall Street 'cult of the mug' – the idea that anyone is fair game – has infected UK financial services as well. It is another way that financial services are corroding what remains of middle-class professionalism.

One of the great mysteries of all this is why so few politicians and economists point out how the privileges of the financial sector are corroding the economy. This is partly because universities are now so dependent on corporate sponsorship that they use their public voice less. It is also because our political classes are still wedded to the doctrine that wealth trickles down when, as we know to our cost, it is actually trickling up. But it is also that the economics profession has been captured by the lure of the financial markets.

The Chicago economist Luigi Zingales looked at 150 of the most downloaded academic papers on executive pay and found that those arguing that top managers should get more were 55 per cent more likely to be published in the top journals. As long as you supported the conventional line – the Efficient Market Hypothesis and all the rest – you could expect the whole array of professorships, conferences, consultancies, book contracts, and so on. 'If you got behind Wall Street, you went to Lake Como every summer,' said Rob Johnson, of George Soros's think tank, the Institute of New Economic Thinking. 'If you left finance alone, you took a nice vacation in California, and if you took on the bankers, you drove a second-hand car.'[29]

Just how deep this fear of heresy runs in economics became clear when the Post-Autistic Economics campaign spread to Cambridge in 2001. It had begun with a revolt by economics students at the Sorbonne, complaining about the disconnect between the real world and what they were being taught. A series of high-profile petitions followed. It was signed by twenty-seven economics MA students at Cambridge, but signed anonymously – if such a thing is possible – for fear that it might blight their future careers.

In 2005, one American magazine even listed John Maynard Keynes's *General Theory* alongside Hitler's *Mein Kampf* as one of the ten most harmful books of the past two centuries. Enough said.

Barings was over two centuries old by Big Bang. The bank had taken part in the frenetic series of acquisitions in the spring of

1984 by buying Henderson Crosthwaite (Far East), intending to rename it Barings Far East Securities. They took over only twenty-five staff, managed by Christopher Heath. During the negotiations, Heath was asked: 'Won't your people just take the money and go home?'

'You don't understand these guys in our world,' he replied. 'Somebody who gets £1 million just wants to make £2 million. These are people who make money, and spend it.' He explained how he judged new recruits: 'If he spends money on parties and racehorses, I say fine, because he will want more.'[30]

It was a different world for the Barings managers charged with overseeing this new approach, so alien to the traditional middle classes. It was the world of derivatives and instantaneous electronic trading, and it was their Far East operations that were to bring about their downfall. When Barings Bank collapsed in 1995 because of the activities of one trader, Nick Leeson – who lost $827 million in Singapore betting on currency futures – it turned out that his London bosses had no idea what he was doing. They didn't really understand the derivatives market that he was trading in, and had seen themselves as rather above finding out.

The tragedy of the middle classes is that they still don't know. They have failed to live up to their responsibility to understand the changing world, increasingly borrowing against inflated assets like their homes to fund school fees or healthcare or holidays, cheerleading the vast switch in resources from the real economy to the financial sector over the past generation.

And now the changes are happening even faster. The ferocious trading in shares, linked to mergers and acquisitions, which galvanized the markets after Big Bang, is less lucrative now because the fees have to be split between such an array of different advisers and lawyers. Increasingly over the past decade, the financial sector has shifted into trading its own assets. The annual value of securities traded in Europe has increased from $38 billion the year that

Barings disappeared to $576 billion before the crash of 2008.[31] The hedge-fund speculators and derivatives are now firmly in the driving seat.

That is partly what has driven the emergence of what Citicorp called 'plutonomy', driving up the wealth of the richest 1 per cent of earners beginning around Big Bang in 1986 and accelerating terrifyingly under Tony Blair at its height from 2003 to 2005. It is not happening in the same way in most continental economies, so it must be the result of political decisions, yet no political party could possibly be elected on that kind of promise. The financial elite – the One Per Cent – are more embattled, but so far they still have the political elite on their side, still convinced that these are somehow wealth creators, despite mounting evidence that the financial sector has evolved into something which siphons wealth away from the middle classes and into the hands of the Masters of the Universe.

This is what Paul Woolley calls a 'perfect storm of wealth destruction'.[32] It is a system that has been created, perhaps unintentionally, to extract wealth, loading down the real economy with debt, adding to the cost of living with speculative bubbles and the constant fees and deductions on every transaction, while governments find themselves forced to underwrite loans to productive business.

The middle classes have noticed the way prices have been rising, have complained about the failure to invest in productive enterprise, but have failed to see why. They are struggling against the rising value of property that is denying homes to their children, but fail to see how the culture of the financial sector is inflating the prices.

But is it corroding the middle classes?

There is certainly a moral corrosion going on. However well you shape your career, however hard you struggle as a professional, then – if you are outside the financial sector or the very top of the biggest corporations – there will always be people around you with Caribbean holidays and summer yachts, who are earning so much more money that your efforts look silly. It is an inversion of the values of thrift and dedication, of the careers of local head teachers or county solicitors, that the middle classes used to represent. It also turned out to be an inversion of the moderation that had suffused the middle classes a generation ago, based on more widespread traditional values that emphasized the very opposite of greed – treating people in such a way that they would do business with you again – and the very opposite of acquisitiveness and credit card-fuelled excess.

Worse, these are the very professionals who have made society safe, who have organized the police forces and the education systems, who have created the conditions where the doyens of plutonomy could operate. Speculation is now so much more profitable than the ordinary business of business that it is increasingly hard to raise money to do anything else. Companies have long since begun to outsource all functions except the finance one. They have begun to hollow themselves out, just as the economy begins to hollow itself out – all sound and fury, signifying increasingly little.

There is also financial corrosion. The bonus culture has pushed up the price of homes, and is still doing so: bonuses may be lower but City salaries are higher. It has fuelled inflation and shifted the attention of the economy increasingly onto satisfying the luxury needs of the Übermenschen. At the same time, the emphasis on financial markets has been lowering salaries elsewhere. The middle classes have seen this shift, believing it was somehow a necessary correction to trade union power, without realizing that it was corroding their own lives too.

The post-Big Bang financial sector no longer sees its main function as raising money for productive enterprise run by the middle classes. It buys, sells and repackages financial assets in a great swirl of useless and corrosive activity, sucking in the money that might play a more useful role just as it sucks in the young, clever and imaginative to waste their lives on the finance roundabout.

But there is something more fundamental. The tidal wave of money which now pours through the computer screens of the world at the rate of $4 trillion a day, and that started as a trickle in the run-up to Big Bang, has made the new financial class – the One Per Cent – extremely wealthy. But huge sums of money roaring through an economy create inflation, so the peculiar side-effect of Big Bang has been to ring-fence this success, to keep down the wages, to constrain the producers, and do anything necessary to make sure this cascade of wealth does not filter down through society.

Of course this affects the other classes as much as it affects the middle classes, but it is new. For the first time, the middle classes have found themselves on the outside of the party looking in, aware that a few of them have been invited, unaware perhaps that it is absolutely deliberate – and perhaps absolutely necessary – that the rewards should not trickle down much further.

Could it have been different? Would it have been possible to modernize the stock exchange without ushering in this corrosive monster? Big Bang, or something like it, certainly had to happen, but those voices that warned about the dangers of the new investment banks, of the conflicts of interest that would result, were clearly right.

Yet throughout that period, and without really grasping how finance was changing, the middle classes remained committed to the idea of finance as a means of securing their futures, and some of their children flocked to the City to make their fortunes. By the 1980s, Barclays alone had more staff than the total of everyone employed by financial services in the UK in 1900.[33] The actor Hugh Grant used to tell a story about his mother's lunchtime friends in Sloane Square, asking her what her sons did. 'One works in a bank,' she told them, 'and the other one is an international film star.'

'How fascinating,' they would exclaim. 'Which bank?'

Yet something has changed. A generation ago, stockbrokers in Orpington or Bristol – in the days when there were stockbrokers in Bristol – were not that different in their rewards and outlook from solicitors in Sheffield. Now there is all the difference in the world. The solicitor remains middle-class. The stockbroker, banker, hedge-fund manager, even the financial analyst, now live on a different planet.

Middle Classes in Figures

Share of UK national income that goes to the richest 1 per cent (1970): 7.1 per cent.
Share of UK national income that goes to the richest 1 per cent (2005): 14.3 per cent.[34]

The New Middle-Class-Values Dictionary

INTERNATIONALISM: I know, this was the class that felt that speaking foreign languages was quite unnecessary, even in the heart of Paris, Madrid and Berlin. Their language skills are still nothing to speak of, but they do pride themselves on their knowledge of 'abroad', their ability to navigate airport queues and foreign menus, to grasp the significance of – and maybe sometimes even enjoy – the culture of other great civilizations, beyond the hotel pool. They regard themselves, unlike some classes they might mention, as *travelled*. Paradoxically, they are also the class that goes on holiday, very expensively, in the UK – which explains the emergence of frighteningly expensive National Trust cafés, serving exotic salad, right on the beach in Dorset.

Dispatches from the Frontline

National Childbirth Trust meeting, Northcote Road, Clapham, Thursday, 3.30 p.m.

'You've just sort of gatecrashed our meeting,' said the NCT organizer guardedly. It was a simple matter of fact.

It is true that I had arrived unannounced at their coffee afternoon in a particularly trendy street in Clapham, all awnings and market stalls, but I had found it a bit difficult arranging to go to an NCT meeting any other way. The various local and national officials were very helpful until they heard what my book was about, then the conversations ended. I also had no baby with me.

Now in the half-light of All Bar One – why do so many wine-bar chains feel like the foyers of expensive hotels? – with the glasses of Smarties along the table and the lines of expensive buggies around us, I tell the mothers what I am writing about. There are peals of laughter.

How do you define middle-class? asked one. It is a good question and I reply as I always have done during the writing of this book, that it is like recognizing an elephant: you know one when you see one. There is more laughter, slightly self-conscious this time.

I used to visit Northcote Road often a decade or more ago, when it was unassuming, edgy and peculiar. Its little cafés have now begun to make way for the big chains as the rents have shot up, driving out much of what made it so authentic before. It is a fascinating example of the downside of middle-class existence: the pension and investment funds that we all own, with their huge property portfolios, tend to throttle the life out of places like this.

I realize, of course, that it is unfair to describe the NCT as a middle-class institution: you can get 90 per cent reductions on the £300 fees for introductory courses if you are on tax credits. But it certainly tends towards the middle-class round here, where its most aggressive and powerful branch stalks the cafés and play-grounds, their buggies lined up along the Common like a flotilla. The mothers around me are also busily pumping middle-class values into the next generation through their breast milk. There is something luxurious about meeting at this time, when the rest of the world is working or doing school runs, and I suspect that most of those around me have wealthy partners among the One Per Cent ('kept ladies', as I have heard them described).

But those I talked to put me right. 'If you're in one of the liberal, non-financial professions, like we are, you're pretty fucked,' one of them tells me.

'I feel it's very unfair that I'm so hard up,' says another. 'It feels unfair that you can get by if you're a banker or accountant or lawyer or maybe a plumber, but for the rest of us to find it so difficult. I went around the temping agencies and not one of them got back to me – not one. I have three degrees, and for the first time in my life I find I'm overqualified and skint.'

5

The fourth clue: the dog that didn't bark

'There must be no retirement. With our backs to the wall, and believing in the justice of our cause, each one of us must fight on to the end.'

Field Marshal Sir Douglas Haig, 1918

Astrid has been an art teacher, an advertising executive, a stand-up comedian and a boxer, among other things. She and her husband are serial entrepreneurs, and have started and sometimes closed down a range of small businesses – and she is rather cross. 'I think we both feel a bit battered and bruised,' she says.

It isn't so much the loss of their small advertising agency, which had provided them with a reasonable income for two decades, though that was bad enough – but it was the way it happened. She describes the decline of the company, sapped by repeated economic downturns, as a 'ten-year train crash'. But the real reason she is cross is the failed promise she believes was made to her generation by the politicians and the financial sector. Astrid's story is about grasping the opportunities for the new middle classes to create wealth, how it turned out wrong – not just for her, but for many others – and how she courageously unravelled the tangled and disastrous web woven by financial services so that she could solve the problem.

'There isn't anything unusual about us. We followed the opportunities we were given, but we were promised more,' she says. 'I think there was a promise – and this goes back to Thatcherism – that just do this, become a small business, and you will be safe for ever and ever.'

Astrid is nothing if not entrepreneurial. She has responded to the loss of the company, with her home mortgaged to the hilt and her credit cards maxed out, with a new career lecturing in the science of fitness, and a new strategy to see the family through into retirement. This is why she is different from other people in a similar situation. She could see what was coming, abandoned the pensions industry completely and invested in property. She and her husband are now £3.2 million in debt. It is a huge amount, and – unless the property market rises hugely – it will never be paid off. But the flats she bought provide a more reliable nest egg than most of us have in the middle classes, and that is an important clue to the pensionless plight currently faced by so many of us.

Astrid was born next to the Austin motor works (now largely disused of course) in Birmingham, which is not exactly a middle-class area, certainly not in the 1960s – but she escaped. 'I didn't want to spend the rest of my life there and I really worked my socks off to get out, and I managed it,' she says. She now lives in a large terraced house on a busy road in north London.

She went to art school, taught at the Brixton Academy during the 1981 riots, moved into advertising and very quickly rose to become a creative director. When she had her first child, she started her own advertising business from home. 'It just suited my personality. I started it from home so as not to be bored,' she says. 'Having children was doing my head in.'

As the business grew, her husband left his job to work alongside her and they ploughed the profits into buying flats as investments. It was a textbook middle-class success story.

She recognizes now how much her generation benefited from state support. 'Sometimes I think I was very lucky to be born in a generation that had lots of opportunities, and I feel like I've used them to the best of my abilities. I was in a new 1960s school. I got a full grant to go to university. We got state help starting a business. We have always been in the right place at the right time,' she says. 'But it does have a downside.'

The first downside was the huge amount of debt that comes from buying properties, remortgaging the family home to pay for a deposit on the first buy-to-let home, constantly gearing up, completely reliant on the economy chugging along effectively – which it has failed to do consistently.

The second downside was the besetting sin of the middle classes in all ages, and the very opposite of thrift:

> I was well and truly part of the middle classes by then, with a house in the right place in West Hampstead, and I know lots of people who followed a very similar path. It meant starting business, and if it was a success, you automatically followed a life path including children at private school, going ski-ing, going to Club Med. We did all the things that semi-successful families did. We all had nannies. These were huge expenses and, if you once start committing yourself to private education, you can't keep changing it.

It was at this point that Astrid made her next shift of direction. She started losing weight, joined a gym – 'another of those ticky boxes middle-class things to do' – got fascinated with fitness, trained as a boxer and then as a boxing referee, and started another small business aimed at middle-aged people and their problems.

By then the recession following the dot.com boom had battered the advertising company, and although it recovered again, each downturn took its toll. 'Every time it takes one of these knocks, it really takes it out of you,' she says. The crunch came after the banking crisis, when they finally reached the limit of what they could mortgage and closed the company. 'It was ten years of awfulness,' says Astrid now. Her husband is back working in the corporate world. What saved them was the flats they had bought in the years of plenty, which paid the mortgage on their home and bought enough food to live on.

'Every time we were really sinking, I've gone to the bank or talked to anyone financial – and it always was men, I don't know if that's got anything to do with it, and they would always say: "Just sell one of the flats." But I dug my toes in and I've been proved right. If we had followed this advice, from these immensely qualified people, we would have had no assets left on the ground at all and would have come to a complete halt.'

And this was the third downside, the miserable failure of the banks to support them effectively:

I used to build up very personal relationships with all the bank managers as individuals, and without exception they have all been brilliant. They watched us go through the good bits and they watched us go through the bad bits and they always tried to help whenever they could. They knew us and they knew we were very serious hard-working people who had genuinely tried to do our best. But at certain points, they had their mouths gagged and hands tied completely. These poor people have been put into an awful position, saying: 'I know you can do this but I can't do anything about it.' Even one bank manager said: 'I don't know what I'm doing here. There's been no point in having me because I can't make any decisions.' The final nail in our coffin was when they took all decision-making away from someone who knew us and put them up to head office, taking all decisions on a spreadsheet, and with no idea about what we could do. It wasn't as if we were completely useless at business. We had made money in the past. We had a track record, but it didn't count.

But this is actually a story about organizing for retirement, when Astrid's difficulties with the company had already led to a rethink about pensions and other financial products. Astrid had already realized her ISAs were losing thousands. 'I thought this was a bit pointless. All this money I put into them was just going on the whims of some twenty-year-old in the City. I thought: what is the point in paying money into pensions?'

She used the ISAs as deposits to buy more property. Next to go was insurance. 'We bought every kind of insurance, key worker insurance, critical illness insurance, we bought every kind of insurance product known to mankind,' she says. 'At one stage, we were paying fifteen hundred pounds a month to Lloyds Bank just on insurance premiums. But we were hustled – and now, when we might actually need critical illness insurance, we haven't got it because we can't afford the premiums.'

So there were Astrid and her husband, £3.2 million in debt, the home on an interest-only mortgage, and in need of a new plan. They decided instead that they would live off her husband's salary, while everything she earns now goes on paying down the debt.

'We are not going to live the traditional middle-class way, but we can live reasonably, and the comfort I do have is that we have options. I compare myself to a lot of friends who have trod a very similar path to us, and who have lost virtually everything and who don't have options – because they didn't get that asset base behind them, because they perceived it as a gamble.'

But of course it was a gamble, but – as it turned out – not as much of a gamble as it was to store money away in a traditional pension. Which is strange, when you come to think about it, because the commitment to pensions used to be what defined the middle classes. The trouble is, it hasn't worked out like that. Astrid's story involves a whole range of dysfunctional financial services, but the real lesson is how difficult it has become – even for entrepreneurs like Astrid – to steer your way to a stress-free retirement.

★　★　★

There is something of a mystery about all this, and I have to admit that researching this chapter sent me into an absolute panic about my own inadequate pension, which I haven't yet resolved. It is uncomfortable to think about, after all. And the worse it all becomes, the more uncomfortable it is to stare into the face of our own future poverty, especially if you are one of those people Astrid talked about who failed to borrow to buy into assets when they could. My latest letter from Standard Life explains to me that, by the time I retire, my pension should be worth around £2,700 a year. This is not comforting.

Once again, everything is not quite how the middle classes fondly believe it to be. Their middle-class parents had comfortable retirements, or at least could have reasonably expected them, and rising house prices to comfort them if not. They had winter cruises and long hot summers on the lawn. Their children reasonably expect the same, but it isn't going to happen. In fact, the extraordinary business of the incredible shrinking pensions is as big a nail as any other in the coffin of the traditional middle classes.

Here is the conundrum. On the one hand, the middle classes have almost been defined over the past centuries by their willingness to save. The terrifying magic of compound interest, brought to bear on middle-class savers – and the sheer security of the occupational pension – became a defining feature of middle-class life in the UK during the twentieth century. Before that, and before David Lloyd George's old-age pensions, the middle classes saved for their annuities at retirement, while the working classes faced the looming poorhouse at the end of their lives.

'We've been together now for forty years,/And it don't seem a day too much,' sang Albert Chevalier with the music hall song 'My Old Dutch', which made the music hall audiences cry in 1892. The reason why it was so emotional was that behind the old couple on stage were the poorhouse entrances marked 'Men' and 'Women', which would part them for ever. The middle classes had the resources to avoid that fate and they saved to do so.

On the other hand, we have been through a generation where the British system of occupational pensions has all but disappeared for the middle classes, and where the institutions created to make it possible to have a comfortable retirement have all but disappeared too. We have entered a new world where people save less than half as much as they used to for their retirement, and where they are systematically fleeced by the financial sector – providing them with future retirement incomes at least 20 per cent and sometimes 70 per cent lower than they were.

And despite all this, hardly a word has been heard in complaint. This is the dog that doesn't bark.

It isn't a complete mystery. Pensions are awkward things to understand. They are disturbing too, because they involve thinking about getting old, which none of us are that keen to do. But there is also more than a hint of the recurring problem which – as we have seen – has so undermined the middle classes over the past generation: an ignorance of the world as it really is. They have believed that the pensions industry was still a middle-class institution and fundamentally on their side. Nothing could have been further from the truth.

There is another peculiar paradox about the middle classes. They represent the only corner of the class system which has traditionally been financially secure. The working classes were not. The upper classes, with their crumbling ancestral homes, were certainly not. But that financial security always felt risky. It bred a paradoxical sense of fear, a sense of insecurity that it might all unravel. This put the middle-class nose to the grindstone. It led to a rat-race mentality of blind loyalty to the firm, and the firms responded. Over the past century, since the 1890s, occupational pensions provided the middle classes with two-thirds of their salary on retirement and for the rest of their lives.

Then two things happened. First, the middle classes responded to their growing security by spreading their wings and having more varied careers. They became less loyal to their employers. They began to progress their careers for themselves and move to where the opportunities or the salaries were higher. They began to go back to university and retrain for new lives. The very word career became a misnomer: all you are really called upon to do these days is to decide what to try next. And every time they changed jobs, they lost the pension rights that went with the old job.

What was happening was that a new kind of middle class was emerging. They were no longer dominated by the word 'thrift' in quite the way that Patrick Hutber had described in 1976. The new middle classes that I described in the first chapter were motivated primarily by independence, or – as the radical marketing theorists called them in the 1980s – 'inner-directed'. They no longer fitted nearly so well into the giant corporate world.

I remember the futurist Francis Kinsman describing an encounter with a manager from one of the mammoth organizations of the 1970s, the Central Electricity Generating Board, after a talk he gave on the rise of the 'inner-directed' approach to life – those people who put independence, health and self-improvement above keeping up with the Joneses. While much of the discussion had been about the benefits to business of independence of mind, the CEGB manager took him aside afterwards to ask how they could recognize inner-directed people on the payroll, in order to weed them out.

Then the other thing happened. By the 1990s, the big employers had begun to change as well. The inspiration was the 1993 publication of the bestseller *Re-engineering the Corporation*, by the mathematician Michael Hammer and computer scientist James Champy (see chapter 6).[1] The new theory suggested that corporate functions needed to be combined in one system, and that meant that middle managers had no real function left. Re-engineering meant that organizations no longer needed to be the great employers of the middle classes, cluttering up their middle ranks with careful, thrifty, sensible and educated types to communicate between the different corporate layers. This was also the defining shift in the class system – the economy, like the corporations, is now run by a tiny ruling elite, with a handful of well-paid managers who do their bidding, and a vast and detachable underclass of drones who man the software and call centres. The middle classes have largely migrated to the public sector, the creative world and the entrepreneurial world of small business.

When the *Independent on Sunday* can talk about the 'casualisation of the middle classes in full swing', that means many things, but most of all perhaps it has meant the end of the traditional middle-class occupational pension.[2]

Here is the shift in a nutshell. When Patrick Hutber was writing in the 1970s, the middle-class employers would pay about 20 per cent of salaries into a pension scheme which specified that it would provide them with a steady two-thirds of their final salary during retirement (known as 'defined benefit'). Now most of them will get instead a retirement savings account which specifies what they should put in ('defined contribution') but is vague about what might come out at the end. It takes some of the income of the middle classes, when they remember and can afford it, and turns it into an unspecified amount when they retire.[3]

This is a bigger difference than it seems at first sight. The old *defined benefit* schemes allowed the risk of fluctuating markets to be shared between a large number of other members. With *defined contribution* schemes, you are on your own. You are an individual saver with no collective benefits, no sharing of the risks, but with higher costs and charges and vastly lower returns – as we shall see. As Peter Morris and Alasdair Palmer put it, *defined contribution* personal pensions are not really pensions at all – they are retirement savings schemes. 'People fail to notice,' they warn. 'They think they have got a house when in reality they have only been sold a tent.'[4]

That is the main explanation for the yawning savings gap – between what people ought to be saving for a comfortable retirement and what they actually are. It now stands at £300 billion, and it falls most heavily on the middle classes.[5] The gap has left them not just far worse off than they were before, but in a state of confusion, unsure what they can rely on and often therefore doing nothing. This is what one middle-class man told the British Social Attitudes survey in 2002:

> I think it's very difficult to plan at all because everybody thought endowments were safe (hurrah I've got one of those as well), then property was fine and then that crashed and it's so difficult to know what you're going to do . . . my plans have spread to so many things and so many different pies, investment's going to go down, property's going to do something soon, it's got to especially down here, it's ridiculous actually.[6]

What went wrong? Partly the change in the structure of the big corporations – defined benefit pensions have declined in nearly every nation in the world, except in Germany and Japan, where people often still have a single employer for life. But there is another reason why the problem is especially acute in the UK, and it goes back to the spring of 1985. It was then that a bitter argument between two of the leading members of Margaret Thatcher's cabinet threatened to derail the government, and led directly to the pensions disaster which was to come. It is a vital clue in the puzzle about the fate that is overtaking the British middle classes. In fact, it may turn out to have been one of the most important blazing rows in their history.

Norman Fowler was one of the ubiquitous Conservative figures during the Thatcher and Major years, as a minister at various departments and as chairman of the Conservative Party. He was a journalist on *The Times* before his election to Parliament in 1970, but he was also in a privileged position. He was one of that successful coterie of Conservative politicians, including Michael Howard and Kenneth Clarke, who all left Cambridge together around 1960.

Fowler's ministerial career began in 1981 when he was made transport minister in Margaret Thatcher's first government, and then – after her triumphant re-election in 1983 – he was reshuffled into the Department of Health and Social Security. The DHSS as it was known, or the Department of Stealth and Total Obscurity in the TV show *Yes, Minister*, was a gigantic and little-loved department of state, covering the whole of the National Health Service as well as the whole of the welfare state – the two biggest items on the national budget – and gathered to itself an exhausting reputation for boneheaded bureaucracy.

Even among the Conservatives, where the DHSS ranked alongside the Politburo as one of the grey citadels of state socialism, any minister in charge would find themselves almost duty-bound to clash with the Treasury. In charge of the Treasury after the same 1983 reshuffle was the ambitious and domineering young Chancellor of the Exchequer, Nigel Lawson, determined to cut taxes now that the last opponents – or 'Wets' – had been excised from the cabinet. Lawson, for his part, was almost duty-bound to clash with the DHSS. He had, as Fowler put it later, 'all the subtlety of a Chieftain tank'.

The stage was set for an almighty disagreement, with huge consequences for the future.

The welfare system was a labyrinthine nightmare at the time, unreformed since the days of Sir William Beveridge, a vast, sprawling, idiosyncratic machine. Not even Sir Keith Joseph, Margaret Thatcher's tame philosopher, had dared to take on a wholesale reform in the 1970s when he was in charge under Edward

Heath, but this was what Fowler planned to do. In particular, he was absolutely determined to look at the pensions system. Ten million people received a weekly pension from his department, administered by 90,000 civil servants. It was beyond tinkering. Someone needed to look at the whole pensions system, and not just at state pensions either. To do so was a huge undertaking – 'lunatic', Fowler calls it now. But that was the objective.

As we have seen, it was already clear that the world of occupational pensions was no longer really suited to people's career paths, as they leapt or were pushed from employer to employer, leaving their pensions behind them every time. There was also the constant battle to break down the divisions between the classes and make people feel more responsible for their own retirement. 'One nation had their own pension, the other nation relied entirely on the state,' said Fowler.[7]

That was the public reason, but there was a private one too: Fowler was still incensed at the fate of his mother after his father died twenty years before, in 1963. His father had been first-generation middle-class, going to night school to train as an engineer and working for the same Essex manufacturing company for thirty years. He really believed in his company pension but, as his son put it later, 'he made the great mistake of not living to collect it'.

There was no transfer to his widow. All she could do was to collect her husband's contributions over thirty years, without the accrued benefits. For Fowler this was a huge injustice that was shared by many millions of people. 'My interest in pensions began with occupational salary schemes and the total inequity of the early leaver's position,' he says now. 'The pension was always regarded as a golden handcuffs. If you left the company, you left your pension: you got your contributions back, but the rest of it – forget about it. All the savings and investment which had taken place counted for nothing. I thought that was a scandal.'

That was Fowler's motivation at the start: to give more rights to the public over their existing pensions. But as soon as the party conference season began, in September 1983, he organized a pensions conference and announced that he also wanted to introduce 'portable pensions'. The pensions industry was appalled.

The idea of personal pensions – portable pensions as they were called at the time – was hardly a new one. The Conservative businessman Nigel Vinson – a man who took the advice given to Dustin Hoffman's graduate seriously and went into plastics – had proposed personal pensions and was campaigning for them noisily in the background. They were intended as a UK version of the American Individual Retirement Accounts, which rejoiced in the acronym IRA – and this was the year before the other IRA successfully exploded a bomb at the Conservative Party conference at the Grand Hotel in Brighton.

Fowler tried to get the pensions debate carried on in public, so it was inevitable that personal pensions should creep onto the agenda. He organized a series of hearings with his review teams – pensions were just one topic – meeting regularly over nine months. By the summer of 1984, immediately before the Brighton bomb, he was ready to set out some proposals about personal pensions, which he said 'extended choice and encouraged personal savings'.[8]

The other issue looming in the background was the future of the State Enrolled Related Pensions Scheme, known as SERPs. This had been introduced by Barbara Castle in the previous Labour government in 1975, without opposition, and had been designed to give the middle classes a second pension through the state. It was increasingly clear that, as the population aged – and uneasy accountants were just catching on to the implications – SERPS would rapidly become unaffordable. By the 2020s it would cost the exchequer a vast £36 billion a year, about twice the cost of the

NHS at the time. Yet in one Gallup Poll at the time, only half the population had ever heard of it. It was ripe for the chop.

'My view was that most people would prefer a pension that was theirs by right rather than being dependent on decisions of government,' said Fowler later. 'A pension of your own could have the same appeal as a house of your own.'[9]

Fowler and advisers dispatched themselves on a fact-finding trip to Switzerland, and never forgot the system they found there – a state system providing basic pensions and a private system to top them up. But he was also becoming aware of how disruptive this would be to the status quo.

'One of the issues then became a battle with the National Association of Pension Funds, who simply were the defenders of the final salary scheme,' he says now. 'That was OK for those who were in a final salary scheme, but about half the population weren't. That's why we put forward personal pensions.'

Months of debate went by inside government, and through the snow-covered January 1985 Fowler's review teams withdrew to the Foreign Office mansion at Wilton Park to put the finishing touches to their proposals. The idea was that SERPS would be abolished, but the new pensions – which would get some tax relief – would be made compulsory. It was the Swiss solution and it would guarantee an extra pension for everyone.

Fowler disappeared to his constituency in Sutton Coldfield to write up the green paper and get ready for the stressful business of presenting it to a special cabinet committee. Set up especially for the purpose, this was christened 'MISC 111' and was to be chaired by Margaret Thatcher herself. It was all going very well: the indications were that she was behind Fowler's findings (though she short-sightedly vetoed any idea of raising the retirement age).

It was then that the trouble began. Nigel Lawson turned out to be implacably opposed to making private pensions compulsory.

Nobody ever accused Lawson of being a social reformer, but he was gripped at the time by his own radical agenda – to cut taxes and make enough savings in government spending to make that possible. And to do so as quickly as possible. The Fowler pension reforms had the whiff of something that would cost money. He began to search for objections.

The first meeting of the cabinet committee was due on 6 February. The papers had already gone out and were sitting in the red dispatch boxes of ministers ready for their long journeys home by ministerial car. On the last day of January, Fowler was at 10 Downing Street for a meeting of the full cabinet and a group photograph, now that John Wakeham and Norman Tebbit were back at work after recovering from their injuries from the Brighton bomb. As the ministers were filing upstairs for the photo, an 'agitated'-looking Lawson tapped Fowler on the shoulder. 'It won't do,' he said. He said he had seen the draft and that proposals involving National Insurance were his business at the Treasury and nobody else's.

Without waiting for further explanation, Fowler lost his temper. As the cabinet processed upstairs, past the pictures of prime ministers gone by, the two of them clashed. Fowler explained furiously that he had been working on the review for a year. If Lawson was right, and National Insurance was outside his remit, then he might as well forget the whole thing. The photograph required silence from both of them, so, by the time they had come back downstairs and sat down at the cabinet table, tempers had begun to cool. But there was worse to come.

There were arguments inside the government about the idea of abolishing the second state pension. The full cabinet meeting to discuss Fowler's reforms was set for the end of April, but everything was thrown up in the air again by a leak to the economics correspondent of the *Daily Telegraph*, Frances Williams. She reported that the cabinet was split over the future of SERPS. The

Labour opposition put down a censure motion in the House of Commons accusing the government of the 'callous dismantling of the welfare state'.

This was tough for Fowler. He would have to defend his plan, even before it had the backing of his cabinet colleagues. He was rescued by leaks from Labour's own social security review, under his Labour opponent Michael Meacher, which was discussing abolishing mortgage interest tax relief. Instead of his own humiliation in next day's news, the headlines included 'Meacher gets a grilling'. But he wasn't out of the woods yet.

Lawson had been dealing with the budget and the sterling crisis in the early months of 1985, and it was only now that it occurred to him just how expensive abolishing SERPS might be, because it involved giving tax relief to compulsory pension schemes – to everyone, in fact. It was like reducing National Insurance across the whole population. He asked his officials at the Treasury if they had worked out what it might cost. 'I discovered to my horror that they had done no work on this at all,' he wrote later.[10] Now it was Lawson's turn to be furious. 'Sheer incompetence' was very rare among his officials, he wrote, but 'in all my time as chancellor, this was the worst'.

The senior Treasury official Peter Middleton and his team worked through the weekend of 20/21 April. On Monday morning, Lawson read their conclusions at his desk. He began to draft a note to cabinet colleagues, explaining that the whole idea of compulsory second pensions was unacceptable.

His spanner in the works wasn't revealed for thirty-six hours. On Tuesday evening, the phone rang at Fowler's London home while he was having dinner. It was his private secretary, Steve Godber. It transpired that Lawson's memo was trying to reopen the whole discussion about SERPS, and this was the first Fowler knew of it. Lawson wanted the whole issue to be shelved until the next election. The trouble for the Chancellor was that, although abolishing SERPS would save a great deal of money in a quarter of a century's time, giving people tax relief on new pensions would mean extra spending right now – just as he was struggling to slash taxes. Fowler spent a furious night and went straight round to the Cabinet Secretary the next morning, withdrawing his proposals from discussion. 'I got as close to resigning as I ever did,' he says now.

Then it was round the corner to the Treasury. 'I have rarely been angrier than I was that day,' he wrote later. 'What angered me was the last-minute timing of the intervention.'

'I have never seen Norman so cross,' Lawson admitted later.[11]

Worse, rumours of the argument began to leak out. 'The cabinet was in disarray last night over the biggest shake up of the welfare state in 40 years,' said the Daily Express.[12]

It wasn't until the following Monday that the ministers got together with the Prime Minister to resolve the problem. To Fowler's relief, Margaret Thatcher was still apparently on his side. It was well known, she said, that Switzerland had chosen a system of compulsory pension provision very similar to the one Fowler recommended. But Lawson had a shot in his locker, and this was the moment to use it – aware that suspicion of continental ways and habits loomed large in the Thatcher breast.

'But Prime Minister,' he said. 'It is well known that, in Switzerland, everything that is not forbidden is compulsory.'[13]

Switzerland was not used as an argument again.

The compromise agreed was that officials on both sides would get together and agree what the costs might be. To Lawson's horror, the bill looked like an increase in borrowing by £1 billion the following year. He shot off an urgent note to Thatcher, and to her deputy Willie Whitelaw, pointing out that people would have their take-home pay cut by £300 million, all going into their pension whether they liked it or not. 'It would be more than a banana skin: it would be evidence of an electoral death wish,' he wrote.[14]

Fowler agreed to meet Lawson halfway. They would exclude self-employed people from the new pension scheme. Then, believing he had won, he disappeared to the Isle of Wight with his family, dictating the final changes to the green paper to his DHSS team from a telephone box in Sea View.

Through the summer and early autumn of 1985, the debate on pensions raged, and it turned out that he hadn't won at all. In fact, he was in a crumbling position. Not only had the pensions industry come out against his plans, but so had the employers' organization the CBI, afraid that its member businesses would have to pay too much if everyone had a pension. The National Association of Pension Funds called the proposed 2 per cent National Insurance sweetener 'a gross misappropriation of public funds'.[15] When MISC III met for the last time on 15 October, Normal Fowler had to bow to the inevitable. 'We had next to nobody on our side,' he said.

He decided that he could not deliver the controversial aspects of the package against this combined opposition. SERPS would be kept, at a reduced rate, everyone would be given the right to contract out of SERPS and take out a personal pension of their own, and there would still be a 2 per cent National Insurance incentive to anyone joining. But that would be that: nobody would be forced to save anything. The personal pensions would be just that – they would be individual, without any of the benefits of clubbing together, as they could have done if the entire workforce had been enrolled.

The Treasury opposition melted away. The CBI and the pensions industry went quiet. As long as they would not have to shell out for everyone to have a pension, as long as the dreaded word 'compulsory' was dropped from the bill, the major players were happy. 'I was not paid to preside over disasters – however noble the cause,' wrote Fowler later. 'I had to think again.'[16]

The media were less impressed. 'Norman Fowler calls his

white paper on social reform *Programme for Action*,' said the *Daily Express*. 'It should have been called "Gone with the Wind" . . . *Programme for Action* is hesitant where it should have been decisive; timorous where it should have been bold; blinkered where it should have been imaginative . . . It is the same old fatal pussy-footing again.'[17]

The new law sailed through the House of Commons the following May with a majority of 128. Lawson congratulated himself that 'the compromise now in place has removed an intolerable burden from the shoulders of future generations'.[18] Once again, the dog didn't bark.

In fact, the compromise would have huge repercussions. If the schemes were not going to be compulsory, then – all too often – people would simply shelve the problem of saving for retirement. If it was all to be voluntary, then the new pension schemes would have to advertise, and that meant that their costs and charges would rise. As we will see, this would have a dramatic effect on the new pensions. But there was another effect as well. Because these were no longer compulsory schemes, the government would feel less responsible for them – either for the way they were sold or for the kind of pensions they produced in the end.

Without any kind of compulsion, not even an assumption that people would take part – and with a right to opt out – the possibility of those gold-plated defined benefit pension schemes for a new generation was drifting out of reach. The new personal pensions would leave those paying into them at the mercy of the markets, of an overcharging pensions industry, and of the pensions roller coaster that was about to begin.

It was not that somehow Fowler had planned for anything except personal pensions, but the failure to press home the idea of making them compulsory ruled out any kind of middle way between the old occupational pensions and the new individual ones. More than anything else, the cabinet row and the intense opposition to compulsory pensions would dramatically slash the retirement earnings of millions.

A story used to go round Wall Street during the booming 1920s that chimes with the spirit of Hans Christian Andersen's story 'The Emperor's New Clothes'. It describes how a visitor to downtown New York City was taken from Wall Street to Battery Park and was shown the luxury yachts of all the bankers and brokers, swinging at anchor, their shining brass and spotless decks a fanfare to the careers of their owners. The visitor took on some of the naive wisdom of the little boy in the tale when he said: 'But where are their customers' yachts?'

The question passed into Wall Street legend when a trader called Fred Schwed – not Fred the Shred, I may say – used it as the title of his 1940 book about Wall Street, recently republished to coincide with our own crash. Schwed had to contend with the Wall Street Crash in 1929, shortly after starting his career. He then carried on waiting for the recovery until finally giving up to write the book. 'Shortly after that I left Wall Street, and I believe it was the next day that stocks began going up; they have continued to go up, with all but negligible interruptions, ever since,' he wrote fifteen years later.[19]

Schwed had something of Michael Lewis about him, carving out a successful career in the American magazine world based on his career as a trader, and basing his commentary on the other jokes circulating about New York's financial district during his period there, at the tail end of the 1920s boom. 'Wall Street . . . is a street with a river at one end and a graveyard at the other,' he wrote. 'This is striking but incomplete. It omits the kindergarten in the middle.'

But the question remains. Where *are* the customers' yachts? The traders and money managers have made themselves extraordinarily rich arranging the financial affairs of the middle classes, but their clients are poorer than they were before. In fact, the middle classes have been their obsessive and enthusiastic customers over the past generation or so, relying on the burgeoning financial services sector to fund their retirement while at the same time watching their pensions unravel – without realizing quite how far they had unravelled. At the same time, those responsible for shepherding those pensions safely home grew ever more wealthy. It was no coincidence that the number of yachts sold in February 2010, at the height of the recession, was double that of the month before, because that was the month that the banks paid out their bonuses.

Back in the final years of the 1980s, the middle classes embraced financial services just as they embraced the idea of portable pensions. What was particularly tragic about it was that some people swallowed the idea so enthusiastically that they flung away their gold-plated pensions in their enthusiasm. The perfect storm was brewing. The first effect of the new Social Security Act 1986 (Section 15, in fact) was that the former opponents of the whole idea of personal pensions, the insurance companies, began selling them with great verve and imagination. After all, nobody would be forced to join their company pension scheme any more. By 1988, when the new law came into effect, Norman Fowler was astonished by the energy that went into selling the new alternatives. 'I suddenly saw buses with slogans saying "Buy Personal Pensions", by people who only a few months before had been telling me that it was a disastrous thing to do,' he says.

Despite all the forecasts, inside and outside the government, no one had predicted how trendy the new personal pensions were going to be. The government had budgeted for about half a million people taking them out within the first couple of years. In the event, 3.2 million people signed up in the first year. The trouble was that, as it turned out, they were often abandoning far better company schemes to do so.

When it came to the reckoning, it was clear that about a third of those people had taken out personal pensions when they should have done no such thing. Nurses, teachers, police were all among those encouraged to contract out of their valuable occupational pensions by the fearsome salesmen from the insurance and pension companies. Investigations were beginning by the end of 1988, and the mis-selling scandal grew. It eventually led to £12 billion being paid out in compensation.

By the time the new law was in effect, and the new pensions were being mis-sold, Norman Fowler was chairman of the Conservative Party (he is now Lord Fowler) and had other problems to contend with. But he watched the scandal unfold with mounting horror. 'I always thought, for God's sake, what was my department doing not noticing that they were selling personal pensions to teachers?' he says now. 'The answer was that we handed over responsibility. I do remember in the committee stage thinking: "Who is going to police it?" I was given strict instructions that I shouldn't say too much about this, because it is a matter for the DTI [Department of Trade and Industry]. If only it had been.'

The idea of personal pensions was designed to solve a particular problem, but the voluntary element was catastrophic. The compromise that followed the fatal argument between Fowler and Lawson gave people the excuse to shelve decisions. It was not that people decided *never* to take out a pension. They took no decision at all, because it is easier that way.

'As long as I live, I will regret having to abandon our plans to give an occupational pension to every worker in the country,' wrote Fowler later. 'It was the worst decision that I ever had to take in government. That is not to say that it was the wrong decision. Given the position in November 1985, there was no other decision for a politician to take.'[20]

One of those who were keen at first on the idea of personal pensions was Robin Ellison, now one of the top pensions lawyers in the country. He is a leading light at Pinsent Masons, which houses the biggest team of pensions lawyers in the world. He now looks back on the whole personal pensions episode as a disaster, particularly for the middle classes.

He was working for his father in a small specialist legal practice in Manchester in the mid-1970s, when one of their clients – an actuary – wanted to set up a special kind of pension that would put money in a separate pot that you could reinvest in your own business. These days, they are called Small Self Administered Schemes, and they remain very successful. But designing a legal framework for them also had the effect of catapulting Ellison into the pensions world.

He was offered a place for a year at Wolfson College, Oxford, and decided to use it to carry out a comparative study of pensions law across Europe. In the turmoil that was to come, that study launched Ellison into his life as a critical legal resource for pension companies. But the past few decades dismay him.

'Pensions are for the middle classes,' he says now. 'Poor people live on the state; rich people don't give a toss. It is people in the middle who really need a pension. How are they going to maintain even a fraction of their income after retirement? But the truth is that pensions have been destroyed in a fit of benevolence by successive governments, by good intentions promoted by diatribes in the Daily Mail. Every time something goes wrong, they pass a law to stop it happening again, and when you do that you stop good things happening as well. It is a history over the past thirty years of unintended consequences – in spades.'

The key mistake was not so much Fowler's compromise, he says. It was the decision to go down the route to personal pensions in the first place.

'It is very hard as a private individual to provide enough for your retirement. Collective provision in old age is hugely efficient. We do it through the state, though very badly, and we used to do it exceedingly well for the middle classes. The destruction of the system makes me want to weep.'

From the 1890s to the 1970s, the company occupational pension schemes thrived. They gave individuals the protection of being in a large group. They also provided the capital needed to develop the City of London as a major financial centre. Then, over the past quarter of a century, the whole edifice started to unravel.

People who speak of a pensions crisis usually point to the way that people are living longer. Robin Ellison quotes one company pension scheme that includes seven people aged 107. If they are women, which they probably are, that means they have been on pensions for forty-seven years. No unmodified pension scheme can survive that, but the problem is solvable: it just means we have to work rather longer.

No, Ellison looks elsewhere for the problem. He points to three key events that brought on the perfect storm that destroyed most middle-class pensions. The first was the Fowler reforms and the great argument with Nigel Lawson. He blames those policy wonks who came up with the idea of personal pensions in the first place – those who believed that company pensions were somehow a kind of 'socialism in drag'.

'It sounds right. It's quite plausible,' he says. 'Make people capitalists. The political logic was kind of appealing, and Mrs Thatcher bought it lock, stock and barrel. But you can't do pensions on your own. You need a collective sharing of defence. I was one of the young Turks that said they should be portable and, with hindsight, I was completely wrong.'

The second blast of Ellison's perfect storm began one night in the middle of the Bay of Biscay, when the publishing tycoon Robert Maxwell fell off his yacht *Lady Ghislaine* in the early hours of 5 November 1991. After his body was found, it became clear that his business empire, including the *Daily Mirror*, was in serious financial trouble and that he had stolen £453 million from his company pension funds.

There was political uproar when the plight of the Mirror pensioners became clear (though most of them received most of their money in the end). Something had to be done to ring-fence pensions, and the starting gun was fired on a destructive race to protect the increasingly embattled corporate pension schemes in ways that, paradoxically, brought about their demise.

In June 1992, a group of eminent pension experts and grandees of the financial world met under the chairmanship of Professor Sir Roy Goode, tasked to make sure that the Maxwell affair could never happen again. They decided that occupational pensions needed regulations to make sure they always delivered the pensions that were promised. This was a bigger change than it looked. Before Maxwell, there had always been an implicit promise to make the best efforts to deliver the right pension. But this was considered inadequate: the promise needed to be stronger. No longer would employees ever have to negotiate with an ailing company to make up the difference. It would be a firm, unshakable contract.

There was also a parallel attempt, led by Ellison himself at the National Association of Pension Funds, to simplify pensions tax law. Until the 1950s, this had only been a couple of pages. By the 1980s it had reached an unwieldy 1,300 pages. Ellison's committee boiled it down to a page and a half of what was really needed and submitted it to the government. It took them five years to agree, with the proviso that it might have to be more like twenty pages.

'When it turns up, it's 200 pages,' says Ellison now. 'We say, this is insane, but we can live with it. Then there were another 200 pages of secondary regulations, which they said they wouldn't have. Then, would you believe it, there are 2,500 pages of guidance notes from the regulator. Other countries manage their pension tax law in under five pages – we have 4,000.'

Grinding through the system at the same time was the result of the Goode Committee's deliberations, in the Pensions Act 1995 and then in November 2000 the highly controversial Financial Reporting Standard, known as FRS17, which forced companies to declare their pension liabilities in their annual accounts. It was the complexity and demands of FRS17 that many of the biggest companies in the country blamed for closing their pension schemes. It was just too complicated.

'Once it gets complex, people say "To hell with it." The cost of compliance is very high,' says Ellison now. 'I spend my life with civil servants. They're intelligent. They look after children. They're nice to animals. But they believe that regulation works, and more regulation works better.'

Sure enough, the collapse of the defined benefit company pension schemes – once the envy of the world – followed shortly afterwards. In 2002, the year the new regulations really began to bite, 19 per cent of them closed their doors to new staff. In 2003, the figure was 26 per cent. In 2004, it was 10 per cent. Now only two and a half million people are covered by occupational pensions, and they are still being closed.

You can see why. There is undoubtedly greed involved with the biggest companies, anxious to reduce the amount of money they are investing in the future of their employees. But every month there are usually reports of smaller companies put into administration, not because they are bankrupt, but because there is a hole in their company pension scheme. Under FRS17, and the peculiarities in the new rules for valuing assets, company pension schemes can bring down a business.

There remain a few of the old-fashioned corporate pensions, and there are exceptions to the great decline, notably in the public sector. Ironically, the still generous senior civil service pensions inoculate those responsible for presiding over the decline of company pension schemes from the consequences of their decisions. The other exception is the elite One Per Cent (the average pension of a FTSE 100 director is worth more than £3,200 a week, while their workers get an average of £7,124 a year).[21] Fred Goodwin's pension pot after the collapse of Royal Bank of Scotland was doubled when he left to £16 million. (Twenty former directors of the bailed-out banks retired in 2009 with pensions totalling over £6 million a year between them.)[22]

Even so, the slow throttling of traditional occupational pensions has been hard-fought inside the companies involved. Some companies have sacked staff for refusing to accept the new pension rules. But even as the struggle goes on, new pensions regulations continue to appear in the UK at the rate of forty pages a week – a desperate continuing struggle to close the door after the middle-class pension horse has long since bolted.

Ellison blames the short-termism of politicians. 'It has been government by newspaper, and nobody is prepared to think long-term or think coherently,' he says. 'When you speak to them, they are really intelligent guys – not stupid people at all. But their time horizon is three months or six months, when in pension terms you need a horizon of thirty or forty years. Other countries are bad, but less bad than we are. We are incandescently awful.'

The short-termism of politicians lies behind the third element of Ellison's perfect storm. It is the problem of pension surpluses.

This hardly sounds like a problem, but it was. For one thing, having big pension reserves made companies afraid that they might be the target of corporate raiders, who wanted to get hold of their huge pension pots. For another thing, it was a temptation too far for hungry politicians.

'For twenty years, pensions had surpluses,' says Ellison now. 'The word was a kind of incentive to governments to raid pension schemes. They shouldn't have used the word "surplus"; they should have used a word like "actuarial reserves". "Surplus" made them think there was too much money – which there wasn't, because with hindsight they needed money for the bad years. We had seven fat years; what we didn't do was keep money in storage for the seven thin years.'

That was the irony. The surpluses were not really surpluses at all.

One of the effects of the new pension regulations was that they had to value their investment at market prices (this was FRS16). It sounded like a good idea at the time, a version of the market rigour then so popular. In practice, it meant the value of pension schemes shot up and down in the wake of the wild markets. It meant huge surges up and down. The Royal Mail famously has a pension deficit of £5.6 billion, but for ten years it had such big surpluses that they paid nothing in. The food giant Unilever had seven years of pension holidays and also took the surplus back into the company's balance sheet (£270 million), and redistributed it in extra dividends to shareholders. Now it has a pensions deficit – not that it stopped them from giving retiring chief executive Niall FitzGerald an extra £3 million to add to his existing £17 million pension pot in 2004.

The problem was that, deep down, politicians of both the Labour and the Conservative parties hated the pensions industry. To the Thatcherites of the 1980s it looked like a form of corporate socialism. To the Blairites of the 1990s it looked like a corrupt form of capitalism. The temptation for Gordon Brown as Chancellor in 1997 was too much, and he raided the so-called 'surplus' with a £5 billion tax (a precedent set originally by Lawson himself).

The combined effect of the perfect storm has been a tragedy for the middle classes in particular, says Robin Ellison. 'What we've done is destroyed what used to be the jewel in the crown. People used to come from all over the world to see how the British ran their company pensions schemes. People you talk to in big companies now are very concerned that they are about to reap a harvest of very badly pensioned retired people. I speak to my legal peers, and they are sweating – really sweating. Because not only are pensions dysfunctional in the UK because of the short-termism of policymakers, but because we are being hit by different but similar policies that are robbing the middle classes.'

All this happens to coincide with a period when, for many good reasons, interest rates are being kept artificially low. If you are lucky enough to have a pensions pot of £100,000, it might now buy you an annual pension of £2,500, when normal interest rates might have produced a pension of between £5,000 and £8,000. The interest rates are being held down to benefit younger people, to help them buy homes in the dysfunctional property market, but it massively shrinks the pensions of the older generation. It is precisely the opposite phenomenon of David Willetts's book *The Pinch*.

'Pensions are a long-term project,' says Ellison now. 'You can't fiddle around with it every few years. There has been a Pensions Act virtually every year since 2007, and that's insane. That is because no party has developed a long-term strategy on pensions. They dabble. We don't have a twenty-five-year strategy on anything and certainly don't have it with pensions – and that's why the middle classes have been hammered.'

If the middle classes have prospered because of their traditional values of thrift and long-term planning, they have been let down because – in practice – the values of those who rule them are no longer middle-class. Perhaps they never were.

It is only when you get into the nitty-gritty of pensions like this – what they will pay out and when – that the full horror of the position that the middle classes find themselves in becomes clear.

In the mid-1960s, just over 8 million people were in company pension schemes, the so-called *defined benefit* schemes, which meant that they were protected by sharing the risk and knew what kind of payout they would get – usually two-thirds of their final salary. Nor would they have to worry about annuities or investments.

For all the good intentions of Norman Fowler's review, and the optimism which followed it, the pensions industry never tried to recreate something along the same lines for a wider mass of people. Maybe it could have been done if Fowler had won the argument about making pensions compulsory for everyone. In any case, it didn't happen, and the new personal pensions rapidly replaced the traditional schemes – leaving individuals increasingly at the mercy of the financial services industry.

In practice, this was the real problem with personal pensions. Far from innovating to reproduce effective and secure pensions for everyone, the industry provided a means by which individuals could gamble away their savings. Far from providing a choice of charges and competitive rates, the industry colluded within itself to keep charges high and to obscure information about their real costs. But it was worse than that. There is an implacable arithmetic about investing in retirement savings which is now shrinking the middle-class retirement pot.

The main difference is that the mixture of contributions from you, your employer and the government into *defined benefit* occupational pensions used to be about 22 per cent of your salary. For personal pensions, which define your contributions but not what you get out (*defined contribution*), the average is only 9 per cent – even though you might personally be paying exactly the same amount into both schemes. Big difference.

It means that if you pay into a personal pension for forty years, you will get out 41 per cent of what you would have got from a defined benefit occupational pension. But then the implacable arithmetic kicks in. For the personal pension, there are entry and exit charges. There are annual management charges and other hidden charges, some explicit, some not. Imagine that the annual charges are around 1.5 per cent a year. It seems like an insignificant amount, but it builds up implacably. For many people, 1.5 per cent a year over forty years will eat up almost half the contributions you make into your pension pot – a whacking £45,000 from payments of £108,000.

Then there is the cost of an annuity, which is 10 to 15 per cent higher for people in personal pensions. The terrifying conclusion is that your pension will be about a quarter of what it was if you had paid into an old-fashioned occupational pension. A *quarter*. That is a huge difference, and not one that was ever mentioned during that whole debate a generation ago.[23] Another dog not barking.

For many of us, four years are enough anyway. Something happens, we stop paying in, the pension scheme falls dormant and our next employer starts up another one. We end up with multiple pots of money, each one leeching money in charges, unclear how to pool them, with no clear disinterested advice (I have three; my wife has eight).

What seems to me to be most outrageous, and a potential answer to the big question – where are the customers' yachts? – is the high charges levied, rather furtively, by the financial services industry on middle-class thrift. Other kinds of investment are in some ways even worse, and again – if you dare to invest as an ordinary punter – the implacable arithmetic of the investment world counts against you.

The American mutual fund innovator John Bogle has done more than almost anyone else to lift the lid on the way the system extracts money from savers. Bogle is an extraordinary man, a pioneer of the idea of index-linked funds, one of those Wall Street giants that have always shunned Wall Street, and – like Warren Buffett – he has kept up a sceptical commentary about the excesses of his own sector. We miss people like that in the City of London, where the grandees tend to stick together. He spent the years before 1977 struggling for control of the mutual funds he ran before finally getting the wriggle-room to try out his own ideas. He called his fund Vanguard after Nelson's flagship at the Battle of the Nile (Bogle is a huge fan of Nelson and a large portrait of himself dressed as the great admiral, including eyepatch and decorations, hangs in his office outside Philadelphia).

He also turned Vanguard into the first index-linked mutual fund. The idea was that, instead of frenetically bouncing in and out of the stock market, it would simply allow customers to hold all the shares in the Standard & Poor 500 index. There would be no marketing and no sales charges. It now has a vast $1.3 trillion under management. When you invest that way, Bogle says, 'it minimises the extraction by the financial community of the returns generated by business'.[24]

In his short and powerful book Enough, he set out the huge gap between what American investors should have earned from the stock market and what they actually did earn. The average equity fund return in the quarter-century from 1980 to 2005 was 10 per cent. What investors actually earned was 7.3 per cent (a 482 per cent decrease). If investors had just bought all the shares in the Standard & Poor index, and hung on to them for twenty-five years, they would have earned a return of 1,718 per cent. The fees earned by the US investment industry during that period were $500 trillion, creamed off the pensions and investments of the nation.

'The gross return generated in the financial markets, minus the costs of the financial system, equals the net return actually delivered to investors,' writes Bogle, and it is an important calculation, and not one that has been done in the UK.

Bogle had his own version of the implacable arithmetic of investment. Over the past half-century, the gross return on investment in stocks has been 11 per cent a year on average. If you invested £1,000 half a century ago, it should now be worth £184,600. But that isn't what you get, of course. Again, the fees look quite small – though they are hard to find. They include brokerage commissions, management fees, advisory fees, advertising costs, lawyers' fees and so on. It is never quite clear how much they might be levied over a half a century, but even at 2 per cent a year it has a dramatic effect on the total. It brings it down to about £74,400. The industry has creamed off about half your returns.

That isn't the end. Imagine another 1.5 per cent a year goes in capital gains taxes, that cuts the total down to £37,000 (and if you factor in an average inflation rate of 4 per cent, what you actually get is less than £6,000). It hasn't all gone to the financial intermediaries, but most of it has.[25]

'While the owners of business enjoy the dividend yields and earnings growth that our capitalistic system creates,' wrote Bogle, 'those who play in the financial markets capture those investment gains only after the costs of financial intermediation are deducted – a vast "losers game".' Like problem gamblers, our financial intermediaries – those we have given charge of our pensions – dip in and out of the markets with increasing frequency, constantly going back for more, ostensibly doing so on our behalf, but constantly extracting the croupier's cut.

There is a parallel problem here to the tragedy of the lost mutual banks. Mutual institutions have been despised in the financial sector over the past generation, but they are usually far better at delivering returns for savers. Endowment policies have been paying out 20 per cent more over two decades where they were taken out with mutuals.[26] Once again, the problem with mutuals was nothing to do with their effectiveness for savers and borrowers. Their 'problem' was that they paid less to their top staff and board.

But the real problem with personal pensions is that they flung the middle classes into the hands of the investment industry, and – as so often before – the middle classes naively believed that this was an industry that was emphatically on their side. It represented them. It was staffed by them. It specialized in their needs. Of course they believed that. The trouble was that it wasn't on their side at all. It was on its own side, and it has used the savings of the middle classes, painfully set aside from their income, to fund the new class of Übermenschen that is now the focus of the global economy.

Again, this great mistake is based on the fantasy that financial markets are efficient, and all that frenetic activity – speculating, coming in and out of the markets in ever-decreasing slices of nanoseconds – all costs money, which the investor pays. The investment theorist Benjamin Graham warned that the financial market is a voting machine in the short term, but in the long term it is a weighing machine. Investors capture the long-term returns of business, speculators don't, especially when the average turn-over of stocks and shares every year was 25 per cent in 1950 (Benjamin Graham's heyday) and is now nearer 300 per cent. These huge and growing costs of the financial system fall on the unsus-pecting middle classes, a heavy and ever-growing burden.

So what does all this mean? It means that 15 million people in middle-income groups in the UK (not exactly the middle classes, but including many of them) are heading for a 60 per cent cut in their household income after they retire. Many of them will have to rely on the state pension – the lowest in the world apart from Mexico – for at least half their needs.

It also means that, once again, the middle classes have been deluded about those to whom they delegated the task of looking after their retirement. They believed that the same comfort in retirement awaited them that their parents enjoyed, and if their pensions were failing – as they know they are (they are not stupid) – well, they could always fall back on the amazing increase in the value of their homes.

As we saw before, this may not be open to them. They are also relying on this increase in value to support them through old age, infirmity and social care – and to put their own children on the housing ladder, and many other purposes besides.

Why has this happened? As we have seen, it is partly because of the changing structure of organizations, so that the middle classes no longer have those safe lifetime careers in middle management – even if they wanted them. Partly it has been political failures, and partly the failure of the financial intermediaries to develop pension products that could give reliable hope of retirement in comfort.

But the middle classes need to shoulder some of the blame as well. There is a strange middle-class blindness, which I have to admit I share, about all this. One study showed that 81 per cent of working people think the state pension won't be enough to live on in retirement, yet 40 per cent are paying absolutely nothing into any kind of pension to do anything about it.

It is their fault as well that there was no middle-class outcry about their dwindling pension prospects, and the disappearance of the institutions they needed to make those prospects possible. There was certainly pressure on the politicians to prevent another Maxwell from putting his fingers in his employees' pension funds. There was pressure to buttress the values of the disappearing occupational pensions too, but no pressure at all to rescue those customers of personal pensions from a disappointing retirement. The middle classes are themselves the dog that didn't bark.

It should not be beyond the wit of the British to tackle the problem. Norman Fowler's reforms assumed that the investment sector would innovate, just as they assumed that they would compete on fees. Neither of these things happened. Nor was there any attempt – once Fowler had lost the argument to make them compulsory – to recreate occupational pensions on a much broader basis.

Then there is the usual squabbling. The Financial Services

Agency chair Adair Turner launched his solutions in October 2004, and immediately – as always – came under combined attack from the Treasury and the trade unions, though for opposite reasons. Chancellor Gordon Brown began to discredit the figures even before the ink was dry on the report. It was ever thus.

Lately the dog has begun to bark. New rules will opt people into workplace pensions automatically, though at very low levels (only 2 per cent). New rules will in practice halve management fees, adding about three-quarters of a per cent to the returns. There is also a debate about the narrow conservatism of the way pensions managers understand their legal duties, which seem to bind them into following the herd. But the hard facts still apply: it now requires a pension pot of somewhere around £600,000 if you are going to retire at the age of sixty-five on £30,000 a year.

There is also some pressure now to rescue the remains of the old occupational pensions sector, the tens of thousands of tiny funds bearing the names of long-defunct companies which continue to pay the pensions of the surviving members. This is particularly problematic for the 40,000 remaining public-sector pension schemes some of which only have a handful of members left, and which therefore cost more and more to run. One report suggests that we could save up to £34 billion on administration over five years just by consolidating the public-sector pensions into a few giant pots.[27]

Part of the tragedy of the UK economy is that – unlike foreign pension schemes – these are now too small to invest in housing and infrastructure, which are far more reliable investments than shares. That is why the Chinese own Thames Water, the Canadians own the Channel Tunnel and our ports are owned by Middle Eastern oil potentates. Nor are our pensions practised at investing in the next generation of green energy infrastructure we so badly need to underpin our lives in the next generation.

But something else needs to happen if the middle classes are to claw back any kind of retirement. Over a million of us in the UK are already working beyond retirement, some because we want to, but some because we still haven't paid off our mortgages (the average mortgage debt for pensioners is now £45,300), and one in four pensioners is still borrowing money to make ends meet.

The middle classes know all this. They are all too aware of the inadequacy of their pensions, without perhaps looking too closely at how inadequate. They are all too aware that the magical compound-interest machine, which protected middle-class generations in retirement, has run down. Interest rates barely exist. The clock mechanism has run down. For people like me, a decade or so from official retirement, that is a serious crisis.

It is true that owning their own homes will insulate the middle classes from poverty in old age, compared with those who have to carry on renting. But they still risk an increasingly impoverished old age, eking out the money to pay for fuel bills just like the rest of the population whose incautious fecklessness they used to despise. Those brochures of bronzed couples of a certain age, waggled temptingly in front of those whose jobs did not provide them with the pension they had hoped for, will be so much more of a distant dream. They will just carry on working, like everyone else.

Middle Classes in Figures

Average pension pot in the UK: £25,000.
Predicted annual payout for a pension pot of £25,000: £1,250.

The New Middle-Class-Values Dictionary

EDUCATION: Gone are the days when the middle classes united in their disdain for and suspicion of learning and cleverness. These days, they are firmly committed, not just to education – though not necessarily to exams – but to culture, creativity and catching the occasional Prom. In fact, they regard themselves as a bastion of a society where people still have books in the house. As always with the middle classes, there is an element of *Après nous, le déluge*.

Dispatches from the Frontline

Outside the school gates, Dulwich, South London, Wednesday, 8.30 a.m.
This is a tale of two schools. On my left, Dulwich Preparatory School (fees: £5,000 a term; motto: 'Inspiring excellence since 1885', whatever that means). On my right, Kingsdale Foundation School (proprietor: Southwark Council). Both bang next door to each other in Alleyn Road, with only a white-painted brick wall and tall fence to keep them apart.

Aware of the potential contrast for people like me, the schools have managed to stagger their arrival times, the Kingsdale pupils arriving like a great army dressed in black and red from the bus stops in the direction of West Norwood, with shirts hanging out and iPods firmly in ears, cycling along the pavement (the only sensible way in this street, I assure you). The Dulwich pupils arrive from the other direction, slipping in through the gate from West Dulwich, and looking almost exactly the same except that this is a blur of blue, branded woollen hats, grey flannel trousers and knee socks.

The late arrivals are sped straight in through the gates in a succession of huge black Land Rovers and Range Rovers, the occasional dutiful dog looking straight out from the front passenger seat. Or black Mini Coopers or vast land cruisers driven by tiny women, with ski-racks on the roof. The only discernible difference between the pupils, apart from age, is that the Dulwich prep school pupils also wield a whole orchestra of musical instruments and have bigger satchels on their backs, so big, in fact, that they are usually carried by the parents of the younger boys. They rumble a little from the weight of homework delivered. The lure of Dulwich College itself, all railway gothic and green playing fields, beckons from the other side of the railway line.

But this division is not quite what it seems. Dulwich Prep takes almost a third of its entry on scholarship or assisted places. It can afford to: the shadowy Dulwich estate owns all the land around here. And Kingsdale is not quite what it seems either: it is a transformed place, thanks to head teacher Steve Morrison, a flagship of the Building Schools programme, an 'outstanding' rating by Ofsted plastered outside the gates. There is hardly any sign of its old self – before Morrison's arrival, exclusions were running at over 300 a year. 'This school is a magical place and makes dreams come true,' says a sign outside, quoting from a parent who wrote to Ofsted about them.

There is a huge gap in income between the two schools, but both are highly successful, both oversubscribed, and both are becoming a magnet for different kinds of middle-class families. Different kinds of magical places. Different kinds of magic.

6

The fifth clue: the great education panic

'Their beautiful St Thomas's – a magnet for professional
commuters to Yarvil, who were attracted by the tiny classes, the
rolltop desks, the aged stone building and the lush green playing
field – would be overrun and swamped by the offspring of
scroungers, addicts and mothers whose children had all been
fathered by different men.'

J. K. Rowling, *The Casual Vacancy*, 2012

I first got a whiff of the middle-class panic about education – which
seems to be nearly universal, at least in London – when I went
along to my local primary school to their introductory morning
for prospective parents. It is a peculiar feeling, which begins almost
physically in the solar plexus and then buzzes day to day around
your head, giving you a background sense of panic and inadequacy.
But I didn't know that then: that was before I had really engaged
with what is known as education choice. The government told me
I had the choice – though it is strictly speaking only the right to
express a preference – and I intended to exercise it with all the
discretion, balance and wisdom I had available.

The introductory morning was actually an introductory hour,
but it was an impressive display. Little girls and boys in magenta
uniform greeted me at every corner and politely told me which
turning to take. The head teacher, tall, informal and reassuring,
was impressive too. He made the most of a forty-five-minute

PowerPoint presentation where the school was lovingly introduced, explained in terms of league tables, and illustrated with pictures of children happily baking, reciting, playing the cello and generally having a fulfilling time being educated.

It was, I admit, a kind of middle-class dream. Polite children, musical instruments, creativity, good results, and apparently happy fulfilment on all sides. It certainly felt happy, even in the school hall (though the gym bars on the walls reminded me unpleasantly of my own school days, which made the phrase 'No PE this week' one of the happiest sentences in the language). I had set out to find a school along these lines, as painted by a head teacher practised in the art of appealing to the middle classes, avoiding all the great sins of brutality, conformity and Gradgrindian narrowness.

I glanced around the room at the other parents, mainly mothers, and of all the many races that have found their home in south London, and they seemed to feel the same. Their eyes were full of hope and some of them seemed to be swallowing, as if their mouths had begun to water at this discovery. It was like a sighting of Moby-Dick, a distant prospect of the Great White Middle-Class Dream.

The last fifteen minutes were all questions, and nearly all questions about the same thing. What were the admissions policies? Where was the catchment area? The head teacher brushed all this off, joyfully and politely – it was clear that this exercise in tempting middle-class parents was something that he enjoyed every year – explaining that admissions were the responsibility of the local authority. Not my department, he said.

So there was a nervous fixed grin on our faces as we walked out beside the green playground (there was another rarity: a grass playground). I felt relatively confident, living only eight minutes' walk from the school, that we would fit into their criteria, but others were clearly not. And I began to wonder what the whole ritual had been about: pumping these parents up with desire and determination when the school was heavily oversubscribed already. Most of us would not get the choice.

In fact, my son was rejected, even though he had been in the school's nursery for two terms already. The catchment area had breathed in and the local authority had decided that the path at the end of our road was not an acceptable route to school. The fact that he was in the nursery at the school already was no guarantee of admission.

The panic returned, but I am nothing if not middle-class, so I had some means to tackle it. I went to see the council officer in charge, who told me that I was the person he most expected to see. Unsure whether this was encouraging or not, I began – exhaustingly at first but with increasingly frenetic enthusiasm – to gather the papers I needed to make an appeal. Day after day, as I trudged down the footpath to the school to pick up from the nursery, the letter I would write and the speech I would give to the appeals panel shaped themselves in my head. I measured distances and walking speeds. I took photos of the path and the journey to school. I realized with delight that the council had not adopted our road (their approved route), but they had adopted the footpath. Why had I not been a barrister? I asked myself. This was fun.

When we sat in the waiting room at the town hall some months later, sitting across the table from other middle-class parents, it seemed considerably less fun. It reminded me of the Dickensian court waiting room, and the terrified witnesses waiting in it, on the front of my copy of *Bleak House*, wide-eyed with boredom and fear. The fathers wielded huge lever-arch files of notes. The mothers just looked frightened and powerless.

In the event, I gabbled through my prepared statement (explaining exactly why I never was a barrister) in front of the panel of three – one of whom glared malevolently at me and one of whom seemed to be asleep. They asked a few token questions, and a week later I called up for the result. Our appeal had been upheld, by a majority verdict (clearly the sleeping panel member had come down in our favour), on the grounds that my son was in the nursery already – precisely the opposite of their policy as I understood it.

My first feeling, after the initial satisfaction, was irritation. Why had they upheld the appeal on a spurious reason but ignored all my clever arguments? I soon realized this was extremely silly of me, and I checked myself and found that the familiar panic was back in its basket waiting until it was needed again. Even so, the whole experience left me with a strong sense of the middle-class angst around the whole business of education.

The truth was that my children would probably have been fine in the school further up the road. Even maybe the school further down the road, where one of the teaching assistants told me how their teacher – close to breaking point – had spent most of the previous term hiding in the stationery cupboard. But I had been persuaded that the one way I could best exercise my choice of schools was to pick the school I had been seduced so expertly into choosing.

Secondary school now looms ahead. There is no school in the immediate area, and barely any in the borough, which I can either afford or contemplate sending my children to. So like so many middle-class parents before me, I shall be off. I see that this is deeply unfair, but I don't want my children lost in a factory school, even a school run by a carpet millionaire, and I can afford to move out of London. Most people can't, and I certainly can't afford to move inside London, where the proximity of a good school can put another £400,000 onto the price of a home.[1] I am aware that it isn't really right, and it isn't really choice either.

The panic I describe here is not wholly a London affliction, but it very nearly is. Across the country, 85 per cent of parents get their first choice of schools. There are clearly many of these (estimated at 9 per cent) who make a more 'realistic' choice, because they know they can't actually choose the school they want. But in London it is a disaster, with 800 children still with no places at all, and a predicted 90,000 more pupils than places by 2015.[2] Entry in London as it currently stands is so organized that the choice is often made, not by the parents, but by the schools and the local authorities. Unless, of course, you go private, which is why 21 per cent of school places in inner London are independent (rising to 51 per cent in Kensington and Chelsea).[3]

One of the less attractive attributes of the middle classes is the way they tend to believe they can play the system. They know the ins and outs of how to get into oversubscribed drama classes (volunteer in the office) or into oversubscribed church schools (become an altar server). They always think they know who to talk to and butter up, even if actually they don't.

That slightly superior skill has taken the political edge off the insanity of London's school places. They believe, rightly or wrongly, that they can finagle something, or – failing that – they can move. Sometimes straight after the first positive pregnancy test. 'When we knew kids were on the way we moved to a house which was within walking distance of the best state primary school and Brighton College, our preferred secondary school,' Elizabeth Moody-Stuart told the BBC in 2010. 'It was part of the plan.'[4]

That is how the middle classes have managed the fact that there are too many schools they believe to be bad. One of the ironies of politics is that the Liberal Democrats poured resources into the schools in three south-west London boroughs which they controlled for three decades, only to find that the house prices had soared so much that they barely had majorities any more. Even more ironic, the pressure on school places in Labour Merton next door has been relieved because a third of their primary school children escape outside the borough when it comes to secondary school. The political rewards of investing in schools are not what they ought to be.

The other option is to go private, and 7 per cent of the school population are still at private schools – but the expense can be huge (over £30,000 a year for each child at my old school) and the number of wealthy foreigners in the independent sector rose by 44 per cent last year (which is why there are now more ethnic minority pupils in the independent sector than there are in the state sector).[5] One side effect of globalization and the rise of the new international elite is that the old independent schools are priced increasingly beyond the reach of the middle classes, especially at secondary level, unless they can qualify for scholarships or some kind of support from employers.

All this means that the intensity of panic has been rising, especially if the rewards are now for so few. There is a reminder of this in the annual struggle to get a place at medical school or the best universities, competing now with a growing international middle class (with places going to Chinese students in the UK rising at up to 25 per cent a year). Even pupils with the top AAB grades at A level have required an extra 25,000 places which will not be available to anyone with lower grades.[6] This is not competition to be part of a burgeoning middle class any more, it is a struggle to enter a shrinking elite.

The emergence of a 'choice' between state schools was bound to bamboozle the middle classes and their carefully calibrated arrangements to finesse the system. First, catchment areas began to disappear. One of the drivers of the great education panic is that parents still believe that schools have meaningful fixed catchment areas, but the reality they discover is that – where they exist at all – many of these tend to breathe in and out according to how many places there are. Some councils, like Brighton's, have experimented with deciding school places on the basis of a lottery, on the grounds that it was fairer. Of course, it *was* fairer, but you can understand the rage and fear of those middle-class couples who had already bought their house to position themselves correctly, and then found those boundaries swept away.

Education 'choice' is usually condemned by the Left as a scheme to help pushy middle-class parents, but in practice it was designed as precisely the opposite. It was intended to encourage more families to shop around like the middle classes, but also to break up the cosy arrangement whereby the middle classes colonized a few schools and nobody bothered much about the rest.

These are difficult things to write about, because people behave quite outrageously when they are in the grip of this panic. There are those who use grandparents' addresses to get into the catchment area they want, or just rent a room, or fake their address altogether. There is also no doubt that the middle classes are a pretty unforgiving lot when they catch anyone else at it, as the journalist Andrew Penman discovered when he wrote a book about his own struggle to find a good secondary school in west London:

> I can pinpoint the moment the panic set in. My son Robert was eight and Tim, the father of one of his best friends, had just visited the local comprehensive. A lot of noise was coming from one classroom as he walked past, so he peered through the small window in the door. The next moment, he told me, a pupil yanked open the door, squared up to him and demanded: 'What do you want?'[7]

The school was Rutlish in Merton, once the grammar school which prepared John Major for adult life, and, as it turned out, Major was to play a big role in the rise of the great education panic. Penman looked them up and found that only a third of pupils had managed five or more GCSEs at C grade or above, the government's gold standard. By the time Penman's book was out, Rutlish had turned itself around and that figure was 49 per cent; it demanded a correction in the *Guardian*. The figure is now 74 per cent, so perhaps Penman should have stuck around.

But what really caused the online outcry was his unashamed confession that he had faked Anglicanism – if such a thing is possible – to get his child into the local church school. He was even on the coffee rota, 'which added an extra half an hour or more to the misery'. His wife Pam got onto the parochial church council.

A pretty harsh reaction met his book and accompanying article. Words like 'snobbish' and 'hypocritical' poured out of the online respondents. It was true that there was something that rather stuck in the throat about such blatant gaming of the system. It is one thing for a self-confessed atheist to go regularly to church just to get their children into the church school. It is another to revel in it, claiming that the *only* reason nine- and ten-year-olds were in churches at all was to access school places. But Penman defended himself:

> Hypocritical is how some people have described my behaviour. I don't know why that's the word that's so often used; I've never criticised anyone for doing what I did, so hypocrisy doesn't come into it. I'm just concerned and pragmatic. I care deeply about my children's education and am prepared to make sacrifices to ensure that they get the best I can manage. If that means mumbling 'I believe in one God, the Father Almighty . . .' when I believe nothing of the kind, then so be it.[8]

So the Penmans moved to Woking, and apparently lived happily ever afterwards. But the howls of outrage that greeted his account seemed to emphasize the panic, rather than dismiss it. There are frightening stories of people buying houses close to schools, and waiting to exchange contracts while they appeal against refusal of admission. A friend of mine researched which universities the alumni of all the local nurseries had gone to. At the time, it seemed insane. Now I am not quite so sure.

All the research confirms that clever children will do well wherever they go, and I can confirm from experience that – once you choose a school – you do start fantasizing about just how bad all the alternatives are, which hardly helps to quell the rising panic. Yet it is all too easy to condemn worried parents for their fears. There must be parents who worry about their children mixing with other classes and races, though I have never met them. What I do meet – all the time – is parents who fret about knives, or about force-feeding their kids with a narrow curriculum that squeezes out enjoyment from life. I don't meet parents who really worry about their children picking up the wrong kind of accent. I do occasionally meet parents who worry about their children having to fake a different accent just to fit on.

It is, of course, a far more competitive world. There are few automatic privileges for the middle classes these days, and if you are a competitive parent, then the panic can really ratchet up. Because I live a sheltered life down a dirt track in south London, I don't meet these kind of parents either. But I know they are out there, pumping up their children's CVs with improving activities, dance classes, sports awards, drama, flute lessons, first aid, and the rest of the Tiger Parents' arsenal.

Watching the heavily laden children at the independent school near where I live, bowed down with the weight of extracurricular activities stuffed into their satchel along with voluminous homework, I find myself wondering whether this is really a recipe for a happy adulthood. The trend has reached crazy proportions in the USA, where the Wall Street lawyer Vicki Abeles made a documentary called *Race to Nowhere* in 2010 after the suicide of a high-achieving teenage girl who lived near her family in the San Francisco Bay area. It focuses on the panic attacks, depression and stress-related illness, especially in the increasingly competitive world of American middle-class schools. The key message seems to be: for goodness sake, give yourself a break and spend a bit of time doing nothing at all – the traditional luxury of childhood in all ages.

Perhaps the middle-class worriers should not need to panic quite as much as they do, but the real question is why they feel they have to. School choice and the other education reforms of the late 1980s were supposed to hand power to parents. Why should they feel that they have so much less power than they did? What went wrong?

Go to Tunbridge Wells in Kent if you seek the heart of the Panic Belt. Kent is complicated enough because there are fifteen different types of schools, from academies to grammar schools, and now free schools as well. The rules for getting into each school also vary enormously. Church schools define 'being a member of the Church of England' in terrifying detail: attending church three Sundays a month and at least one adult receiving communion, which rules out all but the most fervent Anglicans.

What makes Kent unusual is the survival of no fewer than thirty-three grammar schools which require pupils to take the old-fashioned Eleven-Plus exam. What makes it the source of such overwhelming panic is the four of these which have become so-called 'super-selectives', taking pupils on academic ability alone. They make up a string of super-selective schools around the M25. If you are a middle-class parent on the verge of mega-panic, then you take your eleven-year-old on a tour of these schools every weekend, taking eight different entrance exams, and hold yourself ready to move near any school they manage to get into.

In Kent, the highly competitive Dartford Grammar School admits no pupils with less than 415 out of a possible 420 points in the exam. Judd School in Tonbridge requires 417.

Then there is Tunbridge Wells. Tunbridge Wells Girls' Grammar is so incredibly popular that you can only get a place there with a good Eleven-Plus result and if you live within 1.8 miles of the school – a staggeringly narrow catchment for a town secondary school. House prices in that 1.8-mile radius carry premiums of around £20,000. Tunbridge Wells Boys' Grammar is also massively oversubscribed, but because it is neither Dartford nor Judd nor Skinners' it is still known dismissively by the most highly strung middle-class parents as 'the tech', though it abandoned its technical school status three decades ago. There is also a new academy in the town, managed by Skinners', on the site of the failing Tunbridge Wells High – and rapidly improving, but not fast enough for the panicking parents.

But it is the poor children who breathe in that panic that you have to feel for, as they open the results of their Eleven-Plus on 14 October and await the school-place decisions two weeks later. There was a time when the pass mark of 360 points would guarantee you a place at a Kent grammar school. No longer.

This is not a panic that affects everybody. Even in Kent, 85 per cent of parents get their first choice of schools, though nearly 500 children get none of their places at all – which is partly because of the influx of children from outside the county (more than 2,000 outsiders take the Kent Eleven-Plus exam).

'It's a nightmare for many parents,' says Peter Read, who has devoted his retirement to guiding them through the labyrinth, and who holds their hands during the appeal process that tends to drag on until the end of June the following year. His website has 300 pages of information for parents embarked on the quest.

Peter Read has an interesting story himself. For fifteen years he was the first-class head teacher of Gravesend Grammar School, until he was forced to retire after a series of strokes. He took up genealogy and became a professional for a few years before losing interest. 'I have a very low boredom threshold,' he says. Then something happened which dragged him back into the world of education.

Some years before, he had admitted the first statemented autistic boy into the school and had to fight a long battle with the education authority. 'The results were wonderful for everyone concerned,' he says. 'The boy changed the culture of the school.'

But then came a problem. The boy won a place at university in Canterbury, but he needed help to get there every morning. Kent County Council had money from the government to make this possible, but they were refusing to pay. 'I spent three months of my life fighting Kent County Council,' Read says. 'Then I got through to the Department of Education and they said they didn't know what the fuss was about, because they were providing the money. But the council said they didn't care. So I had to keep fighting, and I won, but I realized what parents have to go through.'

With that victory under his belt, Read took on the county council over a secret policy to close the special school units for children with learning disabilities attached to mainstream schools. This battle took four months; it brought him into the lonely and intricate business of providing phone support for parents, and he has since fought more than 700 appeals. In the last two weeks of October, after the Eleven-Plus results, his phone starts running hot. Would an appeal be worth trying? Which school should go top of the choice list? What can parents do who are coming back to Kent from abroad?

'I've just advised a lady in New York to buy a house less than a mile from the school, send her child to private school, and hope that she is first on the waiting list – then she just has to wait until someone leaves,' he says. 'She has now emailed back to say that her first choice of school has forty-one on the waiting list, including three siblings. Even if she buys a house a mile from the school, she will still be behind the siblings.'

If you want to appeal against a decision, Read advises you if you are likely to win and where to give up. Many cases end up with the ombudsman. 'I reckon parents get a rotten deal,' he says, 'which is why I give as much advice as I can.'

Again, the real strain is felt by the children. Across the nation, a quarter of all eleven- to sixteen-year-olds saw a tutor of some kind last year, up from 18 per cent in 2005. Some of the tutoring companies, like First Tutors, employ nearly 15,000 tutors and they get inquiries from parents with children as young as five years old. The tutoring industry in west Kent has grown so big that the county council is trying to work out how to make an exam that is impossible to coach. 'There are children being coached in Kent from the age of six,' says Read. 'There are private schools here which have the sole aim of getting children into grammar schools. A lot of the children who are sent there are also coached privately outside the school. What a life.'

It isn't at all clear that forcing children to be hypercompetitive, and cramming them with the curriculum from an early age, is the best way to equip them for a more competitive world – but it is a sign, not just of middle-class panic, but of a growing sense that the future world is one that will have to be taken by storm or not taken at all.[9]

Kent is a peculiar case. It is an example of what happens when good education is rationed, when parents feel they have to send their children to the very best school, rather than just a good school. It is also an example of what happens when the power belongs to the schools and not to the parents. It is part of the fate of the middle classes that, in places like Kent and London, they should have been downgraded from the monarchs of the system to such pathetic supplicants to it – desperately pretending to be Anglicans to squeeze their children into the better schools, or cramming them with facts to within an inch of their sanity with the aid of £90-a-session tutors.

It was never supposed to be like that. Kenneth Baker, the reforming Secretary of State for Education who shaped the new system in 1988, told one group of parents: 'I have given you more power than you have ever had or dreamed of.'[10] But something vital was missing in the new design.

Suave and confident, the very opposite of his cerebral and uneasy predecessor Sir Keith Joseph, Baker kept a copy of J. L. Carr's hilarious diary of a head teacher, The Harpole Report, next to his bed. He liked to feel he had his finger on the pulse of education, and was probably the minister who most fulfilled the dreams of the authors of the so-called Black Papers on Education. These had been launched in 1969 to defend academic freedom, by an English lecturer and a poet, but rapidly became the voice of the old guard against comprehensive education and progressive teaching.

The Black Papers changed the whole direction of the education debate. The whole idea of experimental education became anathema, and there was particular anger – justifiable anger too – that a fifth of the nation still remained functionally illiterate a whole generation after free secondary education. The debate about how to force up standards had begun, and has dominated the discourse ever since. It divided the middle classes along with everyone else, and, as we shall see, its sheer intractability may have stoked the panic even further.

Baker's 1988 Education Act set out the architecture for the education system we have now, and he certainly intended to give the parents more power. It gave schools the right to govern more of their affairs themselves and made sure that parents were on their governing bodies. It made them open their doors to whoever wanted to come – a policy known as 'open admission' – and Baker also developed the controversial national curriculum.

Open admission exploded rather unexpectedly for everybody

the following year when a group of parents from Greenwich sued Bromley Council, next door, to let them cross the borough boundaries and go to the schools nearest where they lived. The parents won and the so-called Greenwich Judgement meant that all schools were now in theory open to anyone. It was bound to disrupt those cosy arrangements which middle-class parents had developed. From now on, anyone could go anywhere – if they could commute that far. If they could get in. By 1992, Bromley was being forced to offer places to children twelve miles away (two-and-a-half-hour round trips).

The first Grant-Maintained school (the forerunners of academies) emerged in 1988 (in Skegness) and did not count proximity as a reason for admitting anyone. More complication, especially in London. They also ran their own admissions systems. 'It really is an absolute shambles,' said Bromley's chief education officer in 1996, and it was.[11]

It is often suggested that letting parents choose schools was the basic problem, but this really isn't so. Children are different. Different schools suit different people, and insisting that they go to the same standard choice fails to recognize this. Nor does 'no choice' rule out choice: those who can afford the inflated house prices around the good schools will always be able to choose, just by moving. Statutory choice simply levelled the playing field. It was confusing and difficult to start with, but none of this explains the level of panic among the middle classes.

No, something else happened. The key to the mystery lies four years after the Baker reforms, in that strange elated period in British politics after the undignified fall of Margaret Thatcher and the handover of power to her thin-skinned Chancellor, John Major.

Major has been unfairly treated by history. It was he who laid the foundations of peace in Northern Ireland (by negotiating with the IRA) and even the huge success of the 2012 Olympics (by starting the National Lottery) He had to lead a deeply fractured Conservative Party, an unpopular government, which was difficult enough, but he also took everything rather personally. Then history gave him a second chance. Few pundits had believed he would last more than eighteen months at the top, so in the run-up to the 1992 election, which he was so widely expected to lose, he struggled to articulate a new approach to public services. He came up with the idea of the Citizen's Charter, and, although it was the butt of humour at the time, the prin-ciples were carried on by Tony Blair and Gordon Brown a decade and a half later.

These were the great days of charters. The Czech dissident Charter 77 articulated the hopes of the anti-communist opposition before the end of the Cold War. The campaign group Charter 88 was riding high with its message of constitutional reform. Major's Citizen's Charter was designed to set out what people could expect from public services, and was pitched deliberately low-key to avoid the hectoring and aggression of the Thatcher years.

But it was still a strange amalgam, actually thirty or more different documents, held together by Major's own white paper in 1991. It seems extraordinary now that one of the guarantees was no more than two years to wait to get a hospital appointment – how did we put up with that? 'In education, I have a simple dictum – the best for every child, the best from every child,' said Major in a speech that summer. 'I make no apology for our insist-ence on higher standards, on testing, and on a return to basics in our schools.'[12]

The reference to Back to Basics rather gives away the spirit of the time. This was Major's short-lived campaign that petered out in a flurry of sex scandals among his ministers, after which the simple old-fashioned morality that tried to stitch it all together looked a bit threadbare. But the Parents' Charter emerged none-theless to put those education ideas into practice. The government paid £2 million to have them delivered, via the schools, to every parent in the country. Most stayed in their original cardboard boxes in the school storerooms.

At the heart of the Citizen's Charter was a very simple idea, and one that would have profound implications in the years ahead: forcing public services to publish information about their performance and then making it public. The main right that parents got under the Parents' Charter, once you stripped away the stuff you knew perfectly well already, was information.

It also raised a number of questions. What happened if you didn't get what the Charter promised? How was it to be achieved when the Treasury had insisted it should be revenue-neutral? And, most important, how could you choose a good school when it was phenomenally difficult to tell the elite from the dross?

This debate had caused problems for years. Rival educationalists battered each other in print in favour or against the various competing theories. It was hard to argue against transparency – that each school should make its exam results available to parents. It was much more controversial to suggest that you should rank schools in order of success. How could you measure it, after all? Would parents understand that middle-class schools would tend to do better without necessarily teaching any better? But despite all the warnings, once Major had scraped home and remained prime minister – to his and everyone's surprise – this was to be the direction of travel.

'Even as I planned education reforms, overgrown schoolboys in the media were engaged in a silly hunt to find out how many O levels I had passed – as if, thirty years on, it mattered a jot.'[13] This was how Major recalled the debate at the time, rather typically remembering the insults more than anything else. Transparency did not extend to his own results, as it turned out. But the man he chose to put transparency into practice in education would not have to worry about his own results: he was a former Oxford don, the geographer and Home Office minister John Patten.

Patten was a classic car enthusiast (they smelled like decaying Wilton carpets, he said) and a collector of art deco. He had taken up with the writer and socialite Lucinda Lambton before settling down with Louise, who became a novelist and successful business-woman. He was well connected, articulate and clever, but his career had become somewhat stuck as a junior minister. Catapulting him into the job of Education Secretary was a major promotion, but Patten was also to be one of the unluckiest cabinet ministers in recorded history. Even Major described him later as 'less self-assured than his rather donnish demeanour suggested'.[14]

Patten had been chosen to lead the assault on poor schools because he had been a teacher himself, at least at Hertford College, Oxford, and because he was expected to represent a more accept-able choice than a hard-line ideologue. But from the outset, Patten took on the vested interests with a disconcerting vigour, signalling that he would not be available to take part in the annual set-piece speeches to the teaching unions. Why should he – just to be booed?

The trouble was that, under his control but not presumably through his fault, the Education Department presided over a stag-gering series of cock-ups. As soon as the 3 million copies of the Parents' Charter were speeding their way to schools it became clear that the smiling children in the pictures – from Oakwood High School in Manchester – had never been asked for permission. It was a warning sign, so that when the time finally came for the school league tables to be unveiled, in November 1992, it was hardly surprising that it proved an administrative disaster.

Part of the problem had been that, instead of relying on the Central Statistical Office to compile the information, Patten's department had brought in two private companies who could do the job cheaper. The result was that they bodged it. The final league tables missed out whole swathes of schools, including nearly all those in Wolverhampton. They also named a whole range of schools which did not actually exist, like the fictional East Gate School, Nottingham. 'Who can have confidence in the government's league tables?' asked Nottinghamshire's education chairman Fred Riddell. 'They have been an absolute fiasco.'[15] Manchester High School for Girls threatened legal action after their 100 per cent pass mark was reduced to 16 per cent.

On publication day, Major clashed with the Labour opposition leader John Smith at Prime Minister's Question Time. The House of Commons was smouldering as Smith rose to his feet, and asked why the government was 'so incompetent it cannot even produce an accurate record of examination results?'.[16]

Major was nettled. 'The education service will never again be able to hide this important information,' he said, leaning over the Dispatch Box. 'This is information that legitimately ought to be available to parents, is now available to parents and ought to continue to be available to parents.'

Smith assumed the voice of a remedial teacher. 'Why don't you take it away and start again and try to reach minimum competence levels?' he shouted across the growing clamour.[17] Speaker Betty Boothroyd had to intervene to restore order.

The exchange brought out the worst in everyone. The Tory MP Robert Dunn took the opportunity to say that the tables 'exposed the mediocrity which the Left introduced into schools in the 1960s'. The columnist Andrew Rawnsley described the scene, adding that the Prime Minister 'will surely wish to set a personal example by finally lifting the veil of secrecy over his own O level results'.[18]

What the tables did show was that there was a problem. The national average of five passes at GCSE stood at only 38 per cent. Southwark Borough Council was bottom of the league, with 15 per cent. The most revealing comment of all came from the head teacher of a school in Leeds where only two pupils had managed to scrape together five GCSEs: 'We have a dreadful problem with truancy and discipline. We have intrusions like motorbikes being ridden into school during the day while lessons are being taught.'[19] The very honesty seemed to demonstrate the scale of the problem, especially as he added that they were the best rugby league school on the country. So that's alright then . . .

The commentators were dismissive too. 'All it tells us is where the middle classes live,' said Simon Jenkins in *The Times*, warning that 'the imprimatur of central government is now stamped on exam passes as the sole criterion'.[20]

Jenkins was right. This was the key problem, and for everyone and not just the middle classes – but especially for anyone who took the education of their children seriously. It wasn't that exam passes didn't matter – it was just that most sane people, and most middle-class families (not the same thing), had far more complicated things they wanted to know than that.

Oddly, this was not the main complaint at the time. By publishing the first exam results league tables, and organizing the first SATs (Standard Assessment Tests), Patten drew down the wrath of the educational establishment upon himself, and for rather different reasons. They believed that league tables unfairly penalized the schools in poor areas and that SATs loaded teachers with extra administration.

The fierce debate was fuelled by a newcomer to the scene. Chris Woodhead had been an education lecturer and an enthusiastic rock climber. His visits to schools as an educationalist had, he said, 'opened his eyes to what was going on', and he had become an outspoken critic of poor teaching. He was one of the trio of academics commissioned to write the so-called 'Three Wise Men' report in one frenetic month over Christmas 1991, which had finally decided the government to go for league tables. Woodhead's basic message was absolutely correct – the failure of successive governments to organize a really high-status technical education, for those who were not academic, had dragged down standards for everybody. But his outspoken comments added fuel to the flames of discontent among the teaching profession, especially after he became Chief Inspector of Schools in 1994.

In the months following the first league tables, Patten, Woodhead and the teachers fought an increasingly outspoken battle in the press. Head teachers obstructed league tables by refusing to reveal key data and to hand over test results. Teachers' unions boycotted the planned exams for children at the age of seven and fourteen. Patten even considered passing a law forcing head teachers to abide by their contracts, but the thought of sending them to jail was too much for the government to stomach. The respected political biographer Lord Skidelsky, the Conservative Party's nominee on the council charged with setting the tests, finally resigned, accusing the Department of Education of a 'bunker mentality'.[21] All political debate tends to be outspoken, but Patten's insults were just too rude. They seemed to have the slightest hysterical edge and it made the debate uncomfortable.

By spring 1993, Patten had managed to take some of the heat out of the situation, commissioning a review by the educationalist Ron Dearing, the former chairman of the Post Office. By the summer, the tests at seven and fourteen had been shelved and the national curriculum – a complicated document that seems to have been written by the cabinet itself – had been simplified. Patten himself finally departed for France on long-term sick leave with stomach problems, clearly brought on by the strain. Even there, he was accosted by a passing English tourist who shouted: 'John Patten! You've ruined our schools. I'm glad you're ill!'[22]

So when Patten came back to work, things still were not quite calm. He insisted on describing parents who opposed the league tables as 'Neanderthals'. Worst of all, a throwaway remark at the party conference fringe meeting got him into serious trouble. He described Tim Brighouse, the respected and energetic chief education officer of Birmingham, as a 'nutter . . . wandering the streets, frightening children'. Brighouse sued and won libel damages of £80,000.

That was the nadir. At the next reshuffle, the following summer, Patten was out, leaving behind a resignation letter devoid of the usual polite flannel. His successor Gillian Shepherd's more conciliatory approach finally persuaded the National Union of Teachers to back down and start toeing the line. School league tables destroyed one ministerial career, and we have had them ever since, though they have been tweaked to try to measure 'value added' by the school.

Immediately before the 1997 election which brought him to power, Tony Blair visited a large inner-city comprehensive and watched the pupils ragging around next to him and asked himself why no one was stopping them. It was an important moment for his own attitude to education and for his decisions about his own children. He sent them to the Roman Catholic school the London Oratory – not exactly fee-paying, but it does ask parents for contributions.

Blair's education reforms carried on in the same direction laid down by Baker and Patten, and the exam results continued to improve, as you might expect when the whole system – from politicians down to pupils – wanted them to do so. Every year, all sides could congratulate themselves. Only Chris Woodhead condemned the ever-improving results as 'corrupting'.

Yet even under Blair, the failure to provide a respected, successful technical route through education, for those who were not so academic, became ever more damaging. Because every time the idea emerged (in GCSEs for example), the establishment moved to derail it, afraid that it was lowering standards. There they remain in the league tables, the gold standard of education, five GCSE passes at grade C and above.

Was this the fault of the middle classes, for failing to value anything except academic excellence? Or was it the fault of the class-ridden political system, which originally turned secondary moderns into dumping grounds and barely managed to rise above that? Or was it something to do with the measures of success themselves, those league tables which purport to show how good a school is but really say so little except that the pupils pass exams?

Probably a little of all three. The middle classes are certainly not blameless, with their touching faith in the academic intelligence of their own children. Withdraw them from the academic streams and send them to do apprenticeships? They would rather drug them with Ritalin.

If you read the academic literature about the middle classes and education, especially by sociologists, you can end up feeling a little self-conscious. Who are these monsters, fiddling the system, occupying the best schools and pushing, pushing, pushing? Racist, snobbish, there is hardly any epithet too bad to describe them – and, worse, let's face it, there is more than an element of truth here.

The racism is pretty debatable. It is equally balanced by studies showing that middle-class parents flock to schools which they can share with other races, especially Asians, because of the powerful force for discipline and education they provide. Snobbery is also a tough way of explaining that many middle-class parents want their children to feel there are some people like them. It would be snobbish to object to the presence of other classes in a middle-class school, but it is something else entirely when your child is going to be the only middle-class child in the school. Nobody wants their children to struggle to fit in.

If the middle classes do have a fault, it is their bizarre faith in the intelligence of their own children. One academic study interviewed 125 sets of middle-class parents who sent their children to inner-city comprehensives, and recorded the word 'bright' 574 times.[23] This is how one of the fathers put it in a parallel research study:

> The nine year old's extraordinarily bright. I wouldn't call him severely gifted or make out any special case for him. But he is very bright. To hear him explaining Einstein's theory of relativity to Miriam when we're both trying to keep a straight face . . .[24]

I have lost count of the conversations I have had with middle-class parents who claim to be weighed down with the burden of their children's intelligence. Perhaps all this is forgivable, but there is no doubt that the middle classes tend to extract the help and support that their children need by getting them labelled as dyslexic or, failing that, on the Asperger's spectrum, when the working classes struggle to avoid the blame from professionals. It is terribly unfair.

What is quite unforgivable is the way that the middle classes tend to project their greatest fears onto other classes – as they always have done – but in such a way that it fuels the great schooling panic. Their pursed-lipped disapproval has led to a strange demonization of working-class culture – as if they somehow fail to talk to, read to, care for or even love their children much. A kind of *Après moi le déluge*, which was encouraged by so many of the New Labour think tanks. As if any upbringing that is not guaranteed middle-class is deeply damaging to the next generation. Undisciplined. Feckless. Drugged on violent computer games. 'I don't know what it is,' said a friend of mine about her children's new school. 'The children just look vicious.' That is the unspoken and unspeakable fear that accelerates the panic when it comes to choosing schools.

Choosing a school is difficult enough as it is, without all these undercurrents of disapproval and fear. It is one of the defining characteristics of the middle classes that they take the decision seriously. But they come up against the biggest problem of all – the main reason, above all others, for their collective panic. The sources of information are so flawed: the narrow and questionable information in the school league tables and the Ofsted reports.

'Where is the wisdom we have lost in knowledge? Where is the knowledge we have lost in information?' asked T. S. Eliot, and that was in the days before anyone had to peer hopelessly at an online Ofsted inspection report. It ought to tell you something useful, but all too often the reports plunge you into the world of bland and meaningless phrases that you realize are actually generated by a computer when the inspector ticks certain boxes. It is possible to understand the reports, yet not derive any useful information from them at all.

This is a growing problem in the education world as teachers increasingly write their own reports on the children using software like ReportAssist or Teachers Report Assistant, where they tick the boxes related to attainments and preset phrases pop up. 'He has required support to understand that labels carry key pieces of information,' said my son's school report. It is like trying to suck meaning through pieces of straw.

Then there are the league tables themselves, and one study shows that only half of all parents can understand them.[25] Just looking at the relative positions of my own local primary schools, it is quite clear that the schools that are higher in the tables are often less rounded, less friendly, less successful educators than the ones slightly lower down, because the higher school has often banished paints, poems, creativity and fun from the classroom in favour of an all-out, Gradgrindian dash for results. Since discovering that, I have been increasingly suspicious of schools that sit too high in the league tables. It doesn't inspire confidence.

None of this suggests that the exam results which make up school league tables do not matter – far from it. But they recognize so little else, and the result has not just been that those other aspects of education, from music to sport and all-round knowledge, have been ignored. Because they are not included in the tables, they are excised altogether and then forgotten. History is rewritten. They never had a part in education. They are gone, disappeared, buried for ever.

It is the official go-ahead for what Anthony Seldon, Wellington College's headmaster, calls 'factory schooling' that is the problem here. The research by Family Lives showed that parents are often suspicious of too much testing, and of results-based league tables, and are desperate for information on the other aspects of schooling that they value, 'like confidence, self-esteem, respect for others, manners, politeness and even an understanding of nutrition, cookery and managing a budget'.[26]

This is the great mistake as far as the middle classes are concerned. It isn't that exam results don't matter, it is that the middle classes want so much more from education and can find so little recognition of it. They also want so much more from their children's school and find it goes unmentioned. The whole concept of choosing schools on any other basis than results is so alien to policymakers that the poor parents come to believe they are strange dissenters in a crazy world.

The research into why people choose one school over another certainly mentions results, but in London the list also emphasizes their child's happiness, the quality of teaching and learning, school security and child safety. This is hardly confined to the middle classes, but it does particularly concern them when they are searching for a good secondary school. They want a school that will push their children academically, but they also want a school that will nurture and inspire them. They are looking for a place where their child will find others like them, somewhere where they can know the teachers, where they won't be bullied or threatened because they know things. Somewhere without X-ray machines for knives, with some respect for culture, history and music – and which won't just train their children to be an online or call-centre drone. And about these things the league tables will tell them absolutely nothing.

So the core of the great panic is not actually snobbery. It is a search for shared values and it is a fear, as much as anything else, of violence, of knives, security guards and hyper-masculine aggression.[27] 'Stick the name of the school into Google along with words such as "vandalism", "knives", "arson" and "metal detector",' advised Andrew Pawson with unnecessary relish, but he has pinpointed the fear accurately. The only way you can use league tables to indicate any of this is by assuming that academic success implies safety, which it may do, but equally well may not.

Otherwise, it is a matter of talking to other parents, meeting the head teacher, wandering the corridors, gossiping. The league tables may not be a bad thing in themselves, but their central place in policy has narrowed information rather than expanded it, and forced those parents who really value education to fly partially blind. Of course the fear of violence is largely misplaced. That isn't the point. The tragedy is that these are not fears that people publicly admit to – because they sound snobbish – and by driving them underground the panic can foster hysteria.

These are real fears, but behind them lies a familiar pattern in this book. Traditional middle-class values have been misinterpreted by politicians and policymakers. They are certainly interested in standards, but they are not obsessed with academic results. And if you doubt it, you can glance as I did recently at the autobiography of Admiral Lord Chatfield, one of the heroes of the Battle of Jutland, where he praises his son's headmaster for his approach to his pupils. 'His main aim was to develop their character, while ensuring adequate school education . . . Never did I make a better decision,' he says.[28] Character, defined as 'self-confidence and high principles', and just enough education. What about the 'learning objectives?', I hear you cry.

Now there is a middle-class aspiration, but try demanding that from your child's school. Yet the odd thing is that character is beginning to make a comeback as an educational aspiration. The American educationalist Paul Tough suggests that it will take your child further than exam results.[29] It may be time the middle classes rediscovered the power of the two elements that Tough pinpoints in the subtitle of his bestseller: grit and curiosity.

Mary Tasker first realized what had gone wrong with education in the UK when she was an education lecturer at Bath University in the 1970s. She had been attached with some of her students to a huge comprehensive in the south of Bristol, with over 2,300 pupils. The staff were brilliant and deeply committed to the cause of changing people's lives. Many of the pupils were clever, but the school itself was on a scale which dwarfed them.

The moment of revelation came when she invited an English lecturer from Oxford University to talk to her O-level class about Wilfred Owen. The lecturer was a good teacher and this was an engaging lesson, but in the middle of it one girl at the back said: 'I want to puke.'

What is fascinating about Mary Tasker's experience is that it began with exactly the same kind of problem that so influenced the Black Paper writers – the failure of the education system to challenge or engage pupils successfully. But the interpretation was different. The Black Paper writers blamed comprehensive education for poor discipline. Some educationalists believed discipline itself was the problem. For Mary Tasker, the key problem was the size of the school. OR THE FEEDER PRIMARIES

'The staff was brilliant in south Bristol, but they couldn't get to grips with the pupils because the school was so big,' she says. 'I used to meet Year Eights crying because they couldn't get from one of those huge matchbox blocks to another. My student teachers said they couldn't cope. They just couldn't get to know the children. And you don't know the children if you have to treat them like digits.'

The monstrous size of UK schools is an issue for secondary schools rather than primary schools, which are generally speaking much smaller and on a more human scale. It provides some explanation for the catastrophic loss of confidence that so many children feel when they move to secondary school, and the reason why so many (40 per cent) make no academic progress at all in that year.

'Being lost in huge factory institutions may have something to do with it,' says Mary Tasker. 'We did get to know some of the children, through the pastoral system. It was still against the odds in a school that size. Children can drop through the gaps very easily.'

She was so struck by her experience in Bristol that she left her job in teacher training and joined a small lobby group called Human Scale Education, and has been campaigning for smaller schools ever since. She now has experience on both sides of the Atlantic experimenting with small schools, and is convinced that the only way to make a difference is to create the conditions for a relationship with the teacher that gives children some kind of support.

'Staff meetings should be small enough to have everyone around a table, so they can see each other's eyes,' she says. 'I've seen staff meetings with an old dog wandering round. That's human. It isn't some regimented industrialized process. If you look at the real indices of success for schools, they are not examinations, they are absenteeism, staff absenteeism, teenage pregnancy and bullying.' One recent experiment in Essex which split a larger school into smaller units was so successful that they no longer needed a budget for supply teachers. There was virtually no staff absenteeism.

This is absolutely central to the middle-class education crisis. The middle classes want a certain kind of school where their children could thrive and succeed. They can often no longer afford private education, which increasingly caters for the international elite. They can barely afford to move any more. Yet the schools they are offered by the state are often arranged on a factory scale.

Most research into small schools over the past generation has challenged the idea that schools are better when they are bigger.[30] Despite this, for the past generation or so most policymakers have insisted that big schools are better, and that somehow comprehensive education required huge institutions. The beginning of this idea seems to have been the crisis in education thinking in the USA after the successful Soviet launch of the Sputnik spacecraft. They persuaded themselves that somehow only huge schools could produce enough scientists to compete with the USSR. It is one of the peculiar ways that Soviet thinking filtered into the West.

The first challenge to it came from Roger Barker, describing himself as an environmental psychologist, who set up a statistical research centre in a small town in Kansas after the Second World War and researched small schools wherever he could find them. It was his 1964 book *Big School, Small School*, written with his colleague Paul Gump, which revealed that – contrary to what you might expect – there were more activities outside the classroom in the smaller schools than there were in the bigger schools.[31] There were more pupils involved in them in the smaller schools – between three and twenty times more in fact. He also found children were more tolerant of each other in small schools.

This was precisely the opposite of what the big school advocates had suggested: big schools were supposed to mean more choice and opportunity. It wasn't so. Nor was this a research anomaly. Most of the research has taken place in the United States, rather than the UK, but it consistently shows that small schools (300–800 pupils at secondary level) have better results, better behaviour, less truancy and vandalism and better relationships than bigger schools. They show better achievement by pupils from ethnic minorities and from very poor families. If you take away the funding anomalies which privilege bigger institutions, they don't cost any more to run.

But why should smaller schools work better? There is some consensus among researchers about this. The answer is that small schools make transformational human relationships possible. Teachers can know pupils and vice versa. 'Those of us who were researchers saw the damage caused by facelessness and nameless- *You* ness,' said the Brown University educationalist Ted Sizer, who ran *CAN* a five-year investigation into factory schooling in the 1970s. 'You *IF* cannot teach a child well unless you know that child well.'[32] *ITS*

Frightening evidence of this came in June 2008, when the *Times* *LITER* *Educational Supplement* reported that 21 per cent of Year 8 pupils *ACY* said they had never spoken to a teacher. 'Talk to the children, if *FOR* you can,' one school volunteer I know was told by the head teacher *U.7's* on their first visit. 'Nobody talks to them these days.' *NOR ME*

Again, the irony was that what motivated Mary Tasker and her colleagues in the 1970s was not that different from what motivated the Black Paper writers at the same time: they were determined to burst free from the stranglehold of low expectations which trapped so many children from deprived backgrounds in dull, low-quality education, leading to dull, low-quality lives. 'We were very idealistic at the time,' she says now.

Both sides were reacting against the legacy of neglect of the *MINE* old secondary moderns, and the emerging failures of some of *WAS* the comprehensives, especially in inner cities. But the various sides *GOOD* in this debate have not listened to each other. On one side, the *BECAUSE* protagonists of GERM (the Global Educational Reform Movement), *INFANT* rigid testing, league tables and core competencies see themselves *SCHOOL* fighting a long-term war against those who believe that education *WAS*

GOOD

ie. TODAY A SCHOOL IS GOOD IF PARENTS ARE 'GOOD'

is primarily about 'lighting a fire'. For ordinary families, and especially those who most value education, those two ends of the debate – which seem so far apart – are actually both necessary. Despite the overwhelming direction of public policy, despite the warring sides of the great education debate, most middle-class parents believe in standards and exams, but they also want their children inspired.

The absolute failure of the education system to meet their largely unarticulated demands is the main cause of the great education panic. *MY PANIC IS SCHOOLS RELY ON PARENTS*

None of the government measures which rely entirely on exam results recognize this, and the evidence suggests that – in practice – league tables actually drive out some of those elements that might inspire some children, from poetry to music, despite the critical importance of creativity to the modern British economy. There was some evidence that children were missing out on any skills not measured in the exams.[33] The halving of the number of school playing fields since John Patten was Education Secretary may not have been his fault, but they were a by-product of a regime that forgets that these things are important.

Worse, schools are actually getting bigger. There is nothing like the 5,000-pupil factories that have had such a disastrous effect on education in the USA, but a new school in Nottingham has been designed for 3,000 pupils. And the official solution to the problem of choice – to encourage the best schools to expand (presumably onto their playing fields) – risks undermining the one element that makes them so successful. Policymakers fall back on arguments about economies of scale, but there are no economies at all if these huge institutions fail to do the job they were designed to do. *A V. SMALL SCHOOL FAILS THOSE THAT RELY ON IT UNLESS*

The parents and pupils at the £10,000-a-year independent King's School on Tyneside were getting ready for the new academic year.

PARENTS DO THE HOURS

last September, ironing uniforms, collecting books and home-work, rescuing PE kit from the washing machine, when the message came. It was only the next day that term was due to start at the school, next to the gentle tree-lined green (Stan Laurel was among its alumni). To their great surprise, they were informed that the school was no longer independent. The governors had been plotting secretly for nine months to opt into the state system. Their fees were no longer required.

The announcement had been held back so that parents and staff could hear the news together. The independent school had merged with the local primary school. Their pupils were down by nearly a third that year, and it was clear that their fees – only a third of those of some independent schools – were now too much of a burden. 'Governors have recognized that the payment of school fees represents a growing issue for many parents,' said their chairman John Evans.[34]

When more than a third of pupils at independent schools are already getting some kind of assistance with fees, there is a problem with the independent sector. Pupil numbers have been falling, at least outside London, since the start of the recession. The growing internationalization is also a clue: they are increasingly looking abroad, to the international elite, for their clientele: Wellington College has even built a replica of its 'nineteenth-century Baroque' pile outside Beijing, complete with the Duke of Wellington's initials on the flagstones. Those which can't go international – and there are worries about the debt levels for increasing numbers of independent schools – face a more uncertain future.

'I couldn't get a school place nearby,' said Andrew, one of the people I interviewed in west London. 'Towards the end of 2009, the local state schools were overwhelmed by all the people pulling out of independent schools.' That is partly a sign of the times, but it has the makings of a long-term trend.

Then there are the church schools, which have managed to

keep their standards by staying small, and are understandably the nectar for buzzing middle-class bees. I am not one of those people who disapprove of this, because it seems to me that a faith background has helped inoculate these schools against utilitarian nonsense. Any move to undermine faith schools would be resisted by most of the middle classes, and it would be a tragedy to lose the possibility of state education with soul. But faith schools must stick to their original purpose, which is providing education from a faith perspective to the whole community, not allowing the faiths to cater exclusively to themselves. No faith school which shirks this duty is worthy of the name. But it isn't really enough for me just to assert this. The drift seems to be in the other direction as the faith schools fend off the influx.

In short, the effective choice for the middle classes – the kind of options open to them without financial or emotional panic – seems to be shrinking. Once again, it explains some of the panic. This is clearly at its worst in London, where there is an urgent need for more school places, not just more places in ever-bigger education factories. So for some time I have believed we needed a bottom-up movement of planting new small schools by parents who felt strongly about education. That puts me in the free schools camp.

The tragedy of the free schools is that they are answerable directly to Whitehall, which leaves them cruelly exposed to the whims of bureaucrats and politicians: a dangerous piece of centralization. They should be embedded, and federated together, like other schools, under light-touch local authority control – another way of reducing the complexity of admissions – and will not be safe until they are.

The free schools are not all going to succeed by any means, but they are injecting more capacity into the system, providing diversity where it is needed – music schools, drama schools, Steiner schools, schools teaching Latin or Chinese. They are also a huge success for the middle classes, putting parents back in charge of education far more successfully than previous reforms. But it is a slow process. *ORPHANS USED TO BE LITERATE.*

In the meantime, and for the foreseeable future, middle-class parents have become powerless supplicants to a system that has failed miserably to understand what they require, shows little sign of learning any time soon, and which has so arranged things that they can no longer even move house to find a school as they once did. No wonder they are rushing round like Corporal Jones shouting 'Don't panic! Don't panic!'

A PARENT CAN BE IN CHARGE OF EDUCATION AT HOME.

MANY OF THESE TRAGEDIES ARE DUE LOSS OF HOURS FOR U-7's LITERACY

Middle Classes in Figures

Rise in the cost of independent schools over the past decade: 68 per cent.[35]

Number of students at university in the world (2012): 150 million.

Predicted number of students at university in the world (2025): 260 million.[36]

The New Middle-Class-Values Dictionary

AUTHENTICITY: Nobody likes being taken for a ride, but the middle classes increasingly regard themselves as immune to the magic of marketing. They increasingly want services and products that are unmediated, unspun, unprocessed, and made somewhere in particular by someone in particular. They are increasingly suspicious of those they regard as slaves to brand, even if they are occasionally slaves to their own kinds of brand.

Dispatches from the Frontline

Waitrose cheese counter, Balham, Friday, 1 p.m.
Camembert, cave-aged Gruyère, Manchego, Dolcelatte, Pecorino di Sardegna, aged Alpine Emmentaler, Petit Pont-l'Evêque, Chaource, Chabichou du Poitou, organic ewe's Slipcote, P'tit Basque, aged Ossau-Iraty. The cheese counter at Waitrose is like

an evocative trip around Europe in itself and occasionally beyond. It is like sitting in a travel agency.

'There's so much choice,' says a voice behind me, looking at the milk selection. It certainly is any colour you like as long as it's white (or yellow or pink).

The question of how the British middle classes managed to drag the obscure produce of Europe onto their supermarket shelves, a process that began in the 1970s, is one of the strange, barely told stories of the past generation. The man who started it seems to have been Marcus Sieff, briefly chairman of Marks & Spencer, who first imported grapefruit and avocados into the UK (one customer complained that avocados didn't go as well with custard as she had been led to believe).

Even in middle-class Balham (it has come a long way since Peter Sellers called it 'Gateway to the South'), there is no obvious way to distinguish the customers from one class rather than another. Perhaps my assumption that those who bring their own canvas bags for the shopping are the middle classes is a sign of outrageous class bias.

Here, standing in the broad, luxuriant, understated aisles of Waitrose, the cheese counter seems to be the apotheosis of middle-class shopping. Waitrose has, after all, taken over the position of M&S in the middle-class heart by sticking to the formula of good design and middle-class prices, rather than trying hopelessly to appeal to everyone.

It is also a mutual, and the smiling staff suggest that this is a successful strategy. There are certainly no security guards obviously peering at you, as you find in Tesco. The UK middle classes have benefited from mutuals so much less than their class fellows in other countries. There is a lesson there.

The only sign that all is not quite well with the middle classes is here at the cheese counter. All the supermarkets have their own-brand budget lines. For Waitrose, it is called *essentials*, packaged simply and affordably (so they say) for those who can't afford their usual products. I can understand Greek feta being packaged for those on low budgets, but when you also get Parmigiano Reggiano, you feel that something else is going on. Basics but with a posh name. Would you ever get 'basics' Parmigiano Reggiano in Sainsbury's? I wonder. Or would they just call it parmesan?

7

The sixth clue: the strange case of the disappearing professionals

> 'In the past the man has been first; in the future the system must be first.'
>
> Frederick Winslow Taylor, *The Principles of Scientific Management*, 1911

Come with me for a moment to the small Hampshire village of Nether Wallop, with its thatched roofs and perfect, photogenic houses. A distant prospect of the ancient hill settlement of Danebury stands out against the skyline across the way. There are council houses there, so Nether Wallop is not wholly middle-class, but it might as well be – and middle-class in a particularly privileged way. There is no doubt that the proportion of people from the City and the population of retirees is growing, certainly in the time I have been going there. They can afford it, after all.

Here are the retired major generals in their faded red corduroys. Here are the black Labradors. Here the faint whiff of overheating Agas. It is a village straight from the pages of Joanna Trollope, and none the worse for that. The trouble is that it has been sliding over the decades slowly into the realm of unreality. The village still has a primary school, which anchors it in authenticity, despite this subsidence into fiction. There is still the occasional bus, though sightings are becoming rarer. There is an energetic and effective woman vicar. But the other services and institutions that keep a place from being so picturesque as to lose touch with reality have been slowly disappearing. We have grown used to the idea that it is poor, working-class places which lose their shops and institutions, but middle-class places can lose them too.

Of course the array of Women's Institutes, horticultural clubs and amateur dramatic associations which keep middle-class places alive are still here, so this is not quite a crisis. But look at what has been happening. Half a century ago, Nether Wallop boasted two village shops, a post office, two pubs, a butcher, a village policeman and police house, a doctor and district nurse, a railway station a short bus ride away, and a multiplicity of postal deliveries. That was in the austerity years of the late 1940s. Now, when we are incomparably 'richer', all that's left is one pub, some groceries available in the wine merchant's, and that very occasional bus.

For the local shops, the emergence of Tesco and Sainsbury's is enough of an explanation. Those with cars just drive to do their shopping these days, and there is no doubt that it is more convenient than the terrible queues and narrow choices of the 1950s. But why the rest? Why can we no longer afford those post offices, police stations and courts? Whatever happened to them, and the middle classes that used to manage them?

Take Aldeburgh on the Suffolk coast. These days it is a middle-class mecca, a living shrine to the music of Benjamin Britten, but in the 1830s – the first decade or so of the middle classes – it was a small fishing village, with a market on Wednesdays and Saturdays. In those days it had eight inns, six shoemaker's, four grocer's, two haberdasher's, three baker's, two chemist's, two tailor's, three milliner's, five blacksmith's, a saddler, a coachmaker and a hairdresser.

It was a bustling economy managed by those who were rising out of the peasantry, even if they were not quite middle-class. It worked because the spending power tended to stay circulating locally. As the century wore on, the grocers and shoemakers – who had been artisans who made their own wares – became professional shopkeepers who stocked things made elsewhere. The brands were emerging. You could get the same tins in Aldeburgh, Nether Wallop and everywhere else. The shopkeepers became increasingly middle-class, and they were joined by a whole range of middle-class professions: solicitors, vicars, stock-brokers, bankers, local government officials, teachers, magistrates and many more.

This was the world that I was born into in 1958. You could go to university and aspire to be one of these professionals, and be paid enough for a comfortable life and live out your days with status and job satisfaction. It didn't matter if you lived hundreds of miles from London SW1 or EC1, there were all around you middle-class professionals living relatively comfortable lives, having reached as far as they could go in their career.

My godmother's husband was a stockbroker in Bristol in the 1950s. Paul Woolley, the City thinker we met in chapter 4, was a stockbroker in Birmingham in the 1960s. There were teachers, solicitors, factory managers, cinema and brewery owners and newspaper editors. There were bank and building society managers in every community, and regional grocery chains with their managers. There were doctors, dentists and magistrates dotted around the country, a very visible middle class, but by the time I was born the process that would displace them was already well under way. The local stockbrokers are long gone and the local bank managers have mostly disappeared as well, to be replaced by risk software taking decisions in regional offices (see chapter 3). The vicars are increasingly scarce, in rural areas at least. The middle classes who populate the rural areas outside the London commuter belt are increasingly there because they have retired there. Like Nether Wallop, so many middle-class places have become strange fictional dream worlds. Others still cling to life.

Whatever happened to all those middle-class jobs?

We have already seen how the twentieth-century multifunctional corporation, which had emerged, first at General Motors, in the 1930s, began to shed its middle-class layers. But there have been other forces at work as well, and partly what has become known as 'digital Taylorism'. The reference is to the efficiency pioneer Frederick Winslow Taylor, of whom more later. It indicates the way that companies are increasingly codifying the knowledge used by their skilled or professional employees so that their work can be done anywhere in the world.[1]

First the manufacturing was outsourced abroad, but now increasingly it is the middle-class functions as well – the design, the planning, and the programming know-how. It is a process which is hollowing out corporations, leaving a footloose core of financial services, but it is also hollowing out the future prospects of the middle classes. They increasingly have to compete with middle-class professionals worldwide, who are usually on considerably lower salaries. There is a narrow but ferocious 'efficiency' about this aspect of globalization, which may not actually be very efficient when it comes to spreading wealth, and which corrodes the middle classes and middle-class institutions, just as it has corroded working-class institutions before.

We are still living in a period when UK universities lead the world and attract the brightest and the best, but that will not go on for ever if the prospects for professional employment in the UK begin to dry up. It was always assumed, as companies like Marks & Spencer destroyed what remained of the UK textile industry, that somehow the 'clean' professional jobs would stay in the UK.[2] That is no longer quite so obvious. The digital revolution will also create jobs, but they may not be very good ones. 'It is a continuation of the hollowing out of the middle class which we have seen,' said Professor John Van Reenen from the London School of Economics.[3] 'People will find it harder to support a middle-class family.'

Other middle-class jobs, the middlemen functions like estate agency, look set to disappear altogether. Why do we need estate agents if we can do it online?

Globalization is only part of the huge increase in competition among professionals back home. There are now twice as many lawyers in the UK as there were two decades ago, with a handful at the top taking the lion's share of fees.[4] The number of doctors has been squeezed into the same ever-tighter pyramid, by decades of dysfunctional hospital mergers, so that if all the doctors currently training go on to be consultants, as they would have done a generation ago, there would be 60 per cent more senior doctors in the NHS.[5]

The increasingly competitive business of getting into the top UK universities, requiring the very top A* grades at A level, is just the start of what is to be a fierce competitive struggle throughout a professional career. There are also implications for our chances if we need to access senior legal or medical experience and skill in the future. Competition works both ways, after all, and all we may get access to are semi-trained juniors or, worse, software that boils down their skills online.

It is no coincidence that 97 per cent of the new jobs created in the USA over the past generation have been local, the kind of tasks that you simply could not outsource, like education or healthcare – what we would call public-sector jobs.[6] It is no coincidence that most of the job growth in the UK in the early part of this century was in the public sector too, or local in other ways, like retailing. At the same time as a toxic kind of globalization has been trans- forming good middle-class jobs into digital proletarian ones, a similar process has been taking place locally too, to the public- sector professionals and the middle-class shop owners.

That is the great fear for the middle classes, that their jobs and contracts will be replaced with uncertain short-term contracts, or enforced self-employment, tied to the clock, measured and moni- tored in their every action, cowed by the fallow periods without income into silent, resentful obedience. In short, that they will become working-class, and experience the very same erosion of security that the lower-paid working population is now facing.

Aldeburgh went off in its own direction, unlike anywhere else. But you can see where this process ended up today thirty miles away in the Suffolk town of Hadleigh. Jan Byrne is chair of the Hadleigh Society, a local civic society, and from that position she has watched over the way her own town has been changing. It remains a thriving place, and – as more and more people come to retire there – increasingly middle-class.

The local shops selling ready-to-wear clothes have long gone. People who want to buy shoes have to go to Ipswich. There were still a few butcher's and baker's when Jan arrived in the 1960s, and the Co-op has been a fixture since the 1880s. The handful of florist's, pet shops and ironmonger's are hanging on in the high street, but there are new arrivals too – the farm shop selling seasonal vegetables which are, as she puts it, 'wet with the dew'. The police station hangs on as well, open a few hours a day. The post office is still there, and so are the doctor's surgery, the library and the primary schools. The railway disappeared in the 1950s, but two local newspapers still cover the area.

In short, Hadleigh survives. But a threat is looming, and Jan Byrne has been at the forefront of the struggle against a planned Tesco supermarket on the edge of the town which she believes would wreck the careful balance that has kept Hadleigh's high street alive. Morrison's is there already, in a former repair shop for bren-gun carriers on the edge of town. There are three other Tescos within twelve miles, two more within fifteen. There is an Asda and a Sainsbury's within eight miles.

Hadleigh has more than doubled in population since Jan arrived there from London in the 1960s, part of the twists of history that have brought it from a wealthy medieval weavers' town, to a bankrupt former weavers' town in the eighteenth century, and back to a thriving place again in the twentieth. You can see why Tesco wants to be there, why they first put in a planning application for a supermarket by the water meadows back in 1998. They came to the Hadleigh Society to talk to them early in the process, but the meeting didn't go well. 'They were so arrogant they had our backs up even before we started,' said Jan.

In the fourteen-year struggle between the locals and the Tesco machine, she constantly takes reporters along the River Brett and says: 'Stand a moment and listen: what can you hear?' Then she asks them to imagine the supermarket car park next door. Otherwise her main weapon has been to go through the planning submissions, point out the mistakes, and then take photos of the other places in Suffolk which Tesco boasts about, and put on show all the pictures of closed and abandoned shops in the local high streets.

The Hadleigh Society reckons that Tesco may undermine about 200 jobs in the town (Tesco say they will also create 200), and that doesn't count the middle-class livelihoods – shop owners, local suppliers, producers and other support services. Just as in the digital economy, the replacement jobs are not responsible or flexible ones; they are the new drones of the retail behemoths. That is why three referendums in Hadleigh have voted overwhelmingly against Tesco, and why the local council voted against the most recent plans. 'The company has already been and gone from Hadleigh when it suited them,' she says. 'The part of the . . . site owned by Tesco for many years, has been allowed to deteriorate to such an extent that any proposal could be presented as an amenity improvement. The site is wrong, no matter how Tesco try to position the level of support otherwise through their in-house marketing team and PR consultants.'

This kind of struggle has counterparts all over the country – supermarkets very rarely give up on a site – and increasingly so as people's awareness grows that supermarkets can sap local economies as well as support them. It is a sign also of just how nervous people are about the survival of local life and the institutions that underpin them. This is a campaign that motivates the middle classes, but not just the middle classes. Ironically, the worst-hit places are definitely not middle-class – look at the boarded-up former shops on the outlying estates of Glasgow or in inner-city London. But the blight affects middle-class places too.

We have already seen how hundreds of British banks were reduced by 1920 to just five big ones and a handful of little ones. We have seen how 2,200 building societies in 1900 were reduced to forty-seven now (see chapter 3). One in six bank branches closed over the past decade, and at the rate of one a day over twenty years. As many as 900 communities have no bank branches at all. We have lost ten thousand pubs in the last decade.

New funding regimes are cutting provision to any local school with fewer than 150 pupils. 'We are already losing our library van, public toilets in the village are being closed, funding to help the village hall is being cut and the bus service into Shrewsbury, our nearest town, is being drastically cut,' said Sue Cooke, head teacher of the Stiperstones primary school in Shropshire, under threat again in 2011.[7] Herefordshire next door was then planning to do away with forty small rural schools. Small schools have been closing at the rate of ten a year or so now for decades, even through the days of high public spending.

The number of post office branches has dwindled from 25,000 in 1963 to less than half today, while grocer's have gone from over 200,000 down to less than a quarter. Small businesses with employees are down 29,000 since 2010. In 2010, the Ministry of Justice announced plans to close 54 county courts and 103 magistrates courts, a far cry from the 491 county courts – one within seven miles of the whole population – that were built under the original plans in 1847.

Take a look at the newspaper map of England published in 1926, with thousands of spots covering nearly every community in the nation. Newspaper experts told MPs in 2009 they expected that about half of the remaining 1,300 titles – many of them already consolidated into single papers with different titles – would close within five years.

Taken together, it is a bleak picture which has shown the slow disappearance of those institutions that make life worth living, from playing fields to pet shops. They have fallen victim to massive consolidation, while one government after another turned decades of blind eyes to blatant monopoly power, to outrageously inflationary rent rises, and to successive rounds of public spending cuts.

There are certainly exceptions to this rule. There are now more small breweries than at any time for seventy years, and the number of voluntary organizations is also rising, though probably at the expense of the small informal clubs which used to be such a mainstay of community life – and which were not able to cope with all the hurdles set by the Big Lottery and its predecessors. It is also true that middle-class roles have also changed. There are IT professionals and accountants and NHS managers in practically every street. But most of the new professionals that have emerged are in the public-sector middle class: they are NHS doctors and managers, teachers, court officials, HR professionals, academics. They have also seen their status and their salaries, and now their pensions, systematically shrunk over the past generation, and largely because of another process altogether, which has thrived over the last century, acting to hollow out our local institutions and to constrain their professionals.

To pin this one down, we have to go back to Saratoga in New York State in June 1903.

Frederick Winslow Taylor was a dapper little man, brimful of confidence but with the pugnacious manner of a man who has just been dismissed, when he rose to address the audience at the United States Hotel in Saratoga. The subject of this meeting of the American Society of Mechanical Engineers was 'Shop Management', by which he meant the factory 'shop floor'.

This is not a moment celebrated much by historians, but it was to have hugely important implications for all of us. Taylor's ideas – revealed in public for the first time that night – would have such an influence, first on factories and then on every organization, that today we almost take them for granted. His impact on the lives of industrial workers has been vast, and now – more than a century after that meeting in Saratoga where he first announced his ideas to the world – they are having a profound effect on the middle classes too.

Taylor was only known at the time as a controversial factory manager who was supposed to have worked miracles of productivity at the giant Bethlehem Steel plant in Pennsylvania, churning out armour plating for the world's battleships. Ironically, 1903 was the same year that Henry Ford first experimented with production lines, and the combination of Taylor's time and motion thinking and Ford's assembly lines was described as 'Fordism' by the Italian Marxist thinker Antonio Gramsci.

We are now in a post-Fordist world. The robots have taken over the factories – the masses don't work there any more – but we are definitely not in a 'post-Taylor' one. You can see his ideas, breaking every task down into units, measuring how long they take and setting targets for workers to meet, in call centres, NHS hospitals, probation offices and the battery of statistics by which public services are now run all over the Western world.

Taylor died of flu in 1915, broken and embittered by his treatment at the hands of congressmen inquiring into his methods. Ironically, he died winding his watch, the symbol of his legacy. His formula for efficiency led to job cards, time clocks, inventory control and all the other apparatus of twentieth-century manufacturing. By the First World War, the British car manufacturer William Morris was using what he called 'continuous production', an amalgam of Taylor and Ford, and many of the arms manufacturers were following suit. Morris's rival Austin called it 'progressive production'.[8] In fact, the British pioneer of all this was probably an American visitor to Westinghouse's factory in Manchester called James Stewart, who used Taylor's ideas in 1902 even before he had articulated them himself.

The spread of Taylorism through the UK remains a subject of debate among historians, but there is no doubt that it was part of the campaign for 'national efficiency' which united Fabians like H. G. Wells with some progressive Liberals like David Lloyd George. The impact was felt exclusively by the working classes. Taylor's ideas went further – he created a new middle-class cadre of white-collar experts with clipboards who would roam the factories, trying to make them more efficient. Taylor sired the middle manager.

Opposition in the UK came from trade unionists and radical Liberal industrialists like Edward Cadbury, who described Taylorism as 'reducing the workman to a living tool'.[9] But the impact was soon to be felt on the middle classes too. The American business guru Charles Bedaux managed to combine Taylorism with accounting, and his ideas took British business by storm between the wars. Soon the middle managers were coming under the same kind of productivity pressures, reducing what they did to different parts and measuring every aspect.

Then, as we have seen, the cult of 're-engineering' arrived in the 1990s and the era of the middle manager was over. The middle classes were packed off with their gold-plated pensions, wondering vaguely what their children would do for a living. What had happened was the 1993 publication of the bestseller *Re-engineering the Corporation*, by the mathematician Michael Hammer and the computer scientist James Champy. Hammer had begun his revolution with a typically aggressive article in the *Harvard Business Review* three years before called 'Don't automate, obliterate'. It was a management philosophy for the software age. It said that it made no sense to split up the functions of a company and do them separately. They needed to be brought together in one system, and that meant that middle managers had no real function left.

Re-engineering meant huge redundancies. A third of BT staff lost their jobs in the mid-1990s, with a massive impact on morale. It also carried within it a major IT problem. Re-engineering was supposed to make organizations more flexible, but it didn't happen that way. When the software was written that was capable of drawing all these various organizational functions together, most companies were tempted to split their operations into two. There would be a front-office factory of untrained call-centre staff facing outwards, and a back office of experts who would take decisions and make things happen. It was just as rigid as any of the departments they had all replaced.

A great disadvantage of Taylor's system was its assumption that the workforce were brutish types with no useful ideas of their own. It used their brawn and wasted their brains completely. But there was another problem too. Taylor reduced the different functions of the shop floor down to units, and – although he shed a few – the basic system remained the same. Then he locked it all together with new rules and rates of pay. Re-engineering went further, helped along by Enterprise Resource Planning (ERP) software. The whole function of organizations, minus the middle managers, was to be automated by IT, with a whole range of reporting requirements added at every stage. The idea that any organization might evolve, might find entirely different and more effective ways of organizing things, let alone create new functions, had gone completely. The functions of middle managers had been either automated or parcelled out, at vast expense, to management consultants.

Where the middle classes were left working, in great numbers, was in the public sector, and for decades public-service professionals, from doctors to head teachers, had been immune from Taylorism. They had huge room for manoeuvre, and wide powers to use their best judgement to improve people's lives. There were drawbacks about this, of course, but it did mean that there were still middle-class roles where people could work hard, gain local respect and look back on their lives of public service with pride and satisfaction. It was not to last.

It was the accounting professor Michael Power who first coined the phrase the 'Audit Explosion'.[10] That was the title he used for a pamphlet published by the think tank Demos back in 1994, tracking the emergence of auditing in every area of public life, from schools and hospitals to the environment – and the strange phenomenon whereby auditing failures are greeted by demands for ever more intensive audits.

'The audit explosion is likely to be a passing phase,' he wrote. 'The seeds of change may be there.'[11] In fact, with hindsight, we were back then really only at the very start of an even more all-embracing audit explosion, analysing everything, breaking it down into constituent processes and measuring them, trying to make the work of professionals transparent, assigning numbers and holding people to account. Almost a century after Taylor died winding his watch, his legacy had snowballed into a potent force way beyond factories. The new target was public-service professionals, and they were about to be audited to within an inch of their lives.

Since Power wrote his pamphlet, there have been huge numbers of academic studies which now bear witness to the extraordinary new control demanded by politicians and civil servants over their most distant employees – in fact, over anyone who came within a whiff of public money, and not just frontline workers but professionals too. And especially those middle-class professionals who once could use their judgement to serve their clients as they thought best.

This kind of super-auditing emerged in the years of John Major's Citizen's Charter, and it came with a package of other controls, like super-managers – the small handful of bureaucrats, super-heads or NHS managers-in-chief who could earn really huge sums – as well as league tables, targets and standards. All these together, said one study, were designed 'to restrict the space that many welfare professionals once enjoyed to support services they perceived service users to require'.[12] The result of this modern version of Taylorism is that middle-class public-service professionals came under far greater scrutiny.

This is not an entirely black and white issue. In the days of unfettered professional freedom, there was a whole range of ways in which professionals used to abuse their power – from the architects who designed brutal public housing to imprison the poor to the hospital consultants who refused to touch cases which failed to interest them. We don't want to go back there. Nor do we want to revisit the overwhelmingly middle-class Dr Harold Shipman, who managed to murder his own patients for years without challenge. But something serious has happened as well, to the school-teachers, librarians, senior police people, university teachers, health service managers, court officials and magistrates, the remaining middle-class professionals outside financial services (though GPs managed to negotiate themselves a series of bizarrely generous pay packages, so constitute something of an exception).

One extreme example was that of Richard Elliott. For two years until 2003, he ran the Drugs Action Team in Bristol. It was a responsible professional job which meant managing a £3.5 million annual budget and coordinating all the different agencies in the city to bring considerable resources to bear on the problem.[13] Before he resigned, he had already taken on the job of his deputy, the coordinator, one of four local drugs action team coordinators who were off sick at the time. There was certainly a great deal for his six staff to do, with a client group of 25,000 local drug users and 12,500 addicts.

But this was a job so heavily constrained by auditing that it became impossible. He had to keep his eyes on forty-four different funding streams, nine different grids and eighty-two different objectives imposed on him by managers, funders and the government. His annual plan was sixty-eight pages long. Before his resignation memo, which he called 'the ravings of a burned-out mind', he reckoned that he and his colleagues spent less than 40 per cent of their time actually tackling drugs issues. Elliott compared his management regime to a kind of addiction inflicted by the obsessive and narrow measurement of his performance. 'Monitoring has become almost religious in status, as has centralized control,' he said:

> The demand for quick hits and early wins is driven by a central desire analogous to the instant gratification demands made by drug users themselves . . . We tie ourselves in knots with good-practice guidelines and monitoring. It's like trying to fight with one hand tied behind your back, a boxing glove in the other and strict instructions not to punch.

The problem was endemic in professional life. The government quite reasonably demanded proof that things were working, but their demands were so insistent and so intrusive that the business of proving it soon became the central task of the job. Elliott ended up juggling the fifteen different agencies across Bristol, swapping referrals and assessments, and managing the output figures round and round. It was hardly surprising then that only 5 per cent of the money for drugs action that year was being spent on rehabilitation across the nation. There was no shortage of money. There were huge dollops available, but only to be spent on very specific issues, on condition it didn't seep out anywhere else, that it was spent within months, and was fully audited.

The disease spread everywhere over the past decade. We tested children in schools so intensively that they were simply taught to pass the tests. They were tested on comprehension passages rather than taught to read stories. We congratulated the NHS on the rise of prescriptions it issued, without asking whether that was related to health. It all seemed very modern, but was also reminiscent of the great tradition of the Victorian statisticians who tried to measure the morality of children by counting the number of hymns they knew by heart.

Part of the problem was that this kind of auditing fell foul of what has become known as Goodhart's Law: however incompetent staff may be, they will always be smart enough to make targets work for them rather than against them. Take the rule that patients shouldn't be kept on hospital trolleys for more than four hours. In practice, some hospitals got round this by category shifts: they put them in chairs. Others bought more expensive kinds of trolleys and redesignated them as 'mobile beds'.

It is a delusory world where nothing is quite what it seems, where outputs count more than achievements, where every department or voluntary group had targets imposed by funders who have their own miserable yoke of targets to deliver as well. Where big fleas have little fleas upon their backs to bite them. And each time the bites were passed down, they bit harder. So while the Treasury could be relatively relaxed about the standard of proof they required before acting, those Whitehall targets descended via funder to funder, until they reached the bottom flea – the poor charity which has to make something happen on the ground – by which time they became a Gradgrindian nightmare which bore no relation to practical needs.

It was a new world that corroded the values of the professional middle classes and reduced them to number crunchers, desperately dreaming up new ways to massage the figures, looking inwards rather than outwards at the people who needed their support.

So it was that the targets culture, which had been ushered in on both sides of the Atlantic by McKinsey and other management consultants, was welded onto a related culture of corporate re-engineering. It was powered by enormous IT investment and massive call centres, regulated by ERP and CRM software. IT can be used to enable human relationships, but in practice that isn't what happened. It was used to divide people – professionals from customers, experts from people with problems – because it looked efficient.

This is how it still works. The software teams look in detail at all the processes, just as Taylor urged, find the best employees and watch what they do. Then they turn that into the processes staff are led through on the screen. They also build in onerous reporting, box ticking and measurement systems to satisfy managers that the performance of every part of the process can be measured. 'These are the assembly lines of the digital age,' wrote Simon Head, one of the few academics to give this upheaval in work culture the attention it deserves, 'complete with their own digital proletariat.'[14]

A similar process was going on in the USA, though they came out the other side faster than we have in the UK. The American reform writer David Osborne, a trenchant critic of command-and-control, estimated that 20 per cent of American government spending was devoted to controlling the other 80 per cent, via armies of auditors and inspectors. When Vice-President Al Gore led the National Performance Review in 1993, they found that one in three federal employees was there to oversee, control, audit or investigate the other two. The wage bill for one in five of UK public-sector staff is around £48 billion. The audit explosion comes with a hefty price tag.

The new coalition which took office in 2010 was keen to abolish targets, but all too often replaced them with payment-by-results contracts, which enshrined targets even deeper – and made the consequences for the inevitable massage of figures that much more onerous. The fraud scandals are only just beginning. This is, in a way, the memorial for the professional class, one step ahead of the auditors if they are lucky – desperately trying to make things happen on the ground, reduced by turbocharged Taylorism to a kind of proletarian existence of everlasting measurement. The audit goes on and on.

'Every day, year in and year out, each man should ask himself over and over again, two questions,' said Taylor in his standard lecture:

> First, 'What is the name of the man I am now working for?' And having answered this definitely then, 'What does this man want me to do, right now?' Not, 'What ought I to do in the interests of the company I am working for?' Not, 'What are the duties of the position I am filling?' Not, 'What did I agree to do when I came here?' Not, 'What should I do for my own best interest?' but plainly and simply, 'What does this man want me to do?'

That is how Taylor wanted his workforce: unthinking, phlegmatic, biddable – mere machines. They are there to deliver the demands of their bosses in every detail. Judgement barely comes into it.

There is a hint of this Taylorist control in the approach used by Michael Barber, the father of what he called 'deliverology', and the man most associated with the cast-iron targets of the Blair years. 'What is in the mind of the ministers must be delivered to the child,' wrote one academic, trying to characterize his approach.[15] He was, in effect, telling education professionals to get their judgement out of the way.

Barber was brought in by Tony Blair during his second term to find a way to get to grips with public services, and to exercise more control over his colleague and former friend Gordon Brown, who was then champing at the bit in the Treasury waiting to succeed him at 10 Downing Street. The lineage of this big idea which has so corroded the middle-class professional – don't think, just do precisely what you are told – clearly goes back to Taylor, if not before. There is no doubt that it emerged in UK public services from the American 'New Public Management' fad during the John Major years. But let's be really specific. There was something about the relationship between Gordon Brown and Tony Blair which really boosted the corrosion.

In fact, the real moment of truth for the middle classes, the moment which sealed the fate of public-service professionals, probably goes back to that furtive meeting between the two men to sort out between them what they were going to do, after the death of the Labour leader John Smith in 1994 – the famous meeting between Blair and Brown in the Granita restaurant in Islington.

What passed between them has never been revealed, though Peter Mandelson drafted a kind of agreement afterwards. It was an awkward meeting, and Blair had a horror of awkwardness, which may be why Brown seems to have left believing that they had agreed that he was the chosen successor. That is what the historians have speculated ever since. But it was what else was discussed that counted here. The other key agreement was that Brown wanted control over economic policy, and major areas of social policy too – including public services. Brown ate little and disappeared shortly afterwards back to Westminster for a second dinner, with his campaign team at Rodin's restaurant, but the die was cast.

The extraordinary centralization of public services in the UK may not have been a direct result of the Granita agreement – though that is certainly the way civil servants at the heart of government saw it – but it laid the foundations. It meant that, to make sure he had real control over services, Brown must design a new system to deliver control.

Some of those ideas already existed in the New Public Management and the league tables pioneered by John Major, who was ejected from office by Blair and Brown three years later in 1997. But there was also another idea floating around in those days in more radical circles, and known as alternative indicators. This was an idea I was involved with at the time, and it was based on the economist John Kenneth Galbraith's famous maxim that 'If it isn't counted, it tends not to be noticed.' If you wanted to escape from money as the ultimate bottom line, then you needed to measure something different.

This was key knowledge, but it was to have unexpected side effects, especially on what turned out to be a formidably utilitarian administration under Blair and Brown. Brown used the idea of PSA (Public Service Agreement) targets to increase his control over local administration, and what had been distinctive local indicators of success were soon a battery of centrally imposed targets – covering everything from hospital waiting lists to the tooth decay of sailors in the Royal Navy. Just three years into the new Blair government, there were ten thousand new targets.[16] This was the Taylorist nightmare that was eventually to corrode middle-class professionals.

Fast-forward four years, and the second Blair election victory in 2001, and things looked very different from 10 Downing Street. Brown's budget was now seriously in surplus and he was ready to pour money into public services, but not to relax the iron control. The 2000 Spending Review was already sceptical about targets. The Audit Commission, which had moved from the details of public money to their detailed 'Best Value' inspections, was causing furrowed brows in Whitehall. One select committee talked about being 'alarmed at the current and future impact of a developing culture for over-inspection in the public sector'.[17]

There were even doubts inside the Audit Commission at the staggering amount of time each Best Value inspection was taking

– a vast inquiry into the management of the public lavatories in Scarborough became particularly notorious. And since the inspections director at the Commission insisted on signing off all the reports personally, a huge backlog was beginning to build up. Most reports took a staggering two years to finish.[18]

At the time, Blair was only too aware that little seemed to have changed in public services, despite all that measurement. As soon as the 2001 general election was out of the way, his closest allies took a deep breath and decided to start again. The new local government minister Nick Raynsford decided he would dump Best Value. The Audit Commission, desperately trying to salvage its reputation, decided to stop its Best Value inspections and do simple 'Comprehensive Performance Assessments' that could boil the whole lot down to fit on a postcard.

The whole idea was bundled into a new white paper with the revealing title *Strong Local Leadership, Quality Public Services*. The title was a masterpiece of doublethink. The rhetorical commitment to strong local leadership was really just hot air, as was the rhetoric about empowering public-service staff. Nothing that was in the white paper seemed likely to achieve that.

But the real shift was happening at 10 Downing Street. Blair had decided that his first term of office had been squandered. It was time to claw back some of that control over public services he had signed away at Granita, and he was preparing to wrap Brown's targets in a whole system of tight control of his own, again with the intention of boiling everything down onto postcards. The man he chose to do it was the man who gave the name to deliverology. Michael Barber had been an education professor at Keele University and was then the civil servant in charge of rolling out Literacy Hour in schools (hence the Taylorist slogan about delivering things to children). He was given a team of thirty civil servants.

Ironically, Barber had been able to see the whole idea of targets

NOT ENOUGH

quite clearly some years before. He quoted a British Railways senior official about how they met their punctuality targets: 'It's simple really. Every time we think a train is going to be late, we cancel it.'[19] But that was seven years before, and his faith in the numbers had been renewed.

He took up his new position as head of the new Prime Minister's Delivery Unit within weeks of the election, squeezed between the Department of Health in Whitehall and the Red Lion pub, joining an influx into Downing Street from the management consultants McKinsey (motto: 'Everything can be measured and what can be measured can be managed').

Barber soon invented himself as the driving auditor at the heart of the government machine. 'No-one in Whitehall was as obsessed as I was with minor shifts on graphs,' he wrote later.[20] He told his daughters that he was the Prime Minister's graphs drawer. Not for nothing did Simon Jenkins describe him as a 'mole-like figure'. Four months after he set up his office, all the permanent secretaries in Whitehall had been sent letters demanding plans for delivering change. These were followed by a string of irritating management quotations: 'If everything is under control, you're not going fast enough.'

For Barber, *deliverology* meant bringing internal political pressure on senior civil servants from each department, highlighting their failures to reach their target figures by using traffic lights – red, green, orange – and reporting back to Blair with the comforting news he craved. If not, the hapless ministers and civil servants would be hauled in, with Barber and his graphs at the other end of the table, to explain themselves. By 2003, it all seemed to be working. All the graphs were going in the right direction, except for street crime, congestion and rail reliability (this was really no coincidence: they were harder for frontline staff to manipulate).

By the end of 2004, the permanent secretaries had learned – along with those below them – to finesse the traffic lights, and Barber was able to present an impressive display of greens to the cabinet. But journalists had a growing sense that the figures they were given were illusory. Barber himself describes his presentation in a warm room in the Cabinet Office in 2004. When each graph came up, one of the tabloid journalists at the back whispered to himself 'Bullshit.'

The tragedy of deliverology was that Barber seemed not to have understood the power of Goodhart's Law. The graphs he sweated over were illusory. Millions of tiny shifts in definition and procedure by every minor civil servant, NHS worker or policeman were making the figures meaningless. It is hardly surprising that the graphs seemed to be going in the right direction. That is what happens when you put intense pressure on the permanent secretary and it filters down the system.

The real problem was assuming that every public service was simply a version of an assembly line and could be tackled by standardizing responses and turning the professionals involved into automata. So every time the system tightened up, the chances that those professionals could make things happen were that much more constrained. It has been a sad tale of reduced effectiveness bought in the name of efficiency – and at the cost of the cadre of middle-class professionals who used to make the wheels of the system turn. It is hardly surprising that their status has waned, sometimes disastrously so.

Caroline runs a medium-sized nursery school in the Home Counties. She lives in a small detached house not far away, worth – according to the local estate agents – about £275,000. She is very obviously a middle-class professional, born in Amersham and brought up in Essex. Her father went to public school and ran his own business doing technical writing. She studied social anthropology and psychology at university.

'My dad wanted me to do business studies,' says Caroline. 'He wasn't at all enamoured of my first choice of social work. But I couldn't think of anything more boring. I ended up working for him because he asked me and I hadn't got anything else to do. Then I ended up having kids.'

More recently she trained as a therapist, though she is not actually working as one now. 'I did it more for me. It is fascinating and helps with whatever you do. It gives you a different way of looking at things.'

Instead, after her marriage broke down, she got a job running a nursery school. 'I was taking one of my kids over there one day and they were looking for someone and so I applied. I got the job and then the person running it left and I took over. It wasn't particularly what I intended to do, but the older you get the harder it is to move into something else.'

Now she is the supervisor. There are twenty-six children at any one time, most of them paying using public money. There are six or seven staff, depending on the age of the children in the class (the rule is 1:8 children over three, and 1:4 children under three). It is a responsible job. The buck stops with Caroline, not just for the safety and education of the children, but for delivering the government's onerous and complicated Early Years Foundation Stage framework, which she does for thirty-five hours a week.

Now, here's the shock. She earns just £17,000. It isn't a poverty-level wage, by any means, but it is below the national average and below what most people need to live an independent middle-class life.

'We can't afford holidays,' she says. 'I haven't had a summer holiday since 2005. By the time I've paid the running costs of the house and sorted out the things the children need, there's not much left. My mum, bless her, has bought all my daughter's college stuff. But it shouldn't have to be like that. It's not that I'm not working or anything.'

Of course, early years is notoriously badly paid, like home care – another responsible area of the public sector where even the professional managers are paid very little. But these are not the only areas of professional life to be downgraded. Flick through any local newspaper and you will see other similar jobs, on forty hours a week, paid an annual salary of £13,000, or council jobs on £15,000. It is as if the huge edifice of auditing, the hollowing out of professional jobs – offspring of the rivalry between two successive prime ministers – has so undermined their status that those doing these responsible professional tasks can now command only a pittance for their qualifications and effort.

But they still must do the auditing, which is why you see so many clipboards around nursery schools these days – and wonder why the staff don't just show the children how to climb a frame or interact with each other, rather than waiting to capture the moment and tick the box.

'We have to evidence what we are doing in line with the foundation stage curriculum,' says Caroline. 'People come in and check what we're doing – county council early years advisers, Ofsted – we have to show we have looked at the learning styles and characteristics of each child and cater to them all. Someone at head office wants to justify all the money they are spending on early years and they want to see all the documentation. But at the end of the day, parents really just want their children to be happy mixing with everyone and getting on with them.'

The technocratic early years curriculum has been controversial, though it is simply the extension of Taylorism into nursery schools. 'I'm not prepared to struggle on month after month hoping a petty bureaucrat will say this school can continue as it is,' said the head of one Steiner school in the *Times Educational Supplement* in 2009.[21] You can see their point.

Yet despite all this work, and all the professional experience required, the financial rewards for professionalism are few and far between.

'I don't think I should have to get tax credits,' says Caroline. 'At the end of the day, they want the early years staff to be more professional, but they don't put the money into it. I am paid as much as they can possibly afford to pay me. If I didn't get tax credits, I wouldn't be able to run this house. You end up with the situation that nobody buys anything because nobody has any money.'

Nor does she have any kind of pension beyond the state pension. 'I have four kids; I don't have money to put into a pension. I've had to do little bits here and everywhere and I can't afford to pay into a private one. And a lot of people I know are in exactly the same position. I'm not the only one at all. Money is an absolute pain in the bottom sometimes.'

And like so many people, she wonders how her children will cope in the future.

'I bought my first house for £19,500. It was a long time ago, but it was doable. I could get a mortgage for three times my earnings. But I don't know how any of them are going to do it now, especially owing university fees,' she said:

None of these youngsters are going to be able to afford a house. They've got no chance of getting a deposit. How do you get a mortgage for a property like this? How do you get to the point when you are earning enough, even if you have a deposit? And if you're renting, then how are you going to save up for one? The bungalow over the road, with two bedrooms, is rented out at £900 a month; if you're paying that amount on rent, you're not going to be able to buy. There are more and more properties for rent round here. It just means a bigger divide between those that have and those that don't.

The idea of middle-class homeowners down on their luck has a horrified fascination for the newspapers at the moment. There is near-lascivious interest in the idea of company cars and foreign holidays at one moment, and £67 a week job seeker's allowance the next.

'The middle-class unemployed are pretty invisible,' wrote Jane Simmonds in the *Daily Mail*:

> We don't riot, we don't draw attention to ourselves, and we often don't show up in official unemployment figures. We don't qualify for benefits, free school meals or tax credits – we have to use up our savings first, and sell our home . . . Some friends of ours were terrified of traumatising their children if they admitted that Daddy didn't have a job any more. So each morning he'd dress in a suit and head for the station, take a train to London and spend the day in a library.[22]

One story was particularly horrifying:

> A friend told me recently about a middle-class family who'd told no one their finances had reached breaking point. The marriage broke up, the husband moved out. Eventually their 13-year-old daughter told a teacher that she needed help because her mum was ill. When friends went around to the house, they found the mother lying in bed, her face to the wall. She wouldn't speak to them, she was engulfed in despair. There was no food in the house. They'd quietly run out of money altogether, and were too ashamed to ask for help.

The sudden impoverishment of the middle classes has a kind of moral to it. It is fascinating because it seems to be about pride and falling, but is actually just the traditional middle-class horror that everyone shares to some extent – the repossession, the sudden fall from grace and favour, the looming gutter.

But it also misses the key point. It isn't sudden middle-class impoverishment by unemployment that is really the most important story – though it happens in economic downturns of course – it is the slow impoverishment of middle-class professionals, the constriction of their room for manoeuvre, their status and then their salary too.

The political thinker Francis Fukuyama caused a storm of intellectual excitement after the fall of the Berlin Wall in 1989 by proclaiming 'the End of History'. He became, rather reluctantly, part of the intellectual underpinnings of a new kind of deregulated ideal, the one that fell to pieces in the banking crash of 2008. These days, he finds himself in rather different company, and has recently begun a defence of the embattled American middle classes.[23] What he described as 'happy talk about the wonders of the knowledge economy', hailing a new economy based exclusively on service and finance, was actually a 'gauzy veil placed over the hard facts of deindustrialization'. The rewards of technological and financial innovation go overwhelmingly to a very narrow group of people, he warned, explaining that:

> Americans may today benefit from cheap cell phones, inexpensive clothing, and Facebook, but they increasingly cannot afford their own homes, or health insurance, or comfortable pensions when they retire.

The same is worryingly true of the middle classes in the UK, even though they are defined differently, and Fukuyama's key question applies equally to the UK as well: 'What if the further development of technology and globalization undermines the middle class and makes it impossible for more than a minority of citizens in an advanced society to achieve middle-class status?'

There are political implications too. Karl Marx has long been dismissed for his predictions that the bourgeoisie would eventually disappear and usher in the new revolution. It never happened. Quite the reverse: the bourgeoisie and petit bourgeoisie burgeoned in size, bought their own homes and started reading *Country Homes and Interiors*. But what if Marx's prediction was correct, but just a little delayed, and capitalism were to culminate in the proletarianization of the middle classes after all? What would happen then? Some kind of revolution or, as Fukuyama predicts, some kind of populist uprising from the right? The latter seems most likely at the moment, given that most of Western Europe is struggling to survive a financial crisis brought on, predictably, by the tight constraints of the euro. A thriving middle class would provide an inoculation against that kind of upheaval, but if they are not thriving – what then?

Some of the peculiar backward-looking political movements emerging on both sides of the Atlantic may be symptoms of the corrosion of the middle classes, including the Tea Party in the USA and UKIP in the UK. When the bottom seems to fall out of the middle-class economy, these kind of embarrassingly conservative organizations seem to emerge. We can only imagine the political fallout if these trends continue.

Middle Classes in Figures

Annual income after tax and pension deductions of typical middle-class couple (2008/9): £22,900.

Predicted annual income after tax and pension deductions of the same couple (2020/21): £22,100.[24]

The New Middle-Class-Values Dictionary

TOLERANCE: I suggest this rather tentatively, aware – as we all are – of the counter-examples. But the heady days of Mr Curry and Hyacinth Bucket, and the curtain-twitching disapproval of suburban life, may now be behind us. Despite their reputation, the middle classes have actually presided over a period of unprecedented tolerance in British life, embracing a society that – despite the difficulties – is more and more diverse and multiracial, more and more tolerant of the peculiar way that people live, if they are not harming anyone else. And if this was not led by the middle classes, who was it led by?

Dispatches from the Frontline

Village church, deepest Hampshire, Remembrance Sunday, 11 a.m.
'I hope you will bear with me, but I am also the organist as well as the preacher and the celebrant, so there will be a number of

pauses in the service while I am making my way to and from the organ,' says the man in a suit up by the altar. 'I hope you understand.'

I am at the back of the church looking at the straight backs of all the military men in the congregation, in this whitewashed Saxon church. They have filed past me into the pews already, with their poppies or medals or occasionally both, their women in subdued dark blue coats. Even those not in uniform, and obviously from the local army base, are in subdued dark blue suits.

These are, on the face of it, establishment figures. There are at least two retired major generals, one retired public school head-master, a serving brigadier. As you might expect from this segment of the middle classes, the voices are subdued. So is the mood. But the celebrant's little speech at the beginning obscures something rather important. It all feels so ordinary that you hardly notice it, but the vicar is missing (this is a group parish). The choir is no more. There is no procession with a cross at the beginning of the service. The same man must do almost everything except juggle.

Outside, the November sunshine dries the damp in clouds of steam from the thatched roofs. Inside, we hear one of the major generals reading a list of names from the village killed in the First World War. It is a small village, but a long list, and it is relatively easy to guess which class the names hailed from.

'Is everyone sad?' the little boy next to me asks.

Then the hymn starts up. It is 'O God our help in ages past'.

For a moment, I suddenly get a flash of the closing scenes of the 1942 film *Mrs Miniver*. One of the themes of this Greer Garson film was the corrosion of snobbery in the face of war, but it is the last scene I am thinking of. The congregation are in church, battered and bruised, and they sing a rousing English hymn (actu-ally 'Onward, Christian Soldiers'). Then the camera pans out and you see the church has been bombed and has no roof.

This church still has its roof, the product, no doubt, of decades of raffles and village fetes. The church is cared for and comfortable. It isn't like the bare and abandoned medieval churches you find in France. But there is something of the same sense of embattled yet unacknowledged decay that ended *Mrs Miniver*. It occurs to me that these middle classes, with their commitment and their service, are going to have to learn something from the words of the final hymn. There is a time to cease from mental fight. Maybe even a time to let the sword sleep in the hand. But this isn't one of them.

Following the clues, unmasking the villains

'*The riches which should have brought wealth have brought poverty.*'

González de Cellerigo, Spanish lawyer
and economist, 1600

González de Cellerigo was a lawyer in the chancery who worked in Valladolid, the landlocked city where Christopher Columbus died, feeling disgraced and impoverished, nearly a century before. We don't know much about González apart from that, except through his writings – mainly the Memorials he published that year, and especially the one with the least snappy title, About the policy restoration necessary and useful to the republic of Spain.

Cellerigo's thinking was relevant to the middle classes then. But it is also relevant to our own, because he was one of a handful of economists over the previous four decades who grasped what happens when huge amounts of money flood into a nation, as unimaginable sums had flooded into Spain – gold and, above all silver, in treasure ships from the New World since about four decades after Columbus's voyages. The Spanish monarchs had agonized about why money was losing its value, prosecuting, occasionally executing, people for causing inflation, and now they knew: too much money chasing too few goods causes the value of money to fall.

The staggering influx of wealth into Spain during the previous

STIGLITZ 'Price of inequality'

century had operated rather as the cascade of wealth into the City of London has operated in our own time. Instead of financing production, it was frittered away on interest payments for debt, buying luxury goods from abroad, raising prices and, in the case of sixteenth-century Spain, on the purchase of Eastern luxuries from the Portuguese empire.

By 1660, the amount of silver in Europe had tripled. Spanish money was worth a third of its value in 1505, and most of the massive injection of wealth which had been siphoned off by the Spanish kings had been wasted servicing debts incurred by their incessant European wars. Bankers profited. The Spanish crown did not. Financial services grew ever more complex. Worse, Spain soon forgot how to make things on its own behalf, believing that the import of money itself was sufficient for its economy. As much as 80 per cent of the goods shipped from Spain to its new colonies had been imported from elsewhere in Europe.

The business of money for its own sake, the sophistication of financial services, tends to price other productive businesses out of existence, and that was the ruinous effect it had on the Spanish economy. Renaissance Europe tended to obsess about gold, and conferred on it a mystery all of its own. Columbus used to insist that his men should go to confession before collecting it. Pope Julius II, the man who commissioned Michelangelo to paint the Sistine Chapel, was treated in his final illness with molten gold. This was a fixation that was part spiritual, part economic. It meant that gold – and therefore money – became more important than the wealth it represented. Of course it drove out productive wealth: it seemed more important than that. Also, the more precious metal there was, the more bankers could extend their credit. The more interest-bearing debt there was in circulation, the more power went to bankers and the more prices rose.

This was the Spanish tragedy in a nutshell. A tiny elite emerged to manage this extraordinary influx of wealth into Spain, which paradoxically destroyed the nation's productive capacity.[1] What González de Cellerigo realized, and his predecessors did not, was that this was no accident. The discovery of the wealth of the New World had destroyed the power of the Spanish empire, not through some kind of mistake, but by virtue of economic laws.

This is an idea which keeps emerging as an economic peculiarity, even in our own time, where it is often used to explain why nations which discover oil do not reap the rewards, just as oil in the North Sea drove up the value of the pound and destroyed UK manufacturing in our own time. It is known now as the Curse of Oil. Cellerigo didn't beat around the bush. He articulated what few had really understood before. Spain would have been better off without the Americas. The influx of gold had not been mishandled; it was a disaster in itself. And here is why:

> Our commonwealth has come to be an extreme contrast of rich and poor, and there is no means of adjusting them one to another. Our condition is one where there are rich who loll at ease or poor who beg, and we lack people of the middle sort, whom neither wealth nor poverty prevents from pursuing the rightful kind of business enjoined by natural law.[2]

Cellerigo's diagnosis was that the huge influx of bullion had driven out the true middle classes, leaving behind instead a desperate upper middle class of hidalgos (members of the lower nobility) who were snobbish about work (in fact were forbidden to do anything wealth-creating) and looked desperately to well-paid sinecures in the burgeoning bureaucracies, and a desperate lower middle class who had lapsed into poverty and dependence.

Of course, it is possible to push the parallels with Golden Age Spain and modern Britain too far. There are also debates now about how much the influx of silver from the mines in Potosí was instrumental in causing inflation – the worst Spanish inflation came before Potosí was discovered – but there is no doubt that the influx of wealth, theirs and ours, has helped drive out our respective productive enterprises, if only because they cannot possibly compete with the speculative returns from moneylending and money manipulation. Hence the collapse of local investment and local manufacturing. Hence also the inflationary pressures on house prices that have been tearing the middle classes apart in our own time.

But there are other parallels. After Latin, Spanish was the common European language just as English is now. Spanish universities were the most successful in Europe. Spanish culture was beset with a miserable pessimism and cynicism, just as ours is now. Spanish ports fell one by one into the hands of foreign investors. The only industries to survive in Spain were those catering for the luxury end of the market, like our Bentleys, Burberry and Aga stoves.

The highly sophisticated financial services that Spain developed in the sixteenth century, according to the historian J. H. Elliott, 'might almost have been deliberately devised to lure money away from risky enterprises into safer channels, of no benefit to Castilian economic development'.[3] He meant that the economy was constructed to encourage people to buy government bonds, or *juros*, rather than investing in business. As in our own time, the economy provided a far better return for people investing in money itself rather than productivity.

After the Spanish monarchy collapsed in 1640, the new regime managed to claw the nation back to some kind of prosperity by rebuilding the middle class, the entrepreneurs and bourgeoisie who were able to make things happen. But the fate of the Spanish at their zenith offers us a terrible glimpse of our own future, and still we have not developed the kind of understanding that Cellerigo did from his office in Valladolid, watching the extraordinary decline of Spain, not *despite* the influx of wealth but *because* of it.

Our politicians have not yet seen that the measures taken to make speculation the central purpose of the UK economy – the miscalculations of Big Bang and all that followed – are creating the same small elite and pushing the middle classes slowly into poverty and dependence.

That is what will happen, first for our own generation retiring with our miserable apologies for pensions, and then in the next generation – unable to buy homes and condemned to eking out an existence, in jobs they do not want, just to pay the rent. Unless we learn Cellerigo's lessons ourselves, in our own time, the decline of Spain is likely to herald our own future.

It so happens that the greatest Spanish writer of all, Miguel de Cervantes, lived in Valladolid at the same time as Cellerigo, a few years after Cellerigo was writing his memoirs there. Cervantes was working at the time on his classic tale of an old man, obsessed with a disappearing code of chivalry, *Don Quixote*. It is impossible to know how much he agreed with Cellerigo, but Cervantes's verdict on his own time has some of the same flavour, and there remains just a quixotic hint about it: 'Money is prized rather than worth' ('*Ya no se estima el valor porque/se estima el dinero*').[4]

There is a touch of Don Quixote about the English middle classes today: honest, civilized, cultured, tolerant, clinging half-heartedly to the values of generations gone by, while managing also to set them aside, sadly deluded about the realities of their own time, and above all where money is concerned. But Cervantes's criticism about money could have been a criticism of the English middle classes almost any time. There it all is in *Pride and Prejudice*. 'Pray, my dear aunt,' says Elizabeth Bennett, 'what is the difference in matrimonial affairs, between the mercenary and the prudent motive? Where does discretion end, and avarice begin? Last Christmas you were afraid of his marrying me, because it would be imprudent; and now, because he is trying to get a girl with only ten thousand pounds, you want to find out that he is mercenary.' The same muddle about values and money is part of the middle-class DNA.

Yet if Cellerigo talks about 'the middle sort', we mean something more than that – in Britain at least – when we talk about the middle classes. We are not using the term just to mean people on average incomes, as they do in the USA and other countries. We mean also the whole edifice of values and prejudices bundled together that has characterized the middle classes in our own country, and has done since their invention in their current form in the 1820s.

We are not talking about the descendants of English hidalgos and landed gentry, though they are included, but about the great influx into the middle classes that coincided with the development of the railways. These were not so much gentry as commuters, setting up home away from where they worked, and their arrival coincided with a new kind of society, dedicated to independence from the tyranny of bosses and landlords – as they still are now – but noted also for their extraordinary ability to disapprove.

There is certainly a morality at the heart of being middle-class. Often caricatured, sometimes a caricature of itself, these values were shaped quite deliberately by writers and moralists in the 1820s who saw the new class emerge and were determined that it should strike out in a new moral direction, away from the dissipated aristocracy who gambled, drank, bullied and horsewhipped their way through life.

The radical journalist William Cobbett took the opportunity to write a book of instruction for them to emphasize this point, building the foundations of a society that did not use its money and power to break and browbeat. His book was called *Advice to Young Men, and (incidentally) to Young Women, in the Middle and Higher Ranks of Life*. The middle-class life must not just be about possessing talent, he suggested, any more than the aristocratic life should just be about possessing money:

There must be industry: there must be perseverance; there must be, before the eyes of the nation, proofs of extraordinary exertion: people must say to themselves 'what wise conduct there must have been in the employment in the time of this man! How sober, how sparing in diet, how early a riser, how little expensive, he must have been.'[5]

Cobbett's book was immensely influential, staying in print into the 1930s and still being translated into the languages of the developing world into the 1950s. What he was trying to achieve, according to the historian Ben Wilson, was a 'distinctively middle class culture and morality that would put profligate aristocrats to shame'.[6]

If anything, he was rather too successful. The English middle classes emerged as a rather po-faced bunch, puritanical and disapproving. But through most of the next two centuries or so, and despite constant predictions of their demise, they were also enormously successful in the way they were able to spread their values, and in their ability to shift public policy to support them further.

We know that their presence in an economy matters. There is a growing consensus that economies with a large middle class do better than those that are highly unequal. Their continued existence is vital for our own economic futures, for all the reasons that González de Cellerigo gave four centuries ago. But the English middle classes also stand for something, and even if this is no longer exactly thrift – as Patrick Hutber suggested in 1976 – it is also a series of connected values and ambitions about independence, work, culture, duty and the ability to make things happen. And paradoxically, also about the importance of values beyond money (even though they don't always behave accordingly). Their presence is absolutely critical to a civilized life, not just for themselves, but for everyone.

This book has been written like a kind of detective story. What the investigation shows all the way through, in clue after clue, is that the middle classes have been complicit in their own demise, because they forgot those values. They welcomed house-price inflation without realizing the implications for themselves, the economy and their children. They cashed in on the demise of the very institutions that guaranteed them a place in the economy. They allowed those who rule us to gut their pensions, without really noticing, and were bamboozled by government after government into removing the basis of their professional expertise. Most of all, they naively believed that the rapid growth of financial services, and the money pouring into the City of London, would benefit them – when actually it seems to be destroying them.

The new elite, the Übermenschen, ushered in by the policies of successive governments, have created an inflationary nightmare, allowing a handful to join their ranks and steadily reducing the rest of us to the very dependence on tyrannical employers and landlords that our ancestors began to escape two centuries ago.

When even the society magazine *Tatler* can talk about the 'almost third world degree of disproportionate wealth' in London, you know there is a problem.[7] The middle classes have tended to ignore the rising disparities in wealth around them, blindly assuming that they will be on the winning side. As it turns out, they are not going to be.

So who did kill the middle classes, or at least the prospects for their next generation? Well, the clues seem to point away from one cataclysmic event, one malevolent decision which removed the opportunity for another generation to enjoy the civilization of the middle-class life – the comfortable home, the lawn, the dog, and all the rest of the package. But they do point towards a series of mistakes, often made in the name of the middle classes – a series of unexpected by-products of decisions which go beyond any passing economic difficulties. Here they are:

- The abolition of the Corset which restricted inflationary finance pouring too fast into house prices. The decision may have been inevitable, yet nothing was done to replace it.
- The destruction of the building societies may have been carried out in the name of banking diversity and competition, but it has had precisely the opposite effect.
- The disastrous reforms of the City of London known as Big Bang were organized to protect London's role in global finance, but turned a blind eye to the culture of greed and corruption that followed inevitably in its wake, and ushered in the new elite that is pricing the middle-class life out of the reach of the middle classes.
- The launch of personal pensions was not a problem in itself, but they allowed policymakers to blind themselves to the way that the most effective pension system in the world was unravelling before their very eyes.
- School league tables were an interesting way to make the effectiveness of schools more visible, but the way they were organized has fuelled the bizarre middle-class panic for places.
- And finally, centralized targets were designed to improve public services, but in practice they hollowed them out – together with the status and reputations of the middle-class professionals who ran them.

These mistakes add up to more than the sum of their parts. They amount to a hollowing out of our economy, of businesses reduced to financial functions that outsource everything, of local institutions closed down or reduced to pathetic dependence by targets and tick-box inspections, of banks reduced to speculative machines, and behind them the swirling sound of a global middle class competing for shrinking rewards. The kind of economy that required the middle classes barely exists any more. The kind of society that supports them is being eroded. The kind of morality that they lived by has been turned in on itself, revealed so shockingly in the Lloyd's Scandal and so many times since.

The mistakes also coincide with a fatal crux in economic history – investment yields at an unprecedented low, house prices at an unprecedented high, and the rising insecurity of uncertain economic times. 'The insecurities that were once limited to the working poor have increasingly crept into the lives of middle class – and even the upper middle class of Americans,' wrote the political scientist Jacob Hacker in his revelatory book The Great Risk Shift, and it applies on this side of the Atlantic too.[8] But here is the giveaway. He published in 2006 at the height of the boom.

So it is not primarily our current economic difficulties that are causing the problem – the share of wealth of the middle 60 per cent of the population has been falling steadily everywhere except Denmark.[9] But they may be advancing a process that was already under way.

The clues are all there, but the blame still has to be shared between the policymakers and the middle classes themselves. They made a disastrous political mistake over the past generation. They backed the idea of trickle-down economics that failed to trickle. They cheered the corrosive growth of financial services in the City of London and ignored their excesses. They believed those in charge of their financial institutions had their class interests at heart, when they had nothing of the kind. They did not understand where Big Bang would lead – and where it would inevitably lead: if the middle classes had been allowed to share in the new wealth, it would have caused rampant inflation. They did not understand that policies they supposed would benefit middle-class families and reward hard work were actually enriching a new financial elite.

Joseph Conrad's book The Secret Agent includes an anarchistic doctor who wrote a pamphlet called The Corroding Vices of the Middle Classes. This ignorance of the world as it really is has been the real corroding vice of the middle classes.

Still, although middle-class life may be corroded, the middle classes may have life in them yet. They could yet survive to rebuild their lives all over again for the next generation. Some of them have managed to cling onto the lifestyle as well, despite their terrifying mortgages. It is true that there are still signs of a thriving upper middle class, especially those who can access their housing wealth, or who enjoy corporate salaries, or are working in the financial sector. I have driven down streets in Richmond, Dulwich and Swiss Cottage as I was writing this book and, I have to admit, wondered whether I was right after all.

It is also true that, every time somebody has written a book along these lines before, the middle classes have pulled themselves together and fought successfully for their own survival. Writing books about the decline of the middle classes could certainly be the graveyard of professional reputations, including my own (such as it is). But the trends are more ferocious, the competition more cut-throat, the new elite more privileged, than before.

And there is another paradox. Those books predicting the decline of the middle classes were written in the late 1940s and late 1970s, during periods of very high taxation, under Labour governments with deliberate agendas to squeeze the middle classes. The decline I am writing about, which seems to me to be more fundamental, has taken place during three decades when policy has overwhelmingly shifted – on the face of it at least – towards *supporting* the middle classes. Gordon Brown's response to the banking crisis of 2008 was first to prop up the banks and then to support people paying mortgages. The needs of the middle classes still come first, where they coincide with the interests of the financial world.

This period has also coincided with an extraordinary and deeply unpleasant vilification of the working classes, tracked so compellingly by Owen Jones in his polemic *Chavs*, where mainstream culture and politics alike seem to have become suffused with an unpleasant contempt for anyone who wasn't middle-class, as if the threat to middle-class values came from below and not from above. Websites like Chavscum were reported in the *Daily Telegraph* under the headline 'In defence of snobbery'.[10] As Francis Fukuyama suggested (see previous chapter), the political risks from destroying the middle classes are terrifying.

This 'chavscum' attitude has fed into the extremes of panic for many middle-class parents desperate to choose the right school for their children, and fearing that a feckless, alien culture would somehow steal their security and poison the minds of their families. This panic is at least partly a feature of middle-class imagination, and actually it always has been. One working-class MP told Owen Jones:

> I genuinely think that there are people out there in the middle classes, in the church and the judiciary and politics and the media, who actually fear, physically fear, the idea of this great, gold bling-dripping, lumpenproletariat, that might one day kick their front door in and eat their au pair.[11]

This is true. It is a fear, and the fear is all the more intense because people sense that traditional middle-class life is increasingly fraught.

But the middle classes at their best have always stood for something else. I remember hearing the speech in the House of Lords during the miners' strike in 1984 by the Earl of Stockton (the former prime minister Harold Macmillan), then aged ninety. Even then, his defence of the working classes, in the middle of the bitterness and rage of the strike, had the power to shock and to move. He described it as 'this terrible strike, by the best men in the world, who beat the Kaiser's and Hitler's armies and never gave in. It is pointless and we cannot afford that kind of thing . . . We used to have battles and rows but they were quarrels. Now there is a new kind of wicked hatred that has been brought in by different types of people.'

You don't hear that kind of voice any more, and it is a pity. Because the middle classes have also been able to exemplify that one-nation culture. This is not classlessness, but it is an understanding of our interdependence. When the middle classes resort to fearing the 'other', because of what the artist Grayson Perry calls their 'fragility', then they blind themselves to the real forces that are arrayed against them. When they put aside their fear, they have some chance of tackling the power of what really threatens them.

The real story is not the traditional class war, where we have to line up on the side of one class or the other, it is the way that – despite all the rhetoric about 'hard-working families' and home ownership – policy has actually shifted away from the middle classes and is no longer on their side. No, policy is now designed to support the interests of the global elite, to allow them to take an ever fatter share of the profits, and to make sure that cascade of cash does not filter so far into the middle or working classes that it becomes inflationary. Policy now supports the apotheosis of the richest, under the quite mistaken idea that wealth trickles down – when all the evidence suggests that it actually hoovers up (see chapter 1). For the first time since the Second World War, the interests of working classes and middle classes are now aligned.

The truth is that the middle classes and working classes now stand or fall together. The way out of this for both sides is exactly the same – it is to see the world clearly, to put aside their differences, and to hammer out a political programme capable of rescuing them.

There was just a hint of this in 2011, while the Arab Spring was quickening hearts against their own venal rulers, when the Occupy protesters first put up their tents next to St Paul's Cathedral. You may not have approved of their methods, nor admired their camp or their very obvious lack of focus, but the idea that the protesters represented the 99 per cent was a potent one.

We have been brought up to believe that the Right represents the middle classes and the Left represents the working classes. It is now clear that neither Right nor Left in conventional politics represent the interests of either. The political parties in Westminster are to that extent the 'slaves of some defunct economist', as Keynes put it long ago.[12] They are trapped in a world of policymaking that still believes in trickle-down economics, unable to grasp any other way, and which continues to funnel wealth and power ever upwards.

Margaret Thatcher and Tony Blair rose to power with the support of the middle classes. But the middle classes are at the very beginning of being able to articulate a challenge to that status quo, and to the way they have been treated by the financial forces – handing over the best years of their lives in indentured servitude to pay off the vast mortgage required to live a middle-class life, then finding that up to a third of their pension has been siphoned off in fees.

Experience shows that when the articulate middle classes demand things, sooner or later they get them. That is their best hope. The middle class, mused George Bernard Shaw, 'so clever in industry, so stupid in politics'.[13] That is going to have to change too. + EDUCATION

For all the conservatism in his advice to the new middle classes, Cobbett was a radical, and he saw very clearly in his own time the way that the establishment had organized itself into a great machine of self-aggrandizement that he called 'The Thing'. He meant that great mountain of placemen and aristocratic pensioners paid for by the struggling farmers and labourers of the nation. He believed that Britain was run not so much by a government, but by a financial system which had 'drawn the real property of the nation into fewer hands . . . made land and agriculture objects of speculation . . . in every part of the kingdom, moulded many farms into one . . . almost entirely extinguished the race of small farmers . . . we are daily advancing to the state in which there are but two classes of men, masters and abject dependants.'

Cobbett's analysis is dated, of course, but it is not entirely out of date, because – let's face it – The Thing still exists, and his two extremes, masters and abject dependants, are precisely the division that is happening to the middle classes in our own day. A handful are allowed into the masters category while the rest become abject dependants.

The twenty-first-century Thing covers the pension managers who cream outrageous sums from our pensions, and those at the controls of the speculative machine. But Cobbett's definition allows us to go further. Our own Thing includes public-sector sinecures as well as private-sector ones. This is at its summit when it comes to the banking elite, but it also includes members of the hugely paid quangocracy that runs the NHS or audits local government or runs the vast state databases. It includes the retail elite, clawing in public subsidy, recycling it in bonuses, while making swathes of our local communities poorer and more dependent. It includes the consultants to the quangocracy, the IT and management consultancies who have creamed off such huge sums from budgets over the past decade (over £70 billion to IT consultancies alone) while undermining the effectiveness of our institutions.

Cobbett knew that the emergence of a new middle class depended on them asserting democratic control of The Thing. The same is true today. One small glimmer of political hope lies in the fact that we are ruled by a coalition which is the first government for three decades dedicated to rebalancing the economy away from financial services – the first government that appeared to buy into the idea that the way out is local and entrepreneurial, rather than waiting hopelessly for the riches to trickle down from the new elite. The fact that the coalition seems to have no idea how to achieve this does not take away from the fact that they have, at least, articulated it.

That is the political possibility that can still save the middle classes. The practical hope for them seems to me to lie somewhere along these lines – to remember that they are not hidalgos, and to put aside centuries of nervousness and snobbery about 'trade', and to claw back the economy from the speculators and monopolies. This means taking a leaf out of William Cobbett's book. It means that hard work lies ahead. In fact, given that their place in the missing middle layers of the corporations has now gone for ever, the middle classes have to become entrepreneurs again.

Bridport in Dorset is an unlikely place to choose as the capital of a resurgent entrepreneurial culture. It still has an old-fashioned manufacturing base, specializing in making ropes and nets, as the town has done for centuries. Although it is in a corner of the English county which has grown faster than any other over the past generation, there is a distinct lack of people in their twenties and thirties. Those moving into the Bridport area have been primarily middle-class retirees or middle-class downshifters in search of a better quality of life.

Yet Dorset now has one of the highest levels of self-employment anywhere in the country. There is also an energy about the place which may go some way to explaining why Dorset is riding out the recent recession with less collateral damage than almost anywhere else in the UK, though it remains tough, even in Bridport. And among those at the epicentre of this small revolution is an energetic middle-class downshifter, Tim Crabtree.

Tim moved back to Dorset after leaving for London when he graduated from university. Like many others of his generation, he cut his teeth with charities and pressure groups in London, moved on to start social enterprises in Bristol, and then took his expertise home with him to start a family. One of the unexpected findings of the 2001 census was, as we have seen, that half the population now lived within half an hour of their birthplace – almost certainly a by-product of high house prices. When both parents have to work to pay the mortgage, they need to live near the grandparents to provide childcare. 'I always wanted to come back to Dorset,' says Tim.

The entrepreneurial revolution in Dorset has, until recently, been happening under the radar of the official economic development officials, who have tended to dismiss these new enterprises as 'lifestyle businesses'. It is true that many of them have no interest in growing huge. They have been created in order to sustain a living or to put right some local problem. But the Local Enterprise Partnership has now woken up to the potential of food and drink businesses in this predominantly agricultural economy.

Perhaps this is not so surprising, given that food and drink has underpinned the success of so many of the local enterprises that have managed to grow, and there are now sixty-six restaurants, cafés and food businesses listed in the Bridport area by TripAdvisor. In Bristol, Tim had helped run a social enterprise support agency as well as running his own business training in shiatsu, and starting a local aikido club. But when he joined the team at Dorset Community Action, it was soon clear that food was the great untapped opportunity.

The original problem was that his employer had grants to give away to community enterprises, but no community enterprises to fund. To help rectify this situation, Tim helped set up the West Dorset Food and Land Trust in 1996. The trust also had a trading subsidiary called West Dorset Food Links. Their task was to start farmers' markets and direct marketing or online schemes to provide outlets for the new businesses making local or organic food.

Then there was a string of new organizations and acronyms, vegetable gardens, kitchen spaces and then a basic distribution system. The number of food businesses began to grow. The Food and Land Trust started farmers' markets in Bridport and Poundbury. Soon there were seventy local businesses trading there. Within a few years, Dorset Food Links had started twelve markets across the county.

Tim's own foray into the food business started with a phone call from a local primary school in 2003. Dorset County Council had responded to the deregulation of school food standards in 1981 by closing all their school kitchens. The result had been an influx of junk food. This particular school had taken the heroic step of banning sweets and encouraging children to bring in fruit instead. The result had been problematic. The children used to take one bite out of their apples and pears at break time, and then throw the rest away in disgust. The bins were full of rotting fruit. Something had to be done.

Tim set up a small enterprise sourcing local fruit, organizing volunteers to cut it up and arrange it on plates, and selling the bits in school for 10p each. The project worked. The children liked their choice of fruit and soon other schools were clamouring to take part. Fruit platters were soon being dispatched to schools all over the area. Parents wanted to set up stalls outside the school gates.

There then followed one of those examples that show why government procurement is so often disastrous for local business. The government launched its free fruit scheme. Contracts to provide fruit to schools were organized on a regional basis. Tim tried to get the local contracts for schools, but the county council refused, and the school fruit enterprise went rapidly out of business. The result was that the children were soon eating fruit from Bulgaria and Spain. 'It was a great example about how top-down decisions and contracts actually destroyed a really innovative business,' he says now. They were determined not to make the same mistake again.

It so happened, even in those days before Jamie Oliver's school food documentaries, that the food in Dorset schools was causing some concern. Since the kitchens had been closed, the contract to provide free school meals had gone to Initial Rentokil – purveyors of roller towels – who packed them into individual yellow bags in a kitchen in London and trucked them down overnight. The yellow bags were a stigma for the children, who were increasingly refusing their free school meals. Take-up of free school meals was the basis of local authority grants to the schools, so the schools were getting worried.

Here Tim's Centre for Local Food in Bridport came in useful again. They began providing soup lunches for one school and it was successful enough to attract another. Another enterprise was emerging, and then came a stroke of luck. Political fallout from Jamie Oliver's TV campaign meant that all schools suddenly had to offer a hot meal.

Dorset County Council prepared to drop another brick. They signed a contract for frozen ready meals with a company in Nottingham. Every day they were trucked down 220 miles, reheated in hub kitchens or in microwaves in the schools and then served up. This time, Tim's team was not going to be battered into submission. They held a meeting of eight local head teachers, and they agreed to launch a partnership between them to opt out of the county council contract.

Tim's team suddenly needed a much larger kitchen, and within a very short space of time they had raised £250,000 and recruited staff. Soon they were producing 200,000 hot lunches a year. 'We built up slowly, and six months later we had two hub kitchens, in Bridport and Blandford Forum, twenty-four schools and a turnover of £500,000 a year. And we had begun doing lunch clubs and day centres too,' he said. 'And all from serving cut-up bits of fruit to children.'

While all this was going on, Tim and his colleagues were trying to tackle the other big hurdle getting in the way of new enterprises – the absence of local banking organizations capable of lending locally. In 2001, they set up the Wessex Reinvestment Trust, modelled on a similar organization in Birmingham. It was designed to lend to local businesses and to use local savings to do so.

Go to Bridport now and you will find a bustling town centre with market stalls, tea shops and butcher's, delicatessens and baker's. There is an energy there and it is instantly recognizable as Bridport. This is no clone town. It is home to successful food companies like Dorset Cereals, Organix and Olives et al. But what has been happening here is being repeated in different ways in other parts of the country, and the phenomenon goes way beyond the middle classes, though it is still tough to get jobs in Bridport.

For example, the huge success of the Nottinghamshire micro-providers – in the string of social enterprises providing human-scale social care far better than the dysfunctional care sector. And the pioneering work of Somerset Food Links, which was the template for the one Tim set up in Bridport, or of the Aston Reinvestment Trust or the London Rebuilding Society. Over the last ten years, a social enterprise support sector has also grown up to nurture them, with organizations like Ashoka, UnLtd and the School for Social Entrepreneurs.

It is a good news story, but the new entrepreneurs are stuck in the old political categories. They have a choice of a political tradition that is pro-business, which in practice regards this as backing the ambitions of the biggest businesses. Or a political tradition that is sceptical about business, which in practice promotes the biggest businesses in order to control them. Entrepreneurs have to struggle to explain that their interests are different.

Like so many others in the middle classes now, Tim looks at the future facing the next generation with alarm. 'My father-in-law is probably in the last generation to have been able to take early retirement on a corporate pension,' he says. 'You look at your own children and what faces them and you just think "Oh God!"'

If there is any chance to reverse the trends that are killing the middle classes, and of making possible a comfortable, civilized, independent life for the majority of the UK population again, then Bridport may be a kind of template. The middle classes developed a horror of 'trade' in the last century, at least down that huge fault line that runs down the middle of the class between upper and lower, what Grayson Perry describes as 'the Berlin Wall of British taste'. That is a snobbery, if it still exists, which the middle classes can no longer afford.

There is no place for them any more in the middle layers of giant corporations, and even the public services are becoming so hidebound and target-driven that they may no longer provide an honourable haven for middle-class professionals. The new monopolies in every area of business, and especially in public-service contracts, are preparing to truss us up and bind us. The only way out is for the middle classes to claw back their own sector of the economy, by providing themselves and those around them with paid employment.

That is a leadership task which the middle classes are uniquely suited to. It is up to them now to fight their way out of the forces that are crushing them, and remake the world.

How are they going to do that? If you recognize yourself from this book, here is a checklist, a twelve-point programme for the middle classes.

1. Accept the realities
Most twelve-step recovery programmes start with an injunction to accept yourself. This means more than the statement: 'I am David Boyle and I am middle-class.' It means accepting the situation for what it is, realizing that nobody is going to rescue you.

All the conventional solutions have been tried – dragging in cheap resources from the empire, relying on clever financial products, dumping traditional values, loading us down with debt. It does not work. Accepting the realities means understanding the way the world is. Being overwhelmingly conservative in their understanding of financial issues, the middle classes still have little idea just how much the speculative tail is now wagging the dog – productive goods and services now make up just 5 per cent of the vast $4 trillion that storms through the ether every day. Once they understand that the world has changed, then the way out becomes clearer.

2. Be entrepreneurial

Nobody is going to rescue the middle classes from the outside. They have to do it themselves, and that means building the kind of economy that can support them, not by waiting around for the government to act or for the Chinese to invest, but by going out there and starting the businesses we need. Traditionally, medieval cities built up their economies by replacing their imports with home-grown industries.[14] These days everywhere is supposed, under the prevailing doctrine of comparative advantage, to specialize in something that only they can do. But, pushed too far, comparative advantage is a recipe for the kind of wrong-headed efficiency which simply favours big over small. The middle classes need to be at the heart of a movement, supported in this case by rising energy prices, which uses local assets – land, energy and people – to rebuild local production and some measure of independence. If we need an economy that actively supports comfortable, secure, independent lives for the mass of the population, and which does not encourage a hurricane of speculation to drive out everything we value about family and community life, the middle classes have to create it themselves.

3. Buy local

One opportunity, paradoxically, is soaring oil prices, which are increasingly making local production more cost-effective. The days of trucking lorryloads of tomatoes down to Italy and back for packaging are coming to an end. We need new businesses to provide for our needs, new financial institutions capable of underpinning the businesses, and we need new infrastructure to provide us with energy in a resource-constrained world. That offers a clear and potentially profitable role for the middle classes. But it does mean that we need to support the businesses that are underpinning the life we want, rather than those that are corroding everyone's wealth but their own, and it means that – above all – we need local institutions capable of supporting that kind of effort . . .

4. Get involved in creating local institutions

So many of our institutions have been hollowed out, and it is clear that the mainstream financial services industry is no longer meeting the needs of most of the middle classes. In the nineteenth century, all these institutions – the friendly societies, co-operatives, insurance societies and all the rest of them – were built by ordinary people, working together. The middle classes are going to have to do this all over again to meet their needs in a way that the over-consolidated banks and insurance companies can no longer do. We need big co-operative institutions to manage pensions, but most of all we need small local ones to look after us when we are old, or look after our children at reasonable cost when we go out to work. We need time banks and co-operative nurseries (like those in North America) that are driven primarily by the time and effort of the people who use them, or bulk-buying consumer co-operatives (like those in Japan) which can survive the economic storms that are to come. The middle classes are good at making institutions, but they have had it all done for them in recent decades. Not any more.

5. Shun the tax avoiders and semi-monopolies

It is impossible to imagine a widespread, comfortable middle class if it takes on the task of paying for the infrastructure we all depend on with its taxes, while the corporate world and the global elite does not. The middle classes need to use their political muscle to close the tax havens, but also to use their economic muscle against the growing power of monopoly. There is no doubt that a Big Ten supermarkets would be more competitive, better for the economy, would spread wealth and encourage suppliers, better than our Big Four. The huge privileges we give the biggest retailers – three months to pay their bills, providing them with a rolling interest-free loan big enough to demolish any smaller competitor – are not compatible with a stable economy and a healthy middle class. What goes for groceries also applies to many other areas of modern life, from the handful of contractors who hoover up most waste contracts to the train operators and other manipulative megalosaurs – Tesco, Virgin, Google – who want us bound and gagged and dependent. All we can do is put our spending money, as far as we can – and it is difficult to do it all at once – with the human-scale, tax-paying businesses that we need.

6. Chop up the credit cards

This is difficult given that providing ourselves with a home we own, in our overvalued housing market, means taking on onerous amounts of debt, to add to the student debt that the next generation seems likely to build up. But debt constrains our life options, forcing us into jobs and activities we don't want, because we have to pay so much in interest or debt repayments. The corrosion of middle-class life is partly a side effect of the credit-card culture, the consumerism and acquisitiveness that came with a delusory sense of prosperity that derived in turn from rising house prices. If the middle classes want to survive, the objective has to be to minimize these constraints by paying off debts and mortgages as soon as they possibly can, and by embracing again the traditional middle-class value of thrift – because, in the new financial world, thrift means freedom.

7. Demand a new approach to business

The founder of the Body Shop, Anita Roddick, used to describe modern corporations as moral dinosaurs – subsuming the civilized morality of those who work there, and able to feel no emotions but greed and fear. It is time that the idea that business owes no duty to anything except profit was recognized for what it was: a naive, simplistic, adolescent fantasy, completely alien to the traditional values of the middle classes, and corrosive of neighbourhoods and families. The banking crisis, and the economic collapse that followed, is a testament to where it leads. Nobody is exempt from responsibility for their neighbourhood, and anyone who behaves as if they are is freeloading on the civilization created tirelessly by people and families all around them. There is a role here for changing the prevailing structure of companies, and there is evidence that those with more co-operative structures and fairer pay scales are more imaginative, more successful and more flexible than those without.[15] But there is also a role for the middle classes to demand improved behaviour from the companies they deal with, and to shun them when they don't get it.

8. Bring down the price of homes

How? Well, it would be disastrous to do it overnight. Our best hope might be to create a parallel housing market which circulates at a much lower level and is protected from speculation. That means persuading politicians to start building homes again, but in order to give them away – or at least sell hundred-year leases in community land trusts at a tenth of current values, on condition those prices remain during that period. If we can build enough, and if it provides a genuine alternative, a parallel housing market, then it may offer a lifeline out of the bizarre and unwieldy pyramid scheme that our homes have become. In the short term, we can limit speculation in homes by using restrictive covenants to limit ownership of homes to owner-occupiers.[16] Otherwise we may just have to go back to building our own.

9. Retire later

New reforms to pensions will make the charges more transparent and will finally bring them down, but we have to kiss goodbye to the idea of retirement at sixty or sixty-five. A new era of low returns from investments also means that yesterday's gold-plated pensions and final salary schemes are going to be difficult to sustain. But there are lessons from abroad that we need to incorporate here as well. We need to merge pension funds to genuinely share risk, including those exclusive ones reserved for the new elite, and so that they have the kind of scale they need to invest in reliable infrastructure, and in particular the new green energy and transport infrastructure we need. We must be able to define the benefits and not just the contributions. We also need to experiment with pensions combined with other kinds of contribution, which require inputs in time helping neighbours, and which will pay out in kind in support from other members when we need it. The middle classes benefit from mutualism in other countries, especially perhaps in childcare and pensions, yet our own middle classes get little further than shopping at Waitrose. And, let's face it, everyone is going to have to retire later.

10. Demand human interaction

Targets and other kinds of destructive central control can survive many things – including being renamed as 'standards' or 'payment by results' – but what they can't survive is constant questioning from the equivalent of the little boy in the story of the Emperor's New Clothes. Yes, the school is high in the league tables, but are the teachers inspiring? Yes, the doctor's surgery is accredited under QOF and QIPP, but will the doctors listen to you? The middle classes need to represent the wisdom of what is really important, none of which is susceptible to mere measurement. But the most important way the middle classes can put a spanner in the works of the machine that wants to reduce them all to numbers, 'rationalizing' people to make them easier to process, is to refuse to take part in it – to demand real people to deal with when it is important, not software or call centres. To refuse to be served by robots in supermarkets. To avoid 'rationalized' systems as far as possible – and often it isn't.

11. Start new schools
The kind of education the middle classes yearn for can be provided far more easily and effectively in smaller institutions than in big ones. This does not mean a new generation of micro-schools but it does mean refusing to send children to factory-style mega-schools, and if that means the middle classes have to set up the schools themselves, then that is what they must do – as long as they take responsibility for the whole education system and not just the sections of it that cater for their own children. The new middle classes' spirit of entrepreneurialism needs to go beyond just starting businesses and embrace starting more new schools, inside and outside the state system and straddling the two. Finessing a place for their own child in a good school is not enough – it increases the sense of panic for everyone else. They have to reshape an education system that creates a future for everyone.

12. Rethink money
This is a difficult one. There must come a point when desperately competing with the Far East and struggling to pay down the unrepayable debt is not enough to cling to those aspects of British life

that make it civilized. Do we dump them in the search for competitiveness or do we try something else? That something else may be to create the money we need to defend our national civilization, aware that – to make that possible without creating rampant inflation – two other reforms will also be needed. The banks will have to be prevented from creating money, as they create most of the money we use now.[17] We will also need to have a much more equal society, otherwise the money will simply flow to the richest again. Whether this inversion of the money-creation status quo would be possible or desirable remains to be decided by debate – but the debate needs to start now.

What most of these twelve points have in common is that they are not just a political programme; they amount to a call to action for the middle classes themselves. They will have to create the businesses and institutions capable of clawing back some kind of future for a civilized life. They will have to take on the monopolies and the new elite, and create the financial institutions they need to drive a new entrepreneurial culture – one that is capable of providing them with pensions and homes and all those other necessities for a civilized life. They are also going to have to do so, not selfishly – just for their own comfort – but on behalf of everyone else.

This is a tough call. The middle classes can no longer trust their existing institutions, political or financial, to look after their interests, because they are dedicated to looking after the interests of a different class altogether. So this is a political battle which lies ahead, but also a practical one – and we are going to have to inculcate the new generation with the tools they will need to make the best of the middle-class life possible in the future.

Perhaps if they manage it, they will be able to look back and say – as Joseph Chamberlain did more than a century ago:

I belong to the middle class and I am proud of the ability, the shrewdness, the industry, the providence, and the thrift by which they are distinguished, and which have in so considerable a degree contributed to the stability and prosperity of the empire.

The word 'empire' dates this rather badly. So does 'providence' and 'thrift'. But the idea is there, that ability and industry are what we need, but in a whole new way. We need to turn a page from the old story, which has grown bloated, wasteful and obscenely over-leveraged, and trust perhaps to providence that there is still another story in the book.[18]

'An Aga features in artist Grayson Perry's latest works!' screamed the headline in a website called *The World According to Lady*. One of the features of the decline of the middle classes is that they have a new tendency to treat themselves like a small village, a tiny minority with its own interests that few can share or understand.

Grayson Perry's new tapestries which describe the class system, created before television cameras for Channel 4, unpicked some of the peculiarities of class in a particularly revealing way. The strange freemasonry of tiny brand differences. The bizarre way in which the middle classes see their own tastes in moral terms. The peculiar multiplicity of subdivisions within the middle classes. 'The important taste divide in British life is not between working-class and middle-class taste but within the different tribes of the middle class itself,' said Perry, and he was right.

English culture revels in this stuff. Most of those who manage our media channels, and our forces of creativity, are themselves middle-class, yet we are not kind about ourselves. We share the very same pretensions we laugh at. We shiver with horror about the dullness of the suburban places we live in. We accept the verdict of the writer Colin MacInnes on the middle classes – 'concentrated mediocrity' – and believe ourselves to be strange exceptions to the rule.[19] We sneer at the curtain-twitching, Waitrose-shopping, garage-filling, lawn-mowing, focaccia-chewing, balsamic vinegar-sweating, old school tie-denying, catchment area-stalking, costume drama-watching business of being middle-class, even when we participate in most of the list ourselves.

You have to wonder sometimes – are the middle classes worth saving? Should we not just pack the lot up and start the class system all over again, but on a more classless basis? It is a good question, and a fair one.

The advantages to having a middle class have been spelled out throughout this book – political stability, economic success – but in the end, the importance of the question about who killed the middle classes is personal. I want the possibility of a middle-class life to stay open – not the pretensions or the snobbery, but the safe space to dream, to create, to make music, to read, or just to sit on the grass, without being timed when you go to the loo (for call-centre employees), or having to hold down three jobs day and night to pay the rent. And without being sedated in a dysfunctional care home at the end of your life.

With a lawn, yes and flowerbeds and dogs even (well, hens in my case), and a bit of greenery, and enough leisure to have a cultural, critical understanding of the world – and a belief that we can shift it – to pass on to my children. Yes, you can ridicule a caricature of lawns, dogs, hedges, mowing machines, big Sunday newspapers at the breakfast table, *Any Questions?*, the Proms, and all the rest. The middle-class life isn't to everyone's taste, but there is a core of civilization to it, and it underpins other kinds of civilization too.

Writing this book has been more emotional than I expected, not because I had a privileged upbringing (though I did). Nor because I want people like me to cling on to the lives they have managed to build (though I do). But because it reminded me that this space for civilization may not be possible for my children's generation, and it made me nostalgic for my own past, and my own grandparents'. Learning the piano. Watching my sisters play instruments in their school orchestra. Reading in the branches of a tree when the sun goes down. Walking through the woods after lunch. Or lying on the grass doing nothing. There is something intensely luxurious about lying on your own lawn, and feeling the green shoots on the back of your hand and, I admit, it breaks my heart to think this may not be possible for my children.

The English middle classes have been extraordinarily lucky to have benefited over the generations from this civilized possibility. But they have given back, in writers, scientists, inventors, composers, entrepreneurs and organizers and, let's face it, in unprecedented tolerance too. Their case for survival is a good one but, in the end and most of all, I want them to survive, not because they are civilized or uncivilized people, but because they are my people.

Communitarian

Tim Lott

Afterword to the Paperback Edition – The Year Everything Changed: 2013

> 'So we beat on, boats against the current, borne back
> ceaselessly into the past.'
>
> F. Scott Fitzgerald, *The Great Gatsby*

Not long after this book was first published in April 2013 I went to a school reunion. We are middle-aged, middle-class survivors, in a sense. Some of our fellow public schoolboys from the 1970s have died, but most of us are still around, largely happy, not always thriving, but settled. What is most unexpected about the small group of us who meet once a year, upstairs in a bar in London's Covent Garden, is how diverse we are.

There are two builders, a furniture restorer, a very successful barrister, a medical consultant, an alternative health therapist, and a writer (me). There is also a garage owner, a fireman, an undertaker, a sales director, and an engineer, among others. We spent our whole schooldays being told how privileged we were, and we were certainly privileged in many ways – thanks in part to that privilege most of us own our own homes, though not all of us. But if you believe the rhetoric about independent schools, on either side of the political divide, you might have expected us to have been a more predictably cohesive group.

But we have certainly benefited from the age we lived in, from free university education and student grants, and from inheriting the first staggering rises in house prices from our parents. Some of us trained as professionals in the days when you had some freedom of manoeuvre, before the combination of McKinsey and Goodhart's Law (see Chapter 7). We don't talk about money much – we are too middle class for that – and our incomes clearly vary enormously (one of us has even retired in his fifties). But we are not the narrow slice of the class system you might have predicted. We seem actually to straddle a huge variety of different kinds of middle-classness, but we all worry about our children, and their ability to survive in the world that is emerging, here and abroad.

We worry, of course, about the new wave of technological developments which are beginning to replace the remaining middle-class jobs. In a *New York Times* column, David Autor and David Dorn looked at the process of replacing careers with technology, even now the jobs of high-income workers, such as professional managers, engineers and consultants.[1] They argued that 47 per cent of 700 occupation types in the USA are now at risk from automation, thanks to the emergence of big data and advanced sensors, which give robots better senses and dexterity, so that they can perform a broader scope of non-routine manual tasks. Algorithms for big data are already taking over tasks which rely on recognising patterns. Autor and Dorn suggest that the way to avoid this fate is to choose to train for careers that require creativity and social intelligence. But then how do you earn enough to get a roof over your head in some parts of the UK?

But in the cacophony of figures about our battered economy, we are going to have to look beyond all this to see what is really happening. Because that is hard to discern sometimes, with all the talk of a 'booming' southern England and a struggling northern England.

The unbalanced economy, which seems to get more unbalanced with every month that passes, has sucked the enterprise out of the north, leaving it with a constrained, shrinking public sector. The middle classes can afford to rent or buy, but their professional room for manoeuvre is seriously limited, and the enterprises, the local papers, local banks, local food distributors and local shops, which gave previous middle-class generations an economic underpinning, have gone.

In the south, it is the other way around. There is work, but it struggles to pay enough to buy or rent because the housing market is increasingly geared to the needs of foreign investors and the mega-rich.

And here we get to the nitty-gritty. Because, behind all the headlines and soundbites, it is increasingly difficult even for middle-income earners in mainstream work, including ever larger chunks of the middle classes, to get by without support from the government in the form of Help to Buy, or housing benefit or council tax rebates or tax credits or all the rest of the state's generosity to its middle-income earners.

Their children are living at home, their pensions have been corroded by the financial services industry. But political parties need the middle classes and they tend to hide these problems away by subsidising home ownership – even though it pushes up prices for our children.

It is easy to miss what is happening when the price of your home increases by £50,000 in a year. But that wealth isn't real, and will be used – if it is useable at all – to replace lost pensions and social care. It also narrows the ambitions and hopes of our children.

Over 80 per cent of homes in inner London are now bought and left empty by foreign investors, who pay a tiny fraction of the local tax they would pay in Paris or New York. But sometimes it takes an outsider to see it clearly. This is what the American journalist Michael Goldfarb, who now lives in London, wrote in the *New York Times*:

> The property market is no longer about people making a long-term investment in owning their shelter but a place for the world's richest people to park their money at an annualised rate of return of around 10 per cent. It has made my adopted hometown a no-go area for increasing numbers of the middle classes.[2]

At the heart of this is a peculiar policy, which seems to have been designed to gobble up middle-class children. Help to Buy was launched by the UK Treasury in April 2013 for buyers of new homes, guaranteeing their deposits so that they can get on the housing ladder. By May, mortgage applications had risen by a third. It was extended in October to cover all properties, and was almost universally criticised by economists and the Institute of Directors, who called instead for 'Help to Supply', as they put it.

Even so, there remained the failure to understand why house prices rise. There will always be a shortage of homes in London and the south-east, though of course we need to build more homes (see Chapter 2). Because, as the Japanese found to their cost in the 1990s, the more schemes that are invented to help people buy homes – extending mortgage terms, guaranteeing deposits – then the more estate agents are able to raise prices to meet the demand.

'We are the party of home ownership and we're going to let the country know it,' said Chancellor George Osborne in September 2013. But Help to Buy is actually a policy designed to *undermine* home ownership, condemning our children to a lifetime working in financial services – if they can get in – if they ever want to own a home or rent one in south-east England. Or it is a policy designed to perpetually prop home ownership up with government money, and ever-increasing sums will be required.

Sure enough, house prices began to rise, precisely as predicted. The price-to-earnings ratio of house valuations was nearly up to the level it reached before the crash of 2007–08, when it was just below 7 (the recent average has been 3.5). And as prices rise, the government becomes increasingly exposed to the housing market, as the US government was immediately before the crash, as taxpayers guarantee the riskiest part of the market.

Some things that Help to Buy fails to do: it fails to make homes sustainably affordable. It fails to take any action against the UK's very own version of subprime – interest-only mortgages that can never be paid off. It also fails to shift bank lending to where it might genuinely help enterprise. Bank lending to small and medium businesses is still falling: when the government chose in the Help to Buy scheme to commit £130bn to mortgage guarantees, it provided just £4bn in capital to the new British Business Bank.

But as well as higher house prices, the first edition of this book also predicted some strange new ways of calculating mortgages – like Japanese-style longer terms. Sure enough, by autumn 2013, Alliance & Leicester, Nationwide and Halifax were all lending mortgages for forty years – fifteen years longer than the traditional twenty-five-year mortgage term. The specialist lender Mortgage Express, part of Bradford & Bingley, now lends over a forty-five-year term in some circumstances. That is an entire working life, and we are well on the way to the notorious Japanese grandparent mortgage, which pushed up house prices in Tokyo to ruinous levels.

The problem here is that those who claim some allegiance to the idea of a property-owning democracy were making the same mistake as the big banks have, and with the same catastrophic results. They think that the problem is the occasional property bubble, from which we are apparently safe. Their memory goes back only a decade or so, at most. They don't see that we are in the middle of a thirty-year property bubble which is corroding people's careers and hopes and undermining the existence of the middle classes.

I had my own home valued recently. It turned out to be so valuable that I ought to keep it in a bank vault instead of living in it. It was worth around £500,000, yet it is only a small three-bedroom affair of the kind you find all over suburban England. It has had only three owners since it was first bought for £700 in 1937. At average rates of inflation, it should now be worth around £45,000. And according to the Prime Minister, this is not a bubble.

So why is middle-class life – and not just housing – becoming unaffordable? As this book sets out, it is partly because of the rise of the monopolies, partly because the economy is geared increasingly to the needs of the mega-rich (see Chapter 5). It is partly because of the economic doctrine of 'comparative advantage' – a sensible economic concept pushed to ridiculous lengths – which has allowed the regional enterprises of the UK to atrophy and die (see Chapter 7).

It is also because the upper tier is now so much richer that the economy can appear to get by just by serving their needs. That is what happens in an economy which is increasingly like the American one, where 95 per cent of the increases in wealth between 2009 and 2012 went to the top 1 per cent, whose incomes increased by 31 per cent. In the UK, average pay remained steady over the year when I wrote and published this book (2011–12), but the average pay of FTSE chief executives increased from £3.9 million in 2011 to £4.3 million in 2012.

It is a dangerous situation, but people do now seem to be taking notice. The British Social Attitudes survey published recently showed that 82 per cent of people now think that 'the income gap is too large', and nearly seven in ten believe it is the government's responsibility to do something about it. Newspaper editorials across the political spectrum are warning politicians that economic growth will not satisfy voters unless living standards rise for the 'squeezed middle' as well as the richest. In Europe, only Turkey and Portugal are more divided, in terms of income, than the UK, and the middle classes are beginning to realise that they are not going to be on the winning side of the divide any more.

Into this uncertainty, rather unexpectedly in October 2013, stepped former prime minister John Major himself (see Chapter 6) in a strange intervention in the debate about energy prices. If the energy companies were increasing prices at the rate of 10 per cent a year, it would mean that more people would have to be subsidised during the cold winter – and it seemed to him that the energy companies should pay those costs.

The proposal sounded reasonable, so reasonable that it threw the government into panic. They had just signed an agreement with French nuclear company EDF to pay twice the expected price for nuclear-generated electricity for thirty-five years, and the last thing they wanted to do was to discourage investment. But clearly something would have to be done about rising energy prices, as Prime Minister David Cameron himself acknowledged after a painful grilling at prime minister's questions a few days later.

What was so interesting about Major's intervention was that he referred during interviews to his own origins: brought up in poverty in Brixton, the son of a former star of the music halls. Major had been identified before with the brand of free-market globalisation that Margaret Thatcher's name is most associated with. Indeed, he was her chosen successor. But even he could see that this kind of free market – though not every kind of free market – privileges the rich over the poor and undermines the ability of the majority to lead independent lives, and he was asking difficult questions. Those questions are only just beginning.

There is one question that I have had to answer, as I gave talks to groups of eager middle-class people, or wrote my articles, and which came up time after time: does it matter? I still think it does.

For one thing, it is important that the middle classes realise that the destruction wreaked on the working classes is now in store for them. There is no economic purpose to their existence, and their jobs are being replaced by software as fast as it can be invented. For another, they provide political and economic stability, and always have done. Their fierce determination to retain some of that independence is a vital underpinning for the liberties of everyone else. Without the middle classes, there is no hope for the poor either.

But the real reason why everyone needs the middle classes – and why this isn't just about whether my own children get a roof over their heads – is that, without them, society will be bitterly divided between a tiny, wealthy elite and a great sprawling proletariat that will struggle for a living, measured and tested by 'efficient' software at work, some of them holding down more than one job just to get by.

Because the alternative to a thriving middle class is not a happy co-existence between rich and poor. It is a new tyranny by the few who own everything, dedicated to a deadening efficiency that leaves no room for culture, leisure or any kind of education beyond that demanded by the elite for those who man and maintain their computers.

That is where we are heading, and it is partly the fault of the middle classes. But there is some evidence that they are waking up.

Throughout the summer of 2013, the BBC ran a series about the rise of the global middle class and, as they did so, there was evidence from around the world of what looked very like a middle-class revolt, first in the Middle East, then Turkey, then in Brazil. What appears to be happening is that the global middle classes are emerging only to discover how far the current economic system renders them powerless – and how far it threatens their continued existence. Whether it is the loss of a public park in Ankara, or a bus-fare hike in Rio, each revolt escalates quickly into mass rallies on the streets. But actually both the park and the bus fares became symbols of an underlying powerlessness.

What made them middle-class revolts is not that they were defending middle-class privileges. It was that the global working classes no longer have the time, the space or the power to organise any kind of uprising. They are measured and controlled by tyrannical employers when they work, and – when they don't – they are preoccupied with the business of survival. This is not just a crisis for the middle classes, of course. It is a crisis for the current economic model, because it appears to be driving out the possibility of ordinary life.

The Slovenian philosopher Slavoj Žižek has drawn parallels between the democratic reformers in the Middle East and the economic reformers in Latin America, arguing that they are both making a stand against different kinds of fundamentalism, both of which deny the importance of their humanity, and that they recognise the parallels between them. It may be religious fundamentalism which clings to a bizarre belief in the literal truth of every sentence of holy scripture. Or it may be market fundamentalism, which clings to a bizarre belief in the objective reality of market values and the bottom line. It is at heart the same thing, and accepting that is no criticism of either religion or the market.

I find this idea compelling. It points to a similar crisis in economics and theology, and demands a humanistic response to both kinds of spiritual impoverishment. Neither religious nor economic fundamentalists see the world as it really is. In theological terms, both put narrow simplifications above complex truth – which theologians used to call 'idolatry'. To make this comparison doesn't mean rejecting genuine, complex religion, any more than it means rejecting markets. It means rejecting inhumane simplifications, single bottom lines, one-dimensional measures, and all the other nostrums that have been allowed to drive out complex and humanising middle-class values.

Perhaps it also sheds some light on one of the things that has been confusing me. Where is the spark of revolt against the market fundamentalism which is impoverishing the UK, where the middle classes are cowed, the working classes are powerless, and where political debate is so staggeringly narrow and constrained?

Watching the new Pope Francis developing his pro-poor mission in Latin America, I have been wondering whether the spark of change is going to come from the Church in its tolerant form. Watching the Archbishop of Canterbury taking on the usurious payday lenders, using rhetoric not heard from the Church since Jesus cleansed the Temple – 'we will drive you out of business' – I have wondered whether there is some parallel. It may be that only the Church is independent enough to see the problem clearly, and to recognise fundamentalism when it sees it.

We need to hear that voice: uncompromising, determined and aggressive on the side of what is right.

But although there is no middle-class revolt in the UK, unless you count the atavistic longings of UKIP, there is evidence of the kind of middle-class fightback we need. There are moves to cap the charges financial services use to corrode personal pensions. There are the first signs of small banks emerging again in the UK, as they will have to for the revolution in enterprise that we need. I suggest in Chapter 3 that we slit open the stomachs of the big banks, as the woodman did to the wolf, and let the little banks out. Since then, TSB and William's & Glyn's have both jumped free. Metro and Aldersmore, Handelsbanken and Shawbrook have emerged. Cambridgeshire County Council has set up its own bank, to use its own pension fund to support new enterprise. So has Salford Council, and Bournemouth Council and a number of others are following suit. And developing as a result, perhaps, is an energetic, innovative food enterprise sector – just the beginning of the surge of new enterprise that might rescue the blighted middle classes from their fate.

We need new entrepreneurs. We need new institutions. We certainly need more imagination and a new politics prepared to protect the new sectors from the monopolies. But most of all, we are going to need effort, if we are going to claw back the economic purpose for the middle classes. But an economic purpose for the middle classes will have to be local: it requires enterprise and organisation, and actually it always has done.

And so we beat on, boats against the current, to find new ways of keeping alive the values that the existence of the middle classes make possible, for themselves and anybody else who chooses them: broad education, tolerance and independence.

David Boyle, November 2013

Notes

1 The scene of the crime

1 Shona Sibary, 'Stuck in the rent trap', *Daily Mail*, 23 Feb. 2012.
2 Frances Hardy, 'The nouveau poor', *Daily Mail*, 21 Apr. 2011.
3 One fifth of the school places in Deborah's borough are independent.
4 William Leith, 'Have the middle class lost their place?', *Daily Telegraph*, 23 Oct. 2011.
5 *Huffington Post*, 1 Mar. 2012.
6 *Guardian*, 20 Nov. 2011.
7 *The Times*, 22 May 2006.
8 Guy Standing, *The Precariat: The new dangerous class* (London, Bloomsbury, 2011).
9 Guy Standing, 'The Precariat – the new dangerous class', *Policy Network*, 24 May 2011.
10 Resolution Foundation.
11 *Daily Mail*, 23 Jun. 2011.
12 Shelter, online statement, 6 Mar. 2012.
13 UK average: 347 per cent.
14 Daycare Trust/Save the Children Fund survey, Sept. 2011.
15 *Daily Telegraph*, 21 Apr. 2012.
16 PrimeLocation survey, 2011.
17 *Evening Standard*, 27 Feb. 2012.
18 Bloomberg News, 29 Feb. 2012.
19 *Financial Times*, 17/18 Mar. 2012.
20 David Willetts, *The Pinch* (London, Atlantic Books, 2010), xv.
21 Willetts, 81.
22 *New York Post*, 11 Jun. 2009.
23 Francis Fukuyama, 'The Future of History: Can liberal democracy

survive the decline of the middle class?', *Foreign Affairs*, Jan./Feb. 2012.

24 William K. Carroll, *The Making of a Transnational Capitalist Class: Corporate power in the 21st century* (London, Zed Books, 2010).

25 Citigroup, 'Plutonomy: Buying luxury, explaining global imbalances', 15 Oct. 2005, quoted in Edward Fulbrook (2012), 'The political economy of bubbles', *Real World Economics Review*, no. 59.

26 Ferdinand Mount, 'The new few or a very British oligarchy', *Guardian*, 24 Apr. 2012.

27 Adam Raphael, *Ultimate Risk* (London, Bantam Press, 1994), 192.

28 Raphael, 97.

29 Raphael, 13.

30 Raphael, 211.

31 Raymond Williams, *The City and the Country* (Oxford, Oxford University Press, 1975), 9f.

32 Patrick Hutber, *The Decline and Fall of the Middle Class and How It Can Fight Back* (Harmondsworth, Penguin Books, 1977).

33 Hutber, 37

34 Hutber, 30.

35 Hutber, 33.

36 *Sunday Telegraph*, 2 Nov. 1975.

37 Hutber, 37.

38 Roy Lewis and Angus Maude, *The English Middle Classes* (London, Phoenix House, 1949).

39 Lewis and Maude, 9.

40 Quoted in Lewis and Maude, 75.

41 Lewis and Maude, 13.

42 Mike Savage (2007), 'Changing social class identities in post-war Britain: Perspectives from Mass-Observation', *Sociological Research Online*, vol. 12, no. 3.

43 Firstrung (2008), http://www.firstrung.org.uk/, 22 Apr.

44 Future Foundation survey: see BBC website, 5 May 2006.

45 *Daily Telegraph*, 1 Feb. 2012.

46 See for example Tony Bennett et al. (2011), 'Omnivores without borders: two readings on distinction in contemporary culture', *European Sociological Review*, 27(4): 548–54.

47 Paul H. Ray and Sherry Ruth Anderson, *The Cultural Creatives* (New York, Harmony Books, 2000).

48 Martin Stott, *Spilling the Beans: A style guide to the new age* (London, Collins Fontana, 1986), 11.

49 See www.bbc.co.uk/labuk/articles/class/

50 Rosemary Crompton, *Class and Stratification Policy* (Cambridge, CUP, 2008).

51 Cindi Katz (2012), 'Lost youth', *CAM Magazine*, no. 65, Lent.

52 Hutber, 10.

53 Ben Wilson, *The Making of Victorian Values* (London, Penguin Books, 2007), 327.

54 See my book David Boyle, *Authenticity: Brands, Fakes, Spin and the Lust for Real Life* (London, HarperCollins/Flamingo, 2003), 42–3.

55 That is from the Future Foundation's Middle Britain report in 2006. See Simon Stewart, *Culture and the Middle Classes* (Aldershot, Ashgate, 2010), 18.

2 The first clue: the staggering house-price escalator

1 I have borrowed the style of this introduction from David Kynaston's brilliant book *Austerity Britain*, as a tribute to the master of modern social history (just in case anyone thought I was passing this off as my own).

2 www.mortgageguideuk.co.uk.

3 Public Record Office Cabinet Papers, PREM 19/24.

4 Nigel Lawson, *The View from No. 11: Memoirs of a Tory radical* (London, Bantam, 1992), 38.

5 Geoffrey Howe, *Conflict of Loyalty* (London, Pan, 1995).

6 National Housing Federation London, *Home Truths 2011: Fixing our broken housing market* (London, 2011).

7 Judy Hillman and Peter Clarke, *Geoffrey Howe: A quiet revolutionary* (London, Weidenfeld & Nicolson, 1988), 148.

8 Public Record Office Cabinet Papers, Note from Prime Minister to Chancellor, 24 Jun. 1979.

9 I did ask Lord Lawson to let me interview him for this book, but he said he had nothing to add to his published accounts.

10 Quoted in Hugo Young, *One of Us: A Biography of Margaret Thatcher* (Basingstoke, Macmillan, 1989), 157.

11 Lawson, 40.

12 Quoted in Lawson, 38.

13 See draft memo from Bank of England to Treasury, Nov. 1979, Bank of England archives, ref. 5A149/10.

14 Sebastian Cresswell-Turner, 'We used to have it all', *The Times*, 29 Apr. 2007.

15 Quoted in Mark Stephens, 'Mortgage market deregulation and its consequences', *Housing Studies*, vol. 22, no. 2, Mar. 2007.

16 *The Times*, 16 Nov. 1979.

17 Vidhya Alakeson, *Making a House a Home* (London, Resolution Foundation, 2001).

18 HomeOwners Alliance, *The Death of a Dream: The crisis of home ownership in the UK* (London, 2012).

19 *Evening Standard*, 22 Oct. 2012.

20 *Financial Times*, 10 Jul. 2008.

21 Nigel Lawson, speech to the Zurich Society of Economics at the Kongresshaus, Zurich, 14 Jan. 1981.

22 *The Times*, 24 Mar. 1980.

23 *The Times*, 1 May 1980.

24 *The Times*, 8 Oct. 1983.

25 Simon Jenkins, 'This Thatcher mythology condemns her strengths and excuses her failings', *Guardian*, 13 Mar. 2009.

26 *Financial Times*, 27 Jan. 1992.

27 Lawson (1992), 365, 368–9.

28 Bank of England archives, ref. 5A149/10.

29 James E. Thorold Rogers, *Six Centuries of Work and Wages* (London, 1884).

30 *Evening Standard*, 17 Apr. 2012.

31 CABE, *Space Standards: The benefits* (London, University College, 2010).

32 Rebecca Roberts-Hughes, *The Case for Space: The size of England's new homes* (London, Royal Institute of British Architects, 2011).

33 Julian Joyce, 'Shoebox homes become the new norm', BBC website, 14 Sept. 2011.

34 *The Economist*, 20 Nov. 2003.

35 Town and Country Planning Association, 'Residential densities', TCPA policy statement, London, 2003.

36 *The Economist*, 20 Nov. 2003.

37 *Daily Telegraph*, 23 Oct. 2011.

38 Polly Ghazi and Judy Jones, *Getting a Life: The downshifter's guide to happier simpler living* (London, Hodder & Stoughton, 1997), 50.

39 Martin Stott, *Spilling the Beans: A style guide to the new age* (London, Collins Fontana, 1986), 11.

3 The second clue: the strange case of the disappearing banks

1 Forrest Capie and Ghila Rodrik-Bali, 'Concentration in British Banking 1870–1920', *Business History*, vol. XXIV, no. 3, Nov. 1982.

2 Margaret Ackrill and Leslie Hannah, *Barclays: The business of banking 1690–1996* (Cambridge, CUP, 2001), 56.

3 Gillian Tett, 'The banks that politicians can be seen to embrace', *Financial Times*, 18 Feb. 2012.

4 Mark Boléat, speech, 21 Nov. 1985.

5 Mark Boléat, *The Building Societies: The regulatory framework* (London, Building Societies Association, 1988).

6 Nigel Lawson, *The View from No. 11: Memoirs of a Tory radical* (London, Bantam, 1992), 63.

7 Mark Boléat, speech, 7 Feb. 1986.

8 Peter Hosking, 'In the habit of making waves', *Independent*, 16 Jul. 1995.

9 J. Neill Marshall, Richard Willis and Ranald Richardson (2003), 'Demutualisation, strategic choice and social responsibility', *Environment and Planning C*: Government and Policy, vol. 21.

10 John Kay (1991), 'The Economics of Mutuality', in *Demutualization of Financial Institutes*, ed. D. Heald. *Annals of Public and Co-operative Economics*, vol. 62, no. 3.

11 Martin Vander Weyer, *Falling Eagle: The decline of Barclays Bank* (London, Weidenfeld & Nicolson, 2000), 138.

12 *Observer*, 9 Apr. 1995.

13 Ian Pollock, 'Not such a good idea after all?', BBC News, 29 Sept. 2008.

14 Building Societies Association (1996), Annual Report.

15 *Guardian*, 22 Feb. 2003.

16 Pollock, 'Not such a good idea after all?' BBC website, 29 Sept. 2008.

17 *Independent*, 8 Jun. 2001.

18 Alisdair Darling, *Back from the Brink: 1000 days at Number 11* (London, Atlantic Books, 2011), 115 and 199.

19 Mark Boléat, *The Building Society Industry* (London, George Allen & Unwin, 1982).

20 Jonathan Guthrie, 'Rhyme of the credit hungry entrepreneurs', *Financial Times*, 8 Jul. 2009.

21 Will Chen (2006), 'FBI considered *It's a Wonderful Life* communist propaganda', www.wisebread.com, 24 Dec.

22 Federation of Small Business figures, see BBC website (2012), 17 Sept.

4 The third clue: the corrosive explosion of finance

1 Quoted in *Desert Island Discs*, BBC Radio 4, 6 Mar. 1987.

2 *The Times*, 20 Jan. 1980.

3 David Kynaston, *A Club No More 1945–2000* (London, Chatto & Windus, 2000), 624.

4 Hugo Young, *One of Us: A Biography of Margaret Thatcher* (London, Pan Books, 1989), 269.

5 Kynaston, 625.

6 Kynaston, 625.

7 Kynaston, 629.

8 Bernard Attard, 'The Stock Exchange: An oral history', interview with David Hopkinson, 26 Jun. 1990.

9 BBC 2, *The Secret History of Our Streets*, 'Portland Road', 27 Jun. 2012.

10 Andrew Haldane, 'The doom loop', *London Review of Books*, 23 Feb. 2012.

11 http://epicureandealmaker.blogspot.com

12 Quoted in John Cassidy, 'What good is Wall Street?', *New Yorker*, 29 Nov. 2010.

13 Kynaston, 631.

14 Kynaston, 643.

15 Kynaston, 652.

16 Kynaston, 692.

17 *The Times*, 19 May 1984.

18 *Sunday Times*, 1 Aug. 1986.

19 *Sunday Times*, 15 Apr. 1984.

20 Kynaston, 655.

21 Kynaston, 696.

22 Kynaston, 650.

23 Simon Johnson, 'The Quiet Coup', *The Atlantic*, May 2009.

24 Quoted in Paul Woolley and Dimitri Vayanos, 'New light on choice of investment strategy', *Vox*, 18 Jan. 2012.

25 Samuel Evelyn Thomas, *The Macmillan Report, a short summary of its main points* (St Albans, Metropolitan College, 1931).

26 Michael Lewis, *Liar's Poker: Two cities, true greed* (London, Coronet. 1990).

27 Michael Lewis, *The Big Short: Inside the doomsday machine* (London, Allen Lane, 2010), xiv–xv.

28 William D. Cohan, *Money and Power: How Goldman Sachs came to rule the world* (New York, Doubleday, 2011), 15.

29 Quoted in Aditya Chakrabortty, 'Who came up with the model for excessive pay? No, it wasn't the bankers – it was academics', *Guardian*, 30 Jan. 2012.

30 Quoted in Kynaston, 650.

31 Sarah Hall (2009), 'Financialised elites and the changing nature of finance capitalism: Investment bankers in London's financial district', *Competition and Change*, vol. 13, no. 2.

32 Quoted in Cassidy (2010).

33 Margaret Ackrill and Leslie Hannah, *Barclays: The business of banking 1690–1996* (Cambridge, CUP, 2001), 327.

34 OECD figures, see: *Guardian*, 5 Dec. 2011.

5 The fourth clue: the dog that didn't bark

1 Michael Hammer and James Champy, *Re-engineering the Corporation* (New York, HarperBusiness, 1994).

2 Quoted in Simon Gunn and Rachel Bell, *The Middle Classes: Their rise and sprawl* (London, Weidenfeld & Nicolson, 2002), 213.

3 Peter Morris and Alasdair Palmer, *You're on Your Own: How policy produced Britain's pensions crisis* (London, Civitas, 2011), 26.

4 Morris and Palmer, 26.

5 *Guardian*, 22 Sept. 2010.

6 Peter Taylor-Gooby, 'Uncertainty, trust and pensions: The case of the current UK reforms', *Social Policy and Administration*, vol. 39, no. 3, Jun. 2005.

7 Norman Fowler, *Ministers Decide: A personal memoir of the Thatcher years* (London, Chapman's, 1991), 204.

8 Fowler, 211.

9 Fowler, 211.

10 Nigel Lawson, *The View from No. 11: Memoirs of a Tory radical* (London, Bantam, 1992), 589.

11 Lawson, 589.

12 *Daily Express*, 26 April 1985.

13 Lawson, 590.

14 Lawson, 591.

15 *The Times*, 23 Feb. 1986.

16 Fowler, 223.

17 *Daily Express*, 17 Dec. 1985.

18 Lawson, 592.

19 Quoted in Cris Sholto Heaton, 'Where are the customers' yachts?', *MoneyWeek*, 1 Aug. 2006.

20 Fowler, 222.

21 Austin Mitchell and Prem Sikka, *Pensions Crisis: A failure of public policy-making* (Basildon, Association for Accountancy & Business Affairs, 2006).

22 *Independent*, 17 May 2009.

23 This example is worked out in more detail in Morris and Palmer, 25ff.

24 John C. Bogle, *Enough: True measures of money, business and life* (New York, John Wiley, 2009), 30.

25 This example is worked out more clearly for an American audience in Bogle, 42–3.

26 *Observer*, 5 May 2002.

27 Anthony Hilton, 'Here's how to solve the pension problem, Ed', *Evening Standard*, 17 Jul. 2012.

6 The fifth clue: the great education panic

1 *Evening Standard*, 11 Sept. 2012.

2 BBC website, 4 Sept. 2012.

3 *Guardian*, 12 Apr. 2012.

4 Vanessa Barford, 'The great school place sausage machine', BBC website, 2 Mar. 2012.

5 *Daily Mail*, 28 Jun. 2011.

6 BBC website, 18 Apr. 2012.

7 Andrew Penman, 'A real education', *Guardian*, 4 Sept. 2010.

8 Penman (2010).

9 For a distressing account of the side effects of cramming see Tanith Carey, *Where Has My Little Girl Gone?* (Oxford, Lion, 2012).

10 Quoted in Jim Docking, *Education and Alienation in the Junior School* (London, Taylor and Francis, 1990), 79.

11 *Guardian*, 2 Sept. 1996.

12 John Major, *The Next Phase of Conservatism: The privatisation of choice* (Conservative Political Centre, 1992), 9.

13 John Major, *The Autobiography* (London, HarperCollins, 1999), 394.

14 Major (1999), 397–8.

15 *The Times*, 21 Nov. 1992.

16 *The Times*, 20 Nov. 1992.

17 *Guardian*, 20 Nov. 1992.

18 *Guardian*, 20 Nov. 1992.

19 *Observer*, 22 Nov. 1992.

20 *The Times*, 21 Nov. 1992.

21 *The Economist*, 8 May 1993.

22 *The Times*, 8 Oct. 1993.

23 G. Crozier, et al. (2008), 'White middle class parents, identities, educational choice and the urban comprehensive school: dilemma, ambivalence and moral ambiguity', *British Journal of Sociology of Education*, vol. 29, no. 3.

24 Quoted in Val Gillies (2005), 'Raising the meritocracy: parenting and the individualisation of social class', *Sociology*, vol. 35, no. 5.

25 Edge et al. (1996), 'Secondary school choice and involvement in education', paper to the American Education Research Association annual meeting, New York, April 1996.

26 Fiona Millar and Gemma Wood, *A New Conversation with Parents: How can schools inform and listen in a digital age?* (London, Family Lives, 2011).

27 Katya Williams et al., 'He was a bit of a delicate thing: white middle class boys, gender, school choice and parental anxiety', *Gender and Education*, vol. 20, no. 4, July 2008.

28 Lord Chatfield, *The Navy and Defence* (London, William Heinemann, 1942), 232.

29 Paul Tough, *How Children Succeed: Grit, curiosity and the hidden power of character* (New York, Houghton Mifflin Harcourt, 2012).

30 The best collection of evidence on small schools is Kathleen Cotton, *New Small Learning Communities: Findings from Recent Literature* (Portland, Oregon, Northwest Regional Educational Laboratory, 2001). There is a more recent American summary by the Chicago Public Schools System at smallschools.cps.k12.il.us/research.html. The equivalent UK information is available from Human Scale Education (www.hse.org.uk).

31 Roger Barker and Paul Gump, *Big School, Small School* (Stanford, Stanford University Press, 1964).

32 See my discussion on this in David Boyle, *The Human Element* (Abingdon, Earthscan, 2011), 64–7.

33 Andy Wiggins and Peter Tymms, 'Dysfunctional effects of league tables: a comparison between English and Scottish primary schools', *Public Money and Management*, Jan.–Mar. 2002.

34 *News Guardian*, 6 Sept. 2012.

35 Press Association, 27 Aug. 2012.

36 Unesco figures, see: BBC website, 18 Apr. 2012.

7 The sixth clue: the strange case of the disappearing professionals

1 See Philip Brown et al., 'Skills are not enough: the globalisation of knowledge and the future UK economy', *Praxis*, no. 4, March 2010.

2 The sad story of M&S, and the destruction of the textile industry it had nurtured, is in David Boyle, *Eminent Corporations* (London, Constable and Robinson, 2010), 125ff.

3 Chrystia Freeland, 'Globalization, the tech revolution and the middle class', *Reuters*, 21 Sept. 2012.

4 *Daily Mail*, 23 Mar. 2010.

5 *Daily Telegraph*, 7 Jul. 2012.

6 Michael Spence and Sandile Hlatshwayo, *The Evolving Structure of the American Economy and the Employment Challenge*, Council on Foreign Relations Working Paper, New York, March 2011.

7 *Independent*, 21 Apr. 2011.

8 Kevin Whitston, 'Scientific Management Practice in Britain: a History', PhD thesis, University of Warwick, 1995.

9 Edward Cadbury, 'Some principles of industrial organisation', *Sociological Review*, vol. VII, no. 2, Apr. 1914.

10 Michael Power, *The Audit Explosion* (London, Demos, 1994).

11 Power, 41.

12 Gerry Mooney and Alex Law, *New Labour/Hard Labour?: Restructuring and resistance inside the welfare industry* (London, Policy Press, 2007).

13 Nick Davies, 'How Britain is losing the drugs war', *Guardian*, 22 May 2003.

14 Simon Head, *The New Ruthless Economy* (New York, Oxford University Press, 2005).

15 Helen M. Gunter (2010), 'The standards challenge', *Public Administration*, vol. 88, no. 1.

16 See David Boyle, *The Tyranny of Numbers* (London, HarperCollins, 2001).

17 Duncan Campbell-Smith, *Follow The Money: The Audit Commission, public money and the management of publics, 1983–2008* (London, Penguin Books, 2008), 473.

18 Campbell-Smith, 492n.

19 Michael Barber, 'Table manners', *Guardian*, 3 May 1994.

20 Michael Barber, *Instruction to Deliver* (London, Politico's, 2007), 135.

21 *Times Educational Supplement*, 15 May 2009.

22 Jane Simmonds, 'Keeping up appearances', *Daily Mail*, 27 Sept. 2011.

23 Francis Fukuyama, 'The Future of History: Can liberal democracy survive the decline of the middle class?', *Foreign Affairs*, Jan./Feb. 2012.

24 Commission on Living Standards figures, see *Daily Telegraph*, 30 Oct. 2012.

8 Following the clues, unmasking the villains

1 Henry Kamen, *Spain 1469–1714: A society of conflict* (London, Longmans, 1983), 110.

2 Quoted in J. H. Elliott, *Spain and its World 1500–1700* (New Haven, Yale University Press, 1989), 232.

3 Elliott, 233.

4 Kamen, 104.

5 Quoted in Ben Wilson, *The Making of Victorian Values: Decency and dissent in Britain, 1789–1837* (London, Penguin Press, 2007), 315.

6 Wilson, 317.

7 G. Greig, 'Capital gains', Tatler, July 2007.

8 Jacob S. Hacker, The Great Risk Shift (New York, Oxford University Press, 2006).

9 Anthony B. Atkinson and Andrea Brandolini, On the Identification of the Middle Class, Ecineq working paper 217 (2011).

10 Quoted in Owen Jones, Chavs: The demonization of the working class, updated edn (London, Verso, 2012), 113.

11 Jones, 131.

12 John Maynard Keynes, General Theory of Employment, Interest and Money (1936), 383.

13 Quoted in Roy Lewis and Angus Maude, The English Middle Classes (London, Phoenix House, 1949), 75.

14 See for example Jane Jacobs, Cities and the Wealth of Nations (New York, Random House, 1986).

15 Evidence for the link with fair pay scales is in D. Cowherd and D. Levie (1992), 'Product quality and pay equity between low level employees and top management', Administrative Science Quarterly, vol. 37.

16 See Ross Clark, A Broom Cupboard of One's Own: The housing crisis and how to solve it (Petersfield, Harriman House, 2012).

17 See Josh Ryan-Collins et al., Where Does Money Come From? A guide to the UK monetary and banking system, second edn (London, New Economics Foundation, 2012).

18 Quoted in Lewis and Maude, 47.

19 Quoted in David Kynaston, Austerity Britain 1945–1951 (London, Bloomsbury, 2008), 503.

The Year Everything Changed: 2013

1 David Autor and David Dorn (2013), 'How technology wrecks the middle class', New York Times, 23 August.

2 Melanie McDonagh (2013), 'We are being priced out of our city, Boris', Evening Standard, 22 October.

Index